Y0-CYH-476

# Alternative Work Organizations

# Alternative Work Organizations

Edited by

Maurizio Atzeni
*Lecturer in Labour and Industrial Relations, Loughborough University*
*School of Business and Economics, UK*

First published 2012 by
PALGRAVE MACMILLAN

Palgrave Macmillan in the UK is an imprint of Macmillan Publishers Limited,
registered in England, company number 785998, of Houndmills, Basingstoke,
Hampshire RG21 6XS.

Palgrave Macmillan in the US is a division of St Martin's Press LLC,
175 Fifth Avenue, New York, NY 10010.

Palgrave Macmillan is the global academic imprint of the above companies
and has companies and representatives throughout the world.

Palgrave® and Macmillan® are registered trademarks in the United States,
the United Kingdom, Europe and other countries.

ISBN 978–0–230–24140–4

This book is printed on paper suitable for recycling and made from fully
managed and sustained forest sources. Logging, pulping and manufacturing
processes are expected to conform to the environmental regulations of the
country of origin.

A catalogue record for this book is available from the British Library.

Library of Congress Cataloging-in-Publication Data
Alternative work organizations / edited by Maurizio Atzeni.
     pages   cm
  Includes bibliographical references and index.
  ISBN 978–0–230–24140–4
  1. Work environment.   2. Management—Employee participation.
  3. Organization.   I. Atzeni, Maurizio.
  HD7261.A35 2012
  331.2—dc23                                            2012016689

10   9   8   7   6   5   4   3   2   1
21   20   19   18   17   16   15   14   13   12

Printed and bound in the United States of America

# Contents

# Tables and Figures

## Tables

## Figures

# Contributors

**Len Arthur** worked for over 30 years teaching trade union studies and industrial relations. For the last 10 years of his career he was Director of Cardiff Institute for Cooperative Studies. Academically, he is still involved in exploring cooperatives as social movements, how they can reconnect with the labour movement and in developing concepts that may help this process, such as 'deviant mainstreaming' and 'transitional demands and actions'.

**Maurizio Atzeni** is Lecturer in Labour and Industrial Relations at Loughborough University School of Business and Economics, UK. He is also a Research Fellow at CEIL/CONICET, Buenos Aires. His general research interests include the investigation of the role of labour and workers in societies. He has researched and published extensively in books and academic journals on workplace conflict and workers' collective action, on Argentinian trade unionism and workers' self-management.

**Joseba Azkarraga Etxagibel** is a cooperative member and Professor of Contemporary Social Change and Social Economics at Mondragon University. He is the founder of LANKI (Institute of Cooperative Research at Mondragon University) and a researcher there. He was Head of the Department of Social Science at Mondragon University and a member of the Board of Directors. Professor Azkarraga has published several essays and articles on his main areas of research: the Mondragon cooperative experience and social economics, Western development models and the transition to sustainability, and contemporary Basque society.

**George Cheney** is Professor of Communication Studies at Kent State University. Previously he held faculty positions at the universities of Illinois, Colorado, Montana, Utah and Texas. He has held administrative positions or roles in communication departments, a campus quality-of-worklife programme, an interdisciplinary peace and conflict studies programme, a human rights centre and a service learning institute. He has taught, lectured, conducted research and consulted in Europe and Latin America, in addition to holding a position as adjunct professor at the University of Waikato in Hamilton, New Zealand, since 1998. Professor Cheney has published eight books and more than 90 articles, chapters and reviews. His award-winning book on the Mondragon cooperatives is *Values at Work* (Cornell University Press, 1999, 2002). He is the North American book review editor for the journal *Organization* and is a faculty associate of the Ohio Employee Ownership Center at Kent State University.

**Martino Ghielmi** has an MA in African studies from the University of Pavia, Italy. He spent a year in Nairobi taking part in the evaluation of a non-governmental organization support programme for informal workers and currently works in management consulting. His research interests include informal labour, social entrepreneurship and innovation in East Africa.

**Anita Hammer** is Senior Lecturer in Comparative and International Human Resource Management at Leicester Business School, De Montfort University, UK. Her research interests include globalization and its impact on economic development and social change; multinational corporations and international human resource management; industrial relations and social movements; and the political economy of India. She has worked in the industry for several years and teaches on a range of undergraduate and postgraduate management programmes.

**Tom Keenoy** is Emeritus Professor at the University of Leicester and Honorary Professor at Cardiff Business School, UK. He has published widely and has a continuing research interest in organizational discourse analysis, the social construction of human resource management, time and organization, the co-construction of management in cooperative organizations and the changing temper of sensemaking in academic work.

**Camila Piñeiro Harnecker** is a researcher and professor at the Center for the Study of the Cuban Economy, University of Havana, where she focuses on self-management and democratic coordination. She is editor and author of *Cooperatives and Socialism: A Cuban Perspective* (Ed. Caminos, Havana, 2011).

**Molly Scott Cato** works as a green economist, seeking to develop a sustainable and just economy. She is Professor of Strategy and Sustainability at Roehampton University, UK, and a former Director of the Cardiff Institute for Cooperative Studies.

**Russell Smith** is an economist and the Acting Director of Cardiff Institute for Cooperative Studies (CICS), UK. With other colleagues in Cardiff Metropolitan University's Management School, he helped to establish CICS in 2000. He is involved in exploring cooperatives as social movements, human firms and demonstrable radical alternatives to conventional businesses through the concept of 'deviant mainstreaming'.

**Alan Tuckman** currently teaches at Nottingham Trent University, UK. He has researched and published widely on employment relations and the sociology of work, most recently on migrant labour, employee voice and workplace conflict.

**Ainara Udaondo Alberdi** is the Head of LANKI (Institute of Cooperative Research at Mondragon University) and of the Department of Cooperative Training and Development there. She is a member of the Board of Directors of the School of Humanities and Education and has been the Head and a faculty member of the graduate programme of Cooperative Development. She has contributed to the development of educational and audiovisual materials on the Mondragon cooperative experience. In addition, she offers advice and training on cooperative enterprise to the cooperatives of Grupo Mondragon.

**Marcelo Vieta** holds a PhD in social and political thought (York University) and is a postdoctoral research fellow at the European Research Institute on Cooperative and Social Enterprises (EURICSE) in Trento, Italy. He is also a research associate at York University's Center for Research on Latin America and the Caribbean (CERLAC) and sits on the board of the Canadian Association for Studies in Co-operation (CASC). In recent years, Marcelo has been researching and publishing on the historical conditions, the political economic environments, and the lived experiences of the worker-recuperated enterprises of Argentina, as well as on the social and solidarity economies of Latin America. More broadly, he is interested in the prefigurative possibilities for alternative economic arrangements, as well as the socio-technological spheres within which alternatives to capitalism emerge. He has lectured and taught broadly on topics such as the social economy, critical theory and communication. Since 2005, he has been actively involved in helping develop researcher and practitioner linkages between cooperative experiences in Canada and Latin America.

# 1
# An Introduction to Theoretical Issues

*Maurizio Atzeni*

There is a shared view among business people that it is common sense to organize work in a hierarchical, management-led way. Notwithstanding fashionable managerial programmes about employee participation and involvement (which in the best of cases collapse like sandcastles in the storm of economic crises), within capitalism, 'management has the right to manage'. That somebody needs to be empowered in the interests of the business to make quick decisions and impose the execution of these on working people is a principle hardly contested and indeed commonly accepted by workers themselves as the normal state of affairs. This acceptance is further reinforced by a system of work organized on the basis of a separation between planning and execution that concentrates knowledge (and consequently decision-making power) in the hands of a few. This conception about the accepted, effective and thus 'natural' way of organizing work in our societies is so embedded in the way we live that to think about a different, more democratic, equalitarian, less hierarchical and authoritarian way of organizing work is at best treated as a utopia. Thus, in building a convincing argument about alternatives, the first point to make is about the pervasiveness of dominant social relations in shaping the organization of work. This necessarily implies a theoretical effort to criticize the existing organization of work before practical alternatives can be envisaged.

Historical research on the labour movement and on workers' contentious actions provides a good antidote against this dominant view about organizing work and represents a fundamental tool in the process of critique to the existing system. Although with differences in terms of socio-political and geographical context and within a wide range of ideological perspectives, workers with their actions have often reverted to taken-for-granted assumptions about property, management, work organization and wages, and have overall contested, in daily practice, the almost natural character of capitalist work relations while contemporaneously creating alternative forms of work organization. From Owen and the socialist utopians to the cooperative movement of the late 19th century; from the Russian Soviets to the revolutionary factory occupations in Italy in the 1920s; from the spread of self-management in Cataluña during the Spanish Republic of 1936–1939 to the institutionalization of self-management in post-war Communist Yugoslavia; from the promotion of workers' control in industry in the 1970s to the contemporary cases of worker-run production and democratic decision-making at Tower Colliery and Suma in the UK; from the recent experiences of self-management in Argentina born out of an economic crisis to Venezuelan state-supported factories' expropriation and nationalization under workers' control – all these geographically and historically diverse contexts nonetheless represent cases and experiences of workers with alternative forms of work.

What is the theoretical relevance of all these attempts to revert to the 'natural' state of affairs in capitalist work relations? What would an alternative model look like? Will market competition influence this new model? Which type of values will be supporting? Who is going to take decisions in the new organizations? Will there be any leaders? What role, if any, will there be for managers? How will tasks be distributed among workers? These are just a few of the questions that a serious attempt to envisage new, alternative forms of work organization will face.

The in-depth analyses of specific cases presented in this book will help to delve – from different theoretical perspectives, approaches and geographical contexts – into the intricacies of maintaining alternative practices and views about work in a competitive market environment and provide evidence of the ambivalence of state and local institutions in supporting, using or repressing workers' attempts to directly control production. This chapter attempts to insert these issues into a more general theoretical framework.

In the light of this, the chapter first aims to deconstruct accepted views about work organization by reflecting upon the capitalist nature of the labour process. Production within capitalism is rationally organized, both technically and socially, to produce and increase profit. This logic of production changes the nature of the labour process, which from a process, just like any other, in which human labour transforms things, becomes a unity of production and valorization. Management control of the labour process, authoritarian and hierarchical decision-making, a tendency to task specialization, job segmentation and deskilling, and increased individualism and divisions among workers are just a few of the consequences that the need for profitability can impose on the organization of work.

In the second part of this chapter, a number of important theoretical aspects associated with workers' attempts to control production will be addressed. The pervasiveness of capitalist social relations makes exceptional any deviations from the capitalist model of work organization. Historical experiences have nonetheless provided evidence of how it is the existence of structural conditions that favour the emergence of an alternative, and how this alternative is by its own nature transformative of the status quo and thus potentially revolutionary.

Despite this potential, workers' experiments with new forms of organizing work have inevitably always been inserted within the present capitalist socio-economic system and the dynamics of market competition. This has a twofold consequence. On the one hand, the mere existence of a radical alternative in the form of direct control by workers of the whole production and decision-making process has always been opposed by the dominant classes. Workers' control in capitalism is indeed critical. With its emphasis on grassroots democracy, collective property and self-management, it directly challenges the capitalist labour process, giving space to the formation of new, for their nature more radical, forms of workers' organization, the workers' councils or committees. On the other hand, once the alternative remains within the remits of the system, as has been typical of any surviving experience of workers' self-management and of the cooperative movement, the competition in the market imposes the adoption of capitalist managerial rules that limit the extent of democracy and participation within the organization.

The theoretical debate about the fate of workers' attempts to build an alternative within the system has been dominated by the thesis that the incorporation in the market would lead to a degeneration of the potentially revolutionary character of workers' control of production. However, while it is true that capitalism strongly distorts or eliminates any serious attempts to change the organization of work, all experiences with alternative work have represented an advance in terms of workers' emancipation and empowerment. It is from here that we need to start if we aim to make the search for an alternative and more democratic organization of work central to the social science and policy agenda.

## The nature of work within capitalism

There seems to be a coincidence among disciplines in the social sciences about the nature of work within capitalism. Work is generally seen as a negative, alienating and unchangeable condition of life. In mainstream labour economics, for instance, in the last 300 years, work has been described as a pain or disutility and mainly seen as an activity workers would happily avoid for a life of leisure and consumption. As a consequence, rather than looking at the intrinsic characteristics of the work activity itself, labour economists have placed great emphasis on monetary rewards as an instrument to convince workers to work (Spencer, 2009).

That workers need to be motivated to perform work is a view also shared by contemporary human resource management literature. While monetary incentives linked to the monitoring of employee performance remain central to increased productivity, discourses about job satisfaction and enrichment, employee involvement and the mutual gain enterprise have stressed the importance of promoting workers' motivation to work through psychological and ideological incentives (Kochan and Osterman, 1994; Guest, 2002). Added to this, it has been argued that in today's more dynamic and knowledge-based work environment, autonomy, mastery and purpose are the most fundamental motivators of people at work (Pink, 2011). From a different perspective, workplace ethnographic and qualitative studies have often given voice to workers unconformity to work. The degradation of work produced by the repetitiveness of tasks, the intensification of rhythms and conditions of work, management authority and control, its use of race and ethnicity to divide workers, insufficient wage levels and threats to job security are all aspects of work that constantly surface from within the employment relation, structuring collective action and resistance (Linhart, 1981; Beynon, 1984; Fantasia, 1989; Turner, 1995; Cohen, 2006; Sherman, 2007; Mollona, 2009; Atzeni, 2010; Lopez, 2010).

While work represents an important element in the social life of people and it is in itself a potentially creative and fulfilling activity, there is no doubt that workers' compulsion to sell their labour power for a wage – the main social form through which work has been subsumed under capitalism – creates for the majority of workers a negative attitude towards work. Rather than an end in itself, waged work is performed and accepted just because it represents the only means available to reproduce the workers, giving them access, via exchange in the market, to the consumables required to satisfy the variable set of material and social human needs. 'But beneath this apparent habituation, the hostility of workers to the degenerated forms of work which are forced upon them continues as a subterranean stream that makes its way to the surface when employment conditions permit ... it renews itself in new genera-tions, expresses itself in the unbounded cynicism and revulsion which a large number of workers feel about their work, and comes to the fore repeatedly as a social issue demanding solution' (Braverman, 1974: 151).

Marx argued that the double nature of the capitalist labour process, contemporaneously a process of production of a use value and a pro-cess of valorization of this through living labour, and the treatment of labour as a commodity to be exchanged in the market, produces a num-ber of consequences, specific to the capitalist labour process, that affect the material reality of work, and structure the way people think and behave in relation to their work. On the one hand, by entering into an exchange with the capitalist, workers are separated from the prod-uct of their labour and lose control of the labour process. This becomes, with the development of industry, increasingly segmented, repetitive and subjected to a hierarchical system of managerial/technical control, functional to efficiency and profitability, based on the division between intellectual/directive and manual work. On the other hand, these mate-rial changes increase the alienation of workers from their work up to the point that 'the instrument of labour confronts the worker during the labour process, in the shape of capital, dead labour, which dominates and soaks up living labour power' (1976: 548).

In his seminal book *Labor and Monopoly Capital*, Harry Braverman re-framed Marx's theoretical insights into the nature of the labour pro-cess within capitalism to account for the transformation of work that occurred in the 20th century. A number of tendencies were identi-fied within this process of change. The technological development of industry with its extensive use of machines, by simplifying tasks, was increasingly reducing the possibilities of workers' mental contribution to the labour process while at the same time driving management to exert an ever more strict control of each step and operation within the productive activity. 'The novelty of this development during the past century lies not in the separate existence of hand and brain, concep-tion and execution, but the rigor with which they are divided from one another, and then increasingly subdivided, so that conception is concentrated, insofar as is possible, in ever more limited groups within management or closely associated with it' (Braverman, 1974: 125). This tendency was accompanied by the consequent deskilling of the working class. While technological developments and the new division of labour were constantly opening up new areas of specialization based on new skills and knowledge, these were often associated with the management monopoly of science and production methods and thus concentrated in the hands of a reduced number of workers. Moreover, considering the speed of technological developments, these reskilling processes were also seen as short trends within 'the secular trend toward the incessant lowering of the working class as a whole . . . as this continues over several generations, the very standards by which the trend is judged become imperceptibly altered, and the meaning of skill itself becomes degraded' (Braverman, 1974: 129–130).

In the years immediately after its publication, Braverman's work sparked an intense debate – the so-called labour process debate – which focused particularly on the validity of his assumptions about deskilling and control. Fundamentally he was accused of holding a determinist and one-sided view of the labour process that did not account for the role of subjectivity and workers' action in reshaping the whole labour process by resisting deskilling and increased managerial control. More-over, by underplaying the role of subjective experiences of work, he was missing important aspects related to the ideological and cultural sphere of workers' subordination (for an exhaustive treatment of the debate, see Thompson, 1989; for a recent re-evaluation, see Thompson and Smith, 2010: Introduction).

Studies in the tradition of the labour process debate have had the merits to maintain the centrality of the labour process and workplace relations for empirical and theoretical analysis.[1] Management and work-ers are holders of different interests and in a relation of structural antagonism, but they are also in an interdependent, though asymmet-rical, relation in which employers' profitability does not depend just on control but also on workers' consent and cooperation in the labour process (Burawoy, 1979, 1985; Edwards and Scullion, 1982; Edwards, 1986). For more than three decades, empirical studies in the labour pro-cess tradition have also provided important insights into changes and transformations occurring in the world of work, particularly with the new work processes associated with flexibilization and lean production (Delbridge, 1998; Elger and Smith, 1994, 2005), and the new knowledge and service economy (Korczynski, 2002; Warhurst et al., 2004; Bolton, 2005; Taylor and Bain, 2005; Bolton and Houlihan, 2009).

Despite the importance of this body of work in explaining the com-plexity of social processes occurring in the workplace, the framework provided by Marx, and successively Braverman, to understand the speci-ficity of the labour process should be defended (Cohen, 1987; Spencer,

2000; Tinker, 2002). Firstly, the tendencies outlined in this framework have proved to be to a large extent resistant to times, just thinking how valid the idea of deskilling remains if applied to the global production process (Taylor, 2008). Secondly, it is still probably the best model we have to establish linkages between the abstract and the concrete, the theoretical and the empirical. Marx's view of the labour process as contemporaneously a production and valorization process connects the specificities of social relations in the workplace with the general dynamics of a system based on class relations, in which the labour process is set in motion to create profit. This logic tends to shape the entire organization of work but is limited, among other factors, by workers' opposition and resistance to it. This is indeed omnipresent and rational since the exploitation of labour by capital is inherently contradictory and conflictive (Hyman, 2006).

It might be argued that in any social system based on class division, labour would always be coerced and work would always be organized in a way functional to the interest of the dominant classes in appropriating the surplus produced by workers. In this sense there would be nothing specific to the capitalist system, and producers would always perceive work as a pain and a cost. However, as Burawoy rightly shows in his comparison with the feudal system (1979: Chapter 2), there are a number of specificities of the labour process under capitalism that makes this system different and consequently structures subjective attitudes to work. The appearance of the payment of the wage as an equal compensation for the expenditure of labour power, while giving an impression of equal exchange in reality conceals the automatic appropriation by capitalists of both necessary and surplus labour. Unlike feudalism, there is no clear division between the time spent by workers to produce their means of existence (necessary labour) and the time dedicated to produce the surplus. Workers cannot reproduce themselves independently, not just because under capitalism the means of production belong to the employer, who decides and organizes the labour process, but also because, in a social system that 'presents itself as "an immense accumulation of commodities"' (Marx, 1976: 1), workers are forced to sell in the market their commodity – labour power – if they want to obtain the means of their existence. The market is thus the necessary mediator for both the worker and the capitalist, whose relations become dominated by economic rather than political and institutional factors. 'The production of commodities is, simultaneously, the reproduction of the relations of production, whereas, under feudalism, production for the lord is connected to production for the serf through political and legal mechanisms' (Burawoy, 1979: 25). Finally, important differences are to be found at the level of control, coordination and conflict. During feudalism, productive activities were fixed and legally regulated, allowing workers, to a large extent, to keep control of the labour process. In capitalism, due to the indeterminacy of labour power, management control is essential in securing profitability. At the same time, whereas changes to the production model and the organization of work were in feudalism the outcome of struggles at the political/institutional level, the economic nature of the relation between capital and labour imposes a process of constant renegotiation of the effort/reward directly where production takes place. All these specificities, deriving from the nature of the capitalist labour process, act upon the subjective experience of work and shape individual and collective responses to it, creating conditions for the existence of a continuous tension between the opposing interests of capital and labour (Hyman, 1975).

Although the exchange between labour power and wages has become the historically dominant form through which commodity production within capitalism has taken place, different forms of workers' subordination and thus different modes of production/labour processes do co-exist within the same system (Van der Linden, 2008). Producers might be more or less autonomous and independent from selling their labour, they might or might not be the owner of the labour power (as with many forms of indentured or bonded labour), they might be economically or non-economically tied to their employer or they might or might not possess their own means of production (for a full categorization, see Van der Linden,[2] 2008: chapters 1–3). This historical reality has consequences in terms of the practical arrangements regulating the labour process and the efforts/rewards, requiring, for instance, the use of more or less extended forms of direct control and supervision, giving space to different forms of conflict and labour management relations. However important these differences are, within a system globally organized on the basis of commodity production and quite independently of the form through which labour has been commodified, the labour process will continue to remain influenced by the capitalist environment in which it takes place. Even outside 'traditional' wage labour, work will be performed, organized and shaped to produce not just useful but also exchangeable things in the market. Thus the need to realize profit through exchange in the market will tend to continue shaping the labour process, even in those cases in which collective ownership of the means of production and self-management have substituted the more traditional forms of capital ownership and control of production.

The recent case of the recovered factories in Argentina is just the last concrete example of the influence of market forces on workers' genuine attempts to organize work in an alternative, more democratic and participative way (Atzeni and Ghigliani, 2007; Vieta: Chapter 6 in this book). I will, however, consider the extent of these influences and the possibilities for alternative work in the final part of this chapter.

For the majority of people, work under capitalism remains a negative experience. A situation of 'structural unfreedom', to use the expression of the political philosopher G. A. Cohen (1983), is what characterizes the daily conditions of workers under capitalism. Lacking access to the means of production, they are compelled to work and to 'offer' themselves in a labour market in order to guarantee their survival. They need to accept a type of work organization that while functional to profitability tends to impoverish their daily work experience, simplifying and repeating tasks, reducing their intellectual contribution to the production process, increasing the physical and mental exploitation of the worker. At the same time they spend their working day in an environment which is not just limiting their participation in decision-making but is often authoritarian. Furthermore, their job stability and salary levels, on which their living directly depends, are subordinated to decisions taken under pressure imposed by an impersonal market, which is, by its own nature, unstable and uncontrollable.

A world historical perspective on the labour movement provides evidence of workers' attempts to limit these negative consequences on work and rebalance class relations at the level of society (Silver, 2003). However, workers' struggles have tended to remain within the limits imposed by the system. Fair wages and working conditions, rather than workers' control, have indeed been the historical demands that trade unions have put forward as agents representing workers in the negotiation of the price of labour. Why then have workers tended to maintain their struggle within the wage system and, consequently, why have workers' practices of, and ideas with, alternative systems of work been numerically less important in the history of workers' struggles?

Many contingent factors can explain the emergence, and the success or the failure of, experiments with alternatives, as I will attempt to do in the next section of this chapter by presenting an historical overview of the issue. But an answer to these questions necessarily means, to use the expression of Michael Lebowitz, to understand what 'keeps capitalism going' (Lebowitz, 2004). Thus what are the structural conditions that do not allow one to envisage an alternative, notwithstanding workers' negative perceptions of work? Following Marx, three conditions are outlined by Lebowitz: the exploitation of workers is not obvious as this is hidden by the very structure of the wage relation which presents itself on the surface as an equal exchange; capitalism mystifies social relations, capital appears as the producer of all wealth and workers see themselves as dependent on capital; and, finally, workers do not just appear as dependent upon capital – they really are dependent on it for their own survival. Moreover, since capitalism is based on individual capitals in competition among them, workers will be interested in the economic profitability of their own employers and, in the light of this, they will accept economic sacrifices.

Notwithstanding these obstacles, in the course of the last 100 years, workers have contested – from different ideological perspectives and in different geographical and socio-political contexts – the inevitability of capitalist forms of work organization and provided examples of alternatives. It is to the theoretical relevance of these that we now turn our attention.

## The transformative side of workers' control

'Workers' control' or self-management – workers' democratic decision-making power on production and administration – has often been the way in which workers have demanded changes in, or attempted to change, the traditional way of organizing work. In general terms, workers' control can be then considered as epitomizing the search for an alternative. Indeed, with its emphasis on democracy in the decision-making process, on workers' autonomy in the management of the labour process, on solidarity and equality among producers, and on the idea of work as purposive and creative, workers' control stands directly opposite the authoritarian, alienating, job-deskilled, profit-driven reality of a capitalist work organization. For this reason and for the radical view that workers' control conveys, notwithstanding historical variations and meanings of the concept, in this section and the chapter overall, I will be using the term as synonymous with alternative work organization.

The history of the labour movement is rich in examples of workers' control (for a recent review and analysis, see Ness and Azzellini, 2011). But the ways in which this control has been attempted and eventually put into practice have been varied and often contradictory, reflecting the different origins and contexts, political ideals and pragmatic decisions – but also the difficulties inherent in the sustainability of workers' control within capitalism.

Without pretending to be exhaustive, and partly following Bayat's categorization (1991), we could, however, identify six main variations in the concept and forms of control which have appeared and overlapped in different geographical contexts during the last 100 years or so of (mainly) industrial capitalism. The first variation corresponds to workers' control as a means of revolutionary transformation. Linked to the theoretical positions of the different historical streams of libertarian and emancipatory communism (council communism views of the workers' councils, anarcho-syndicalism, Italian *Autonomia Operaia*), workers' control is seen as the organizational pillar for the transition to, and establishment of, a new classless, democratic, communist society. The second variation, exemplified by the activity and debates promoted by the Institute for Workers' Control in the 1970s in the UK, while not directly envisaging a new communist, workers' controlled society, intends control as a means of limiting capital prerogative in the workplace, in what would be a trade union-led strategy for encroaching control. The third variation, mirrored in the history of the cooperative movement, considers workers' control or self-management as the natural consequence of workers' collective ownership of cooperatives. The fourth variation, closely associated with national states' conciliatory industrial relations policies, sees control as a form of workers' participation and sharing in the management of companies. The fifth variation corresponds to the planned and/or implemented workers' control or participation in the management of companies within real socialism planned economies. Lastly, but probably most importantly for its transformative potential, workers' control can be seen as a radical, often spontaneous and unintended form of collective action through which workers defend achieved rights or demand new ones.

These variations should not be considered as clear cut. Very often in the same context, different meanings have been associated with workers' control. Existing ideological or political differences orienting workers' action, the social and economic unstable climate in which workers' control was inserted, the extent of opposition of dominant classes, the need to compete in a capitalist market, but also the unexpected consequences unleashed by the very act of occupying and taking control of factories – all have often resulted in contradictory developments.

However, in an attempt to generalize from historical examples, we could say that the theoretical importance of workers' control lies in its potentially transformative nature. Workers' control is, and has been, transformative in many ways. Firstly, it has often been highly disruptive of the previously accepted systems. Private property, authoritarian workplace management, taken-for-granted patterns of production and distribution, and the entire system of capitalist relations, as in coincidence with revolutionary or political turmoil, have been directly challenged by workers' control of production. For this destabilizing effect, workers' control has always been opposed by the dominant classes and practical attempts to establish this have been shortlived and almost invariably repressed. Secondly, workers' control has been characterized by a high degree of spontaneity, direct democracy, workers delegates' accountability, and independence and autonomy from trade unions and political parties. In this sense the historical manifestation of workers' control has been the proof of alternative, more direct ways of representing and organizing workers' interests that go beyond trade unionism. Thirdly, workers' self-management – workers' democratic decision-making power on production and administration – is transformative in envisaging a capital-free form of work organization built on values and practices radically opposed to those of a traditional capitalist organization.

Most important, however, is that workers' control, with its related transformative potential, is linked to structural conditions of the labour capital relation. Indeed, very often workers' occupation of factories and the following attempts to directly manage production have been the unintended consequences of grassroots collective action based on economistic claims. The most recent and direct example of this can be seen in the cases of the Argentinean recovered factories. Here the occupation of the companies' premises were initially basically defensive, unplanned responses by workers to job losses and unemployment in the midst of a huge economic and political crisis, but these responses then transformed themselves into self-managed production in the course of action. So what started originally as a grassroots defensive action transformed itself into a real, class-based alternative to defend workers' interests, and this process also strengthened the workers' own consciousness.

Structural conditions external to the workplace have often created a fertile soil for the emergence of workers' control. This has been the case with acute and deep economic crises, with periods of revolutionary turmoil or with state's and socialist politics oriented to promote workers' control. This notwithstanding, it has to be emphasised how the conflictive nature of the labour capital relation constantly made possible the reappearance of forms of workers' control and self-management. Driven by the requirement to satisfy basic economic needs, grassroots-based organizations, already existing or spontaneously formed in the course of action, have been crucial in coordinating workers' practical experiences with a new system of work oriented towards direct democracy, equality and diffused decision-making power (Cohen, 2011). Thus the real alternative to the traditional capitalist organization is anchored in the structure of capitalist relations. This, rather than blueprints of alternative work systems, should be the fundamental departure point in evaluating the future perspectives of workers' control.

## Workers' control and self-management as an alternative within capitalism

What we have defined as the transformative side of workers' control is most clearly visible in those cases in which workers' attempts to control production are inserted within a dynamic of workplace or socially diffused collective action. These are the cases in which the disruptive effect of workers' action is most clearly visible and in which a fertile soil exists for alternative proposals. But control of production and self-management has been an historical claim of the working class, finding the most direct expression in the cooperative movement. Producers' cooperatives, in particular – eliminating managerial control of the labour process and giving to each producer/owner equal representation and rights in the decision-making process – represented for Marx a real advance for workers and the 'practical demonstration that capital was not necessary as a mediator in social production' (Lebowitz, 2003: 89), and thus that there was an alternative to the existence of the wage/labour system. However, this emancipatory potential of the cooperative movement has always been the subject of debate, especially among Marxists. The core of the criticism pointed to the limits that market competition imposes on cooperatives since these 'naturally reproduce in all cases, in their present organisation, all the defects of the prevailing system, and must reproduce them' (Marx, 1981: 571). Following from this, Rosa Luxemburg underlined the dual face of cooperatives which were, as small islands of socialism in a sea of capitalism, unable to keep unaltered the democratic principles of their organizations within the market economy. From a revolutionary perspective, cooperatives were then not able to offer a stable, alternative solution. This negative view has long dominated among Marxist writers. Mandel's outright rejection of any revolutionary strategy based on factory occupation and self-management has probably represented the most extreme example of this view (1970, 1974).

By contrast, more recent contributions, while recognizing the limits that even the most democratic experiences of self-managed cooperatives encounter in a capitalist market, have emphasized the importance, in a perspective of social change, of devising strategies for strengthening the role of producers' cooperatives. Thus, while Egan (1990), for instance, has stressed the importance of the existence of a radical self-organizing environment as a way to counteract the degenerating effects of market forces, Baldacchino (1990) has pointed to the need to build an institutional framework to actively promote and defend the democratic practice of self-managed workplaces. In a more reformist vein, other authors, while also acknowledging the limitations imposed by competition, have focused on the positive effects that the expansion of the cooperative sector can have on the market economy, in terms of both generalizing the diffusion of cooperative values (e.g. Mellor et al., 1988; Melnyk, 1985) and inspiring alternative forms of work organization (e.g. Cheney, 2002; Schneiberg et al., 2008).

Leaving aside for the moment the debate about the roles of cooperatives as agents of social change and the strategies that should be adopted in relation to this, what all critical works have certainly underlined is that competition effectively distorts the democratic practices and values adopted by workers in self-managed or cooperative workplaces. What all these experiences show is that there are practical, tangible situations in which market forces influence workers' control and democratic decisions about production, creating a divergence between workers' independent will and existing structural conditions. To emphasize the existence of this distortive dynamic, and how through this the market logic is reasserted, is particularly important in the analysis of cases of self-management because it warns against explanations of changes based exclusively on workers' subjective attitudes. In this sense, independent workers' control and democratic decision-making in self-managed workplaces is weakened not just because workers are, for instance, culturally prone to delegate functions or obey orders. There are material, objective, tangible pressures related to the everyday business of the self-managed company that drive decisions towards centralization and delegation. Similarly, even in those cases in which workers have developed a collective consciousness of the distortive effects of the market on their organization, they will still need to face material obstacles and overcome barriers to assert their own will and control on the organization. To put this in Marxist terms, while workers in the sphere of production can freely and democratically take decisions about the life of their organization – when buying raw materials and resources, selling the outcome of their production or securing their families reproduction (i.e. when they engage in the sphere of circulation) – they will remain exposed to a system based on factors over which they have no, or scarce, control (prices, crisis, offer and demand).

As developed in greater detail elsewhere with reference to the recent cases of factory occupations and self-management in Argentina (Atzeni and Ghigliani, 2007), the pressure of competition can be detected in different forms and at different levels of analysis. It certainly manifests itself in the form of time constraints on the democratic decision-making processes adopted by workers. Delivery deadlines fixed by clients, a quick answer to catch a business opportunity, extended working shifts imposed by the lack of capital – all represent concrete obstacles to the democratic participation of workers in the everyday management of the organization. This democratic deficit leads then to a tendency to delegate and overall to a centralization of decisions. The same time constraints affect the possibility of changes in the labour process. Job rotation – a practice to which many workers would aspire – requires time and resources to retrain workers, but this is in conflict with the need to produce on time and at the required quality level. As a consequence the separation between manual/productive and intellectual/directive work is reinforced. On a different level, labour market competition for skilled workers threatens the equal-salary policy which was adopted by workers at the beginning of their experiences to strengthen solidarity and cooperative values.

Notwithstanding these limitations, the example of the Argentinean self-managed workplaces shows important alternative practices. Favoured by the elimination of managerial/supervision posts and by the central role of workers in the decision-making process, the system of control has been changed and the labour process decentralized. Rather than the top-down style of capitalist companies, workers organize production by communicating through formal and informal channels and this they do throughout the production process. Cooperation rather than imposition seems to be the main motive used to solve problems in a less authoritarian environment dominated by shared responsibility, and in which workers feel empowered and effectively participate in, even if with important limitations, the decision-making process.

The chapters in this book offer a range of examples of alternative practices and of the interplay between market forces, workers' collective efforts to establish a more empowering workplace and the social political contexts surrounding the different experiences. Subjective, cultural or context-based factors have in each case played a substantial role in shaping the outcome of workers' experiences with self-management and control of production. Thus in the famous case of Mondragon (Azkarraga, Cheney and Udaondo: Chapter 4 in this book), there is evidence that the establishment and consolidation of the cooperatives' network and their model of participation and social justice were rooted in traditional forms of governance and community development of the Basque region. Similarly, in the case of Tower Colliery (Smith, Arthur, Scott Cato and Keenoy: Chapter 3 in this book), a coal mine in South Wales, the existence of a strong trade union organization with a militant culture has been fundamental in defending the values and practices of workers' participation in the mine.

However important the combination of one or more of these factors might be in explaining the dynamics and outcomes of self-management in the different cases considered, in an attempt to generalize we have to emphasize, once more, how the existence of structural factors influences different experiences. The exposure to market competition and the effects this has on the organization of work and collective decision-making are unavoidable conditions which any self-managed experience needs, to a lesser or greater extent, to confront on a daily basis. This should then be considered as the point of departure for any future analysis.

## Alternative work organizations in perspective

The path towards the establishment and consolidation of a new democratic, enriching and participatory model of work organization is disseminated with ideological and material obstacles. For workers depending on a wage to live, who grew up in an education system organized to provide skills for a labour market and whose experience of work has always been within a capitalist labour process, it is difficult to imagine a system of work going beyond this and directly empowering them. For the same reasons, despite workers' attitudes towards works having often been negative, rarely have trade unions considered workers' self-management as a way to address these issues, preferring to concentrate on the negotiation of the price of labour. Equally rare – there are only a few cases – has been the role of state institutions in advancing a real participation of workers in the management of companies. Paradoxically, the idea of a more motivating and inclusive work environment, which has been promoted in many industries as a way to capture the knowledge and creativity of workers, has been central to the interests of capital rather than labour.

However, as we have seen, in the history of the labour movement these ideologically built obstacles have often been superseded – in coincidence with moments of local political turmoil, and economic and business uncertainty – by the spontaneous, transformative impetus of workers' struggles. The seizure of factories and the following attempts to produce under self-management have represented the practical alternative proposed by workers to overcome the capitalist organization of work. Shortlived and repressed for their anti-systemic nature, these experiences are the proof not just of the possibility of building a more democratic, empowering and thus alternative system of work but also of how this alternative is rooted in the contradictions of the capitalist system.

While ideological obstacles can temporarily be removed in the course of action, disclosing to workers the possibility of reinventing themselves and their work and then innovating in the sphere of production, material conditions are somehow more solid obstacles in the path towards the consolidation of an alternative system of work. The survival of worker-managed workplaces – as companies generating an income in the market – will in fact be increasingly dependent on the goals of efficiency, productivity and profitability, which will in turn put pressure on the democratic, participatory and more equalitarian values adopted by workers.

The history of the cooperative movement is rich in examples of how workers' genuine attempts to direct and take decisions on production have been transformed and shaped by the necessity to operate in a market. The degree of this transformation has been varied and some cooperatives values and practices, particularly those concerned with the organization of work, have been affected more than others. The size of the companies, the sector of activity, the geographical location, the exposure to the global market, the institutional support, and workers' ideological awareness and commitment to emancipatory values have all been important factors in determining the outcome of these transformations. But certainly the initial emancipatory power common to the majority of experiences of self-managed workers' cooperatives has tended to disappear and to be subsumed under the market logic.

This is a fundamental point of departure in assessing the future of alternative workers' controlled and directed production within the capitalist system. While it does not necessarily imply that all companies that are democratically managed will degenerate into a traditional, authoritarian and centralized capitalist organization, it clearly focuses on material obstacles to the establishment of alternative organizational forms.

Beyond these limits, writing about the experiences of workers' control and self-management tells us, however, of the great potential for transforming the workplace and societies these may have, and of the fears that these transformations have often provoked among the ruling classes. Far from any utopian view, workers have been able to provide real examples of more democratic, enriching and participatory organizations of work, but these have been the outcomes of real class confrontations rather than of smooth negotiations. To the extent that capitalism is an undemocratic but also contradictory system, alternative proposals for the future organization of work in production and the role of work in our societies will recurrently emerge but will also need to be recurrently defended.

## Chapter outlines

This collection continues with Chapter 2 by Alan Tuckman, who offers an historical overview of the factory occupations, workers' cooperatives and alternative productive plans that arose and developed in the UK during the 1970s. The chapter views all these attempts to control production in the more general struggle of workers and trade unions alongside the process of capital restructuring that dominated the decade. The 260 or more occupations and worker-controlled experiences that were registered during those years, from the work-in at the Upper Clyde Shipbuilders in 1971 until the beginning of the Thatcher government in 1979, were generally defensive actions to save jobs. However, in that particular moment of transition from Keynesian state-controlled, mixed economic management to market-oriented neo-liberalism, all these experiences have helped to pose self-management and alternative forms of work and production at the centre of political debate and strategy, as with the Lucas Aerospace plans for socially useful production and the Labour government-sponsored industrial cooperatives of 1975.

Chapter 3, by Russell Smith, Len Arthur, Molly Scott Cato and Tom Keenoy, presents the findings of longitudinal qualitative research on the significance, nature and limits of workers' control during the 13 years of productive life of the Tower Colliery in South Wales. By reconstructing the history of the mine – from the workers' buyout to the following establishment of the workers' cooperative and its operation as an industrial company in the highly regulated mining sector – the authors give a balanced view of the 'strategic tensions' between business commercial success, industrial efficiency and productivity, and the respect of the cooperative values associated with the worker-led buyout. This tension was visible in many areas of participation, work organization and decision-making, as, for instance, with the power ceded by the workers' collective to the whole range of technocrat expertise (finance, marketing, mine management) in the running of the company. However, the maintenance of a high level of democratic organization and collective control remained central during the life of the cooperative. The particularly effective ways through which workers constantly counterbalanced the potentially distortive effects of competing in the increasingly globalized energy market have led the authors to argue that Tower Colliery can be seen as an example of both an alternative, bottom-up form of work organization and a social movement. While apparently following the rules of business and not openly confronting the system, Tower was an example of what might be called a 'deviant mainstreaming' social movement.

Chapter 4, by Joseba Azkarraga, George Cheney and Ainara Udaondo, deals with the case of the Mondragon cooperatives in the Basque Country. The case of Mondragon has been studied many times over the year. It has been described as either a positive example of a progressive form of cooperativism, in which successful business in the market has been maintained together with the defence of social and democratic ideals, or as the case that most evidently shows the degenerative effects of market competition on cooperative values. Drawing on longitudinal extensive research on democratic participation and work organization at Mondragon, and on an analysis of a recent broad-based discussion and reflection process on the state of cooperative values, carried on within each Mondragon cooperative, the authors go beyond the simple disjunctive mentioned above. While the need to respond quickly to the market has reduced the room for effective participation and has installed the dominance of purely capitalist models of management, Mondragon remains a socially complex reality in which power is dispersed and alternative models of work and participation are continually discussed and re-arranged.

Chapter 5, by Camila Piñeiro Harnecker, shifts the focus from Europe to Latin America, analysing issues of democracy and solidarity in newly formed producers' cooperatives in Venezuela. As part of a process of social transformation, inscribed within the idea of 'the socialism of the XXI century' promoted during the presidency of Hugo Chavez, Venezuela is openly supporting workers' democratic and direct control of productive activities oriented to the satisfaction of social, rather than market, needs. This full-scale state intervention, which aims to empower producers and create a more socially and community-based economy, makes Venezuela a particularly relevant case for the study of workplace democracy and solidarity. What methods should be used to guarantee the existence of a substantial, participative type of democracy? How can the interests of producers be combined with those of the community? How can these principles be maintained in the context of competition? These are some of the questions the author addresses.

In Chapter 6, Marcelo Vieta draws on qualitative case study research to give an overview of the process of workers' recuperated and self-managed enterprises that developed in Argentina in coincidence with the severe economic crisis which led the country to declare default on the payment of its debts in December 2001. The case of Argentina neatly resumes both the transformative impact of worker-controlled production, and the constraints and challenges of this as an alternative within the capitalist market, as previously outlined in this chapter. Vieta's analysis helps us to delve into the complexity of these transformations and challenges. The passage from a capital owned to a self-managed enterprise has constantly faced workers with the need to innovate, experiment and, in this process, reinvent themselves and their relations with other fellow workers and the surrounding community. This 'learning by doing' process extended over time has created not just a development of workers' consciousness towards collectivist and solidarity values but the material representation of these values in the organization of the labour process and in the horizontality of the decision-making process.

In Chapter 7, Anita Hammer compares the organizational structure and power relations that exist in two cooperatives operating in India, one in the state of Kerala and the other in the state of Gujarat. As to the development of more democratic and participatory forms of management and the adoption of cooperative values and practices, the comparison shows evidence of important differences between the two cases that can be explained in terms of shifting institutional and mobilization contexts. The chapter argues that while institutions might be normally reproducing dominant social relations, they are at the same time spaces of political contestation highly sensible to social and political mobilization. Thus this dynamic can be seen as having a profound influence in shaping the internal organization of cooperatives, their viability in the market and the social values these defend.

Chapter 8, by Martino Ghielmi, is the result of in-depth ethnographic research on workers' self-help groups in the Nairobi slums. Self-help groups are associations formed by a group of workers around a common economic interest, which might vary from the manufacture of small commodities or the provision of a personal service to a source for financing. Depending on the activity, the group might share the means of production and cooperate in the labour process, coming close to a producers' cooperative, or simply associate in order to pursue a mutual interest. While the existence of these structures is evidence of the workers' self-organizing power and of the continuing possibility of organizing social and economic lives under different principles, the development of self-help groups is limited in many ways by cultural, political and economic factors. The chapter has been intentionally left till the end of the book since it somehow represents – with its focus on alternative forms of work and association in the informal economy – a deviation from traditional studies on workers' control and self-management, which have historically focused on the formal sector. However, this deviation should not be seen as clear cut. Indeed, what Ghielmi's study highlights, following other ethnographic studies of the urban informal sector, is the continuing interconnectedness and porosity existing between these two forms of employment. With the globalization of informality and precariousness, we might see the resurgence of forms of workers' associations and self-organization for production as a distinct possibility in the future.

## Notes

1. This cannot be said for a stream of research that, while originating in the labour process tradition, has shifted away from any concern with structural aspects of work, interpreting workplace relations exclusively from the lens of subjectivist, contingent perspectives. See, for instance, Willmott (1990) in Knights and Willmott Labour Process Theory.
2. From these multiple forms of workers' subordination, Van der Linden draws important conclusions with regard to the concept of the working class. They are not discussed here, however, since they are not directly relevant to the issues raised in the book.

## References

Atzeni, M. (2010), *Workplace Conflict: Mobilization and Solidarity in Argentina*, Basingstoke, Palgrave Macmillan.

Atzeni, M. and Ghigliani, P. (2007), Labour process and decision making in factories under workers' self-managment: Empirical evidence from Argentina, *Work, Employment and Society*, 21:4, 653–672.

Baldacchino, G. (1990), A war of position: Ideas on strategies for workers cooperative development, *Economic and Industrial Democracy*, 11:4, 463–482.

Bayat, A. (1991), *Work, Politics and Power an International Perspective on Workers' Control and Self-Management*, London, Zed Books.

Beynon, H. (1984), *Working for Ford*, Harmondsworth, London, Penguin Books.

Bolton, S. (2005), *Emotion Management in the Workplace*, Management, Work and Organisations, Basingstoke, Palgrave Macmillan.

Bolton, S. and Houlihan, M. (2009), Are we having fun yet? A consideration of workplace fun and engagement, *Employee Relations*, 31:6, 556–568.

Braverman, H. (1974), *Labor and Monopoly Capital*, New York, Monthly Review Press.

Burawoy, M. (1979), *Manufacturing Consent*, Chicago, University of Chicago Press.

Burawoy, M. (1985), *The Politics of Production. Factory Regimes under Capitalism and Socialism*, London, Verso.

Cheney, G. (2002), *Employee Participation Meets Market Pressure at Mondragon*, Ithaca, NY, Cornell University Press.

Cohen, G. A. (1983), The structure of proletarian unfreedom, reprinted in 1988 in a revised form in *History, Labour and Freedom*, Oxford, Clarendon Press.

Cohen, S. (1987), A labour process to nowhere, *New Left Review*, available at http://www.newleftreview.org/?view=229 (accessed 4 February 2012).

Cohen, S. (2006), *Ramparts of Resistance: Why Workers Lost Their Power and How to Get It Back*, London, Pluto Press.

Cohen, S. (2011), The red mole: Workers' councils as a means to revolutionary transformation, in *Ours to Master and to Own. Workers Control from the Commune to the Present*, edited by Ness, I. and Azzellini, D., Chicago, Haymarket Books.

Delbridge, R. (1998), *Life on the Line in Contemporary Manufacturing*, Oxford, Oxford University Press.

Edwards, P. (1986), *Conflict at Work, a Materialist Analysis*, Oxford, Basil Blackwell.

Edwards, P. and Scullion, H. (1982), *The Social Organisation of Industrial Conflict*, Oxford, Basil Blackwell.

Egan, D. (1990), Toward a Marxist theory of labor-managed firms: Breaking the degeneration thesis, *Review of Radical Political Economics*, 22:4, 67–86.

Elger, T. and Smith, C. (1994), *Global Japanisation? The Transnational Transformation of the Labour Process*, London, Routledge.

Elger, T. and Smith, C. (2005), *Assembling Work: Remaking Factories Regimes in Japanese Multinationals in Britain*, New York, Oxford University Press.

Fantasia, R. (1989), *Culture of Solidarity. Consciousness, Action and Contemporary American Workers*, Berkeley, University of California Press.

Guest, D. (2002), Human Resource Management, corporate performance and employee wellbeing: Building the worker into HRM, *The Journal of Industrial Relations*, 44:3, 335–358.

Hyman, R. (1975), *Industrial Relations, a Marxist Introduction*, London, Macmillan.

Hyman, R. (2006), Marxist thought and the analysis of work, in *Social Theory at Work*, edited by Korczynski, M., Hodson, R. and Edwards, P., Oxford, Oxford University Press.

Lebowitz, M. (2003), *Beyond Capital, Marx's Political Economy of the Working Class*, second edition, Basingstoke, Palgrave Macmillan.

Lebowitz, M. (2004), What keeps capitalism going?, *Monthly Review*, 56:2, available at http://monthlyreview.org/2004/06/01/what-keeps-capitalism-going (accessed 4 February 2012).

Linhart, R. (1981), *The Assembly Line*, Amherst, University of Massachusetts.

Lopez, H. S. (2010), Workers, managers, and customers triangles of power in work communities, *Work and Occupation*, 37:3, 251–271.

Kochan, T. A. and Osterman, P. (1994), *The Mutual Gains Enterprise: Forging a Winning Partnership Among Labour, Management and Government*, Cambridge, Harvard Business School Press.

Korczynski, M. (2002), *Human Resource Management in Service Work*, Basingstoke, Palgrave Macmillan.

Mandel, E. (1970), Self-management: Dangers and possibilities, *International*, 2:4, 3–9.

Mandel, E. (1974), *Control Obrero, Consejos Obreros, Autogestion*, Mexico, Ediciones Era.

Marx, K. (1976), *Capital*. volume 1, London, Penguin Books.

Marx, K. (1981), *Capital*. volume 3, London, Penguin Books.

Mellor, M., Hannah, J. and Stirling, J. (1988), *Worker Co-Operatives in Theory and Practice*, Milton Keynes, Open University Press.

Melnyk, G. (1985), *The Search for Community, from Utopia to a Cooperative Society*, Montreal-Buffalo, Black Rose Books.

Mollona, M. (2009), *An Ethnography of Industrial Work and Politics*, New York, Oxford, Berghahn Books.

Ness, I. and Azzellini, D. (2011), *Ours to Master and to Own. Workers Control from the Commune to the Present*, Chicago, Haymarket Books.

Pink, D. H. (2011), *The Surprising Truth of What Motivates Us*, New York, Riverhead Books.

Schneiberg, M., King, M. and Smith, T. (2008), Social movements and organizational form: Cooperative alternatives to corporations in the American insurance, dairy, and grain industries, *American Sociological Review*, 73:4, 635–667.

Sherman, R. (2007), *Class Acts: Service and Inequality in Luxury Hotels*, Berkeley, University of California Press.

Silver, B. (2003), *Forces of Labour, Workers Movement and Globalisation since 1870*, Cambridge, Cambridge University Press.

Spencer, D. (2000), Braverman and the contribution of labour process analysis to the critique of capitalist production, twenty-five years on, *Work, Employment and Society*, 14:2, 223–243.

Spencer, D. (2009), *The Political Economy of Work*, Abingdon, Routledge.

Taylor, M. (2008), *Global Economy Contested: Power and Conflict Across the International Division of Labour*, London and New York, Routledge.

Taylor, P. and Bain, P. (2005), India calling to the far away towns the call center labour process and globalisation, *Work Employment & Society*, 19:2, 261–282.

Thompson, P. (1989), *The Nature of Work*, second edition, Basingstoke, Macmillan.

Thompson, P. and Smith, C. (2010), *Working Life: Reviewing Labour Process Analysis*, Basingstoke, Palgrave Macmillan.

Tinker, T. (2002), Spectres of Marx and Braverman in the twilight of postmodernist labour process research, *Work Employment & Society,* 16:2, 251–281.

Turner, C. (1995), *Japanese Workers in Protest: An Ethnography of Consciousness and Experience*, Berkeley, University of California Press.

Van der Linden, M. (2008), *Workers of the World, Essays Toward a Global Labour History*, Leiden, Brill.

Warhurst, C., Grugulis, I. and Keep, E. (2004), *The Skills That Matter*, Basingstoke, Palgrave Macmillan.

Willmott, H. D. (1990), Subjectivity and the dialectics of praxis: Opening up the core of labour process analysis in *Labour Process Theory*, edited by Knights, D. and Willmott, H., London, Macmillan.

# 2
# Factory Occupation, Workers' Cooperatives and Alternative Production: Lessons from Britain in the 1970s

*Alan Tuckman*

## Introduction

In 1971, following government withdrawal of financial support for the industry, shop stewards announced that they had taken over control of the gatehouses at the four Upper Clyde Shipyards in Glasgow, initiating a work-in. The work-in, as the British Cabinet at the time feared (CM-71, 12 October 1971), served as a catalyst for a wave of workplace occupations – work-ins and sit-ins – by UK workers (Coates, 1981; Sherry 2010). The Upper Clyde Shipbuilders (UCS) proved the inspiration for more than 260[1] further occupations in the following decade, used by workers against the impact of capital restructuring. This capital restructuring, as well as bringing redundancy and insecurity to the labour market, was to represent a major shift in hegemony which saw the decline of traditional industry – and traditional labour organization – alongside the emergence of a more assertive market ideology of neo-liberalism, replacing the idea of a Keynesian economic management of a mixed economy (e.g. Gamble, 1988, 2009). The focus of this chapter will be these occupations staged by workers in reaction and resistance to closures and redundancies; the impact on them of capital restructuring; and particularly the alternative they began to pose, in workers' control and alternative plans, to the increasingly neo-liberal ideology of the restructuring. Instead of the intensified commodification and the increased subordination to the exigencies of the market, this alternative began to articulate an economy based around social utility.

The occupations in Britain in the decade following the work-in at UCS in 1971 were a defensive reaction by workers to the demands of capitalism and could not, compared, for instance, with those in Italy in 1920 (Spriano, 1975; Mason, 2008), be considered a revolutionary threat. However, they did challenge capitalist production, posing debate and experimentation in alternative forms of organization and ownership. Occupation represents the denial of the rationale of capital and the reassertion of labour with workers taking command, if only temporarily, of the means of production. As such, they are not only part of the repertoire of action available to workers to oppose capital but also the germ of an alternative society based around a self-managed economy organized by workers' councils (Gramsci, 1977; Castoriadis, 1988; Pannekoek, 2003).

This chapter commences with a consideration of the context of the labour movement and the post-war consensus in Britain, before considering the wave of occupations. The conditions under which the occupation movement developed are addressed, placing it within and integral to the shifting hegemony of the 1970s. Contrary to the orthodox image of a labour movement engaged in mindless militancy, building on the existing strong workplace organization, workers in the 1970s were able to establish cooperatives and alternative corporate plans, attracting – although briefly – the support of the government for an alternative to redundancy and unemployment. Next, this chapter examines the debate around ownership, especially around workers' cooperatives and workers' plans. These two concerns remained sediment as occupations, and the organized labour movement which generated it went into decline.

## The break-up of political consensus in Britain

By the early 1960s the post-war political consensus in Britain – based around industrial expansion and economic growth, and underpinning greater consumer affluence – was collapsing. While the economy had been expanding, it was at a far slower rate than its industrial competitors. Not only was there increasing foreign competition, with wider penetration of foreign manufacturers into domestic markets and decline of overseas markets, but there was chronic underinvestment, with home manufacture increasingly dependent on the penetration of multinational capital or state aid. The Macmillan Conservative government underlined these problems with the introduction of the National Economic Development Council, containing trade union as well as state and employer representation, to plan economic and industrial development. The Wilson Labour government, taking office in 1964, launched its own more explicit modernization programme which attempted to link with the explosion of popular culture in the wake of The Beatles. The Wilson programme included the extension of industrial and economic planning – launching Britain into 'the white heat of technological revolution' – by attempting a rationalization of key industries to meet international competition. Principally this was to be attempted through the Industrial Reorganisation Corporation (IRC), whose purpose was 'to promote structural change which will improve the efficiency and profitability of British industry' (Hansard, 1968). As we shall see, the IRC made a significant impact with its attempt to rationalize British industrial capital. It brought together large conglomerates which sought to rationalize multi-site operations to achieve their promised economies of scale, creating also large-scale closures and redundancies in establishments often with traditions of strong workplace union organization, and, as such, underpin a growing ambivalence to the state acting as a vehicle for job protection and employment security. This mature labour movement then confronted new circumstances. Full employment of the post-war years was increasingly giving way to heightened job insecurity – even for employees of the state and nationalized industries – of previously paternalistic private sector companies. This appeared most pronounced in companies subject to the rationalization of the IRC.

By the late 1960s there were growing criticisms, from both the left and the right, of the workings of industrial renewal and economic policy. This became fractured by a run on sterling and the government decision, when exchange rates were still fixed, to devalue the pound. Framing their future election strategy, the Conservative opposition formulated a 'quiet revolution' (Bruce-Gardyne, 1974), arguing that the market ought to operate to allow failing companies to fail. The 'lame ducks' of the economy were not to be given state support and so were allowed to collapse. Unemployment was growing and approaching one million, a number considered politically unsustainable. One of the central roles of government, in this environment, was to maintain full employment. Not only this but the very cost of unemployment became a significant draw on the Exchequer. One of the measures introduced by the Wilson government was the Redundancy Payments Act (1965), which, still rooted in the dominant ideology of Keynesianism, sought to assist the mobility of workers made redundant in declining areas in finding work elsewhere. As Fryer (1973) has indicated, this quickly expressed itself not as enhancing mobility but as buying workers out of established jobs. As we shall see, the redundancy payment – in the commodification of jobs – also became the primary focus of trade union negotiations when confronted with job losses, not the mobilization of resistance.

Trade unions were growing in membership, as well as influence, in the new corporate state (Crouch, 1977; Panitch, 1976). Trade union officers were drawn into the state planning apparatus as labour representatives although, simultaneously, there was also a shift to workplace organization with shop stewards acting as unofficial representatives. While basic terms and conditions may have been subject to national bargaining between employers' organizations and full-time officers of trade unions, these were now enhanced or superseded by local bargaining by shop stewards. With the increased significance of multi-plant conglomerates, shop stewards were increasingly establishing cross-site combines for communication and to coordinate strategy.

While appearing as the promoters of conflict within the workplace in popular imagery, the shop steward system had, in reality, minimized open dispute by bargaining a plethora of 'plus payments'. However, such developments were essentially informal arrangements outside of formal trade union and collective bargaining, and opposed by trade union officialdom as much as by employers. An important corollary of the rise of shop stewards was the development of training courses principally emerging in the extra-mural departments of universities. Growing rather haphazardly – and including recruitment, organizing and bargaining skills – the curriculum was sometimes renegotiated annually with tutors to address broader industrial and economic issues and policy. Not only were national officials of trade unions drawn into planning processes of the increasingly corporatist state, but shop stewards were also becoming articulate in representing the interests of the shop floor beyond the immediate terms and conditions of employment. However, they were often encumbered by the bureaucratic framework of trade union and collective bargaining.

It was not only Labour and Conservative Party support which increasingly fractured in the 1960s. The Communist Party had sustained a strong base in the post-war trade unions, but it was hit first by the Khrushchev denunciation of Stalin and then by the invasion of Hungary in 1956, which had seen the revival of workers' councils as a focus for the organization of popular revolt (Anderson, 1964; Lomax, 1976, 1980). A 'new left' began to emerge, exploring alternative models of socialism. Some explored the potential of 'self-management' of the post-war Yugoslav regime. Drawing on this experience, as well as past experience of the workplace organization, this became the touchstone for arguing the need for a return to a concern with 'workers' control'. In an article published in *New Left Review* in 1964 Tony Topham argued that

> the quantitive growth of the shop stewards' strength in industry, the causes and numbers of strikes, (particularly local, spontaneous strikes) are significant factors, and that the whole area of conflict surrounding the rôle of the shop steward is likely to intensify in the near future...whilst the Left's main task should be to assist at the birth of articulate and explicit demands for control at shop-floor level, we must insist upon the need to generalize these outwards to embrace the whole framework of social, economic and political decision-making.
>
> (1964: 4)

A series of conferences were organized involving trade union officers, shop stewards and other activists and academics. In 1968 the Institute for Workers' Control (IWC) was founded. While it is a mistake to generalize about an IWC position or line (Barratt Brown et al., 1975) – with their publications covering an eclectic range of areas and perspectives (Hyman, 1974) – the central academic figures promoted a view of workers' control as 'encroachment' by organized labour into managerial prerogative. While promoting the slogan of 'open the books' (Barratt Brown, 1968), the IWC advocated the development of control bargaining with trade unions, and particularly shop stewards, building confidence and control by encroaching on managerial prerogative into non-remuneration areas around working conditions and work rate. By the late 1960s the IWC had initiated a number of industrial working groups, around the docks, the steel industry and elsewhere, with an early collection of proposals entitled *Can the Workers Run Industry?* (Coates, 1968; see also Topham, 1967). These key figures in the movement were principally engaged in trade union education and plans, and discussion often emerged from classes run for shop stewards in these industries.

With unemployment rising towards a million, blamed largely on closures, there was speculation about an escalation of industrial action to challenge closures. Increasing insecurity in the labour market drew inspiration from the recent experience of student sit-ins and the occupations in France. In February 1969 the BBC transmitted a play, *The Big*

*Flame*, directed by Ken Loach, which portrayed an occupation of the Liverpool docks.

## The occupation in Britain

On 30 July 1971, press waiting at the gates of the UCS heard Jimmy Reid, chair of the shop stewards committee at the yards in Glasgow, announce:

> the first campaign of its kind in trade unionism. [The yard workers]...are not going on strike. We are not even having a sit-in strike. We are taking over the yards because we refuse to accept that faceless men can make these decisions. We are not strikers. We are responsible people and we will conduct ourselves with dignity and discipline. We want to work. We are not wild cats.
>
> (*BBC News* 30 July 1971, cited in McGill, 1973)

The reason for the announcement was the ending of financial support from the government, putting the yards formally into bankruptcy and into the hands of a receiver, whose role was to realize any assets for creditors. The very presence of the press at the gates indicates their anticipation that the shop stewards were to stage some opposition to the closure. However, Reid had distanced the action from a sit-in – a tactic still associated with student action. The words of Reid's statement seemed to infer that shop stewards were to take over the management of the yards. For the following 18 months, the 'work-in' essentially maintained a system of dual power with the receiver's office. The action proved the focal inspiration for over 260 worker occupations in Britain during the following decade. The occupation movement in Britain has been most strongly associated with UCS, as well as with three plants facing closure that transformed into cooperatives – the three Benn cooperatives (Coates, 1976). However, these were far from typical of the more than 260 occupations that occurred in the decade following UCS.

The context of strongly organized and potentially militant workplaces, as well as increased currency of workers' control ideas, meant that there was anticipation that some major resistance to large-scale redundancy was imminent. However, while the occupations in Britain following the UCS work-in were principally associated with large-scale closures of the period, and most of the more protracted occupations were contesting closure, many involved more limited challenges to redundancies or dismissals, or to threat of lock-out. Many tactics in industrial disputes involve workers remaining in the workplace occupation. The very development of a spontaneous dispute may mean some period of uncertainty with the workforce stopping work but not leaving the workplace. While the eviction of management is evidence of worker occupation, as for instance at UCS, it is not a condition.

## In the shadow of UCS

Resistance to closure was anticipated and it was clear in the circumstances that the more traditional industrial action – a withdrawal of labour – would run the risk of precipitating the very outcome being resisted. When in 1969, following the state-sponsored rationalization of the electronics and electrical power conglomerate GEC-AEI (Anti-Report, 1972), the company announced closure at three of its Merseyside plants, shop stewards agreed to resist with occupation. However, with concerns about criminal prosecution – the outcome of Loach's dramatic *Big Flame* – and possible withdrawal of redundancy payments, the action did not materialize (IWC, 1969; Newens, 1969; Chadwick, 1970; Schubert, 1970). It was not until 1971 that the flame was lit by the occupation at UCS, a company created through state intervention, merging civil and naval shipyards on the River Clyde. Government rejection when the company approached for continuing financial support led to threats of redundancies to the workforce. Shop stewards discussed some form of occupation and, when redundancies were announced, they appeared to take control of the yards. Rather than the stewards controlling the yards, 'dual powers' existed for the following 18 months between the shop stewards trying to keep employment and the receiver appointed to realize the capital assets. While the action can only tenuously be defined as an occupation, the UCS work-in mobilized considerable support. Mass demonstrations were held through the streets of Glasgow which attracted senior Labour politicians, most notably their Industry spokesperson Tony Benn, along with trade union leaders. The government worried about any possible social unrest if they attempted to evict the work-in or bar access. Lasting for 18 months, the UCS dispute was the very act of resistance that had an impact on the UK labour movement and particularly in mobilizing occupation.

Perhaps the first incident typical of the UK occupations in the 1970s was at a Plessey plant, just a short distance from Glasgow on the River

Clyde, which started about a month after the work-in at UCS. The work-force at this armament plant had been run down and, when the last 250 workers were told to report to collect their remaining wages, rather than attend for work they jumped the locked gate. The Plessey occupation was to last four months until a deal was reached for a takeover which protected 70 of the jobs.

By the end of the year occupations had spread further south to steel and engineering works around South Yorkshire and into Wales – all resisting redundancies. While occupation was sometimes suggested as resistance to impending closures the actual action tended to be spontaneous. The occupations also tended to be acts of relative desperation at job loss, with no real plan for the future beyond some hope that another owner might be found.

### The Manchester engineers

In early 1972 workers at Bredbury Steelworks took over the plant near Manchester, setting a pattern for about 50 further occupations in the engineering industry. Basic pay and conditions in the industry were determined in long-term agreements between the Engineering Employers Federation (EEF) and the Confederation of Shipbuilding and Engineering Unions (Confed), constituted of the 31 trade unions with members in the industry. However, workplace bargaining had become increasingly important, with shop stewards negotiating local deals which could mean pay of double this in some plants. The union claim was for £25 a week for skilled workers, a 35-hour week and an extra week of holidays – the latter two items as a strategy to counter rising unemployment. When the claim was ruled out by the employer side the unions moved the campaign to the regions.

The Manchester region, perhaps the best organized and most militant, put forward national demands on a plant-by-plant basis. Submission of the claim was often accompanied by the imposition of sanctions – an overtime ban, work-to-rule and so on – to which some employers responded with the threat of lock-out (Chadwick, 1973). Commentators have tended to see the escalation of the dispute into occupation of about 30 plants in the region as being promoted by the integration of the left, predominantly Communist as well as a few Socialist Worker shop stewards and union officials (Mills, 1974; Darlington and Lyddon, 2001). However, it was the organization and discipline of the EEF which targeted a challenge at particular plants where there were, as they saw it, 'communist stewards'. The President of the EEF stressed to employers:

the importance of standing firm in this situation. There's little doubt that a policy of militant plant bargaining... [was] intended to expose the industry to a free-for-all in wages and conditions claims. If the unions are out to test the fibre of our unity, we should leave them in no doubt as to its durability.

(1972)

In plants with shop floor representatives more amenable to compromise with the EEF position the workforce was rewarded with offers of pay increases beyond the national claim but without any other benefits. At Mather and Platts, with a moderate union organization, the offer accepted was for a £5.50 a week increase, significantly more than the national claim of around £4.00, but without any concessions on holidays or hours. While the regions' trade union strategy had been to move to plants and fragment any action the EEF 'took a leaf out of the trade union book' and maintained unity and discipline among its membership, holding the Federation line that plant settlements should only be reached on pay. Most of the settlements that the union claimed had been made with companies outside of the EEF. The few members of the EEF who made agreements also covering holiday and working hours faced expulsion. Not only was this an attack on militant shop stewards, and a support of what the EEF saw as the more acceptable face of workplace representation, it also highlighted what was to become the initial neo-liberal position on bargaining. Collective bargaining should be premised on what a company could afford in the relative market situation of the company rather than the extraneous cost of living and the subsistence of their workers.

By April 1972 occupations spread to the Sheffield region where unions also put in a 'carbon copy claim'; employers at two plants threatened to withhold pay in retaliation to trade union sanctions. Elsewhere, some long-standing grievances gelled with the national claim escalating in a similar way. Occupations around the national engineering claim continued into August. However, the Manchester shop stewards dropped opposition to cash-only settlements, and gradually the national union imposed its own discipline over disputes which had not had explicit union sanction. The EEF loosened its opposition to settlements, including some concession on hours and holidays. In practice the unions, nationally or regionally, never had the control over the spread and development of the occupations. Regional solidarity of the

Manchester EEF, alongside some rogue employers willing to confront their employees over sanctions, dictated the dynamics of the dispute.

## Towards an alternative

The Engineering industry occupations highlight the tensions between not just employers and employees but also among shop stewards, the lay workplace representation and the official union structure. While the shop steward organization gave the organizational foundation for occupation, a capacity being challenged in engineering, this was also to be the basis of the articulation – if pragmatic – to the increasing rationalization of an alternative to the demands of capital. The most significant occupations remained those in response to closure and, in these circumstances, employees needed to formulate their own alternative. In the circumstances, employee representatives had a number of possibilities of either mobilization against closure or negotiation of the terms of redundancy. If closure was resisted, and this tended to be the action of a small proportion of the redundant workforce, they were drawn into formulating their own case. Some sought a new owner for the enterprise, attempting to present a going concern with perhaps a reduced workforce. The reduced workforce usually equated to the number engaged in occupation. In some larger and often strategic enterprises there were sometimes arguments for nationalization. However, the experience of nationalized industries and of the state engagement in the rationalization of industry was increasingly being challenged by arguments from socialists as well as neo-liberals. In this context there was some move towards experimenting, if at first pragmatically, with workers' cooperatives.

Three early cases – Sexton, Son and Everard; Fisher Bendix; and Briant Colour Printing – indicate the range of problems faced by occupations, as well as solutions being explored by workers. In February 1972 Sexton, Son and Everard announced bankruptcy and closure of their factories in East Anglia, which manufactured shoes, making 700 workers redundant. A meeting of the employees voted to contest the closure by means of occupation so they could control remaining machinery and stock (Wajcman, 1983). Before the closure the company was bought by a local developer who guaranteed 500 of the jobs. But among those still to lose their jobs were 45 women workers at a satellite factory in Fakenham. They decided to go ahead with occupation when the first of the women lost their jobs. They had machinery and scraps of leather available, later supplemented by purchases of materials, from which they could produce bags and other leather items for sale locally with the label

*Fakenham Occupation Workers.* The women began to contemplate the prospect of working for themselves in a workers' cooperative. At Briant Colour Printing, workers occupied to resist closure of their East London plant. This became a work-in when occupying workers gained contracts for printing, often for left wing or labour movement organizations. Members of this work-in also seemed to have addressed the possibility of establishing a workers' cooperative but rejected the idea (Inside Story, 1973). Mass pickets were held when the plant was threatened with eviction and, eventually, a new owner was found. However, only 14 weeks after the takeover the plant was again closed.

Fisher Bendix, a motor components plant near Liverpool, had diversified into a range of other products following changes in ownership. In early 1972 there was further talk of redundancies and the shop stewards had been in contact with UCS and Plessey as well as the stewards at the nearby Merseyside plant of GEC-AEI, which had considered occupation in 1969 (see Solidarity, 1972; Clarke, 1974; Eccles, 1981). While there had been discussion of possible resistance to redundancies, the storming of a meeting and eviction of management (with the gates welded shut by the workers taking occupation) was spontaneous and unplanned. Finally, with the intervention of Harold Wilson, the local Member of Parliament and Leader of the Opposition, a new owner was found although, as it turned out, not offering any long-term security for the plant or workforce.

A significant turn towards cooperatives came with the restructuring of the British motorcycle industry. In the 1950s around 70 per cent of the world's production of motorcycles had been in Britain (Smith, 1981); now the industry itself was under threat. This was anticipated as preceding an assault on the far more significant automobile industry, an industry which itself would soon come under state ownership. The motorcycle industry had gone through a series of mergers creating Norton Villiers Triumph (NVT). Plans agreed between the company and the Department of Industry were to reduce the remaining three plants to two – at Small Heath in Birmingham and at Wolverhampton – with a closure of the BSA-Triumph plant at Meriden. The Department of Industry announced that NVT would be receiving £4.8 million under the terms of the 1972 Industry Bill, a bill allowing state aid to industry introduced partly in response to the UCS crisis (see page 37).

In September 1973 it was announced that the Meriden plant would be closed with work transferred to either the Small Heath or Wolverhampton plants; 1,750 workers would be made redundant. The Meriden workforce imposed an embargo on the movement of the plant and motorcycles and, when details of the closure were announced, the workforce evicted the management and continued producing Norton motorcycles until parts ran out and the insurance cover was withdrawn. The work-in became a sit-in which was to last for over a year, holding stock and machinery that NVT wanted to move to another plant. The suggestion was made that the workforce might buy the plant, some production could be subcontracted to them by NVT and that Meriden may become a workers' cooperative. This was originally to be financed by approximately £1 million in redundancy pay from the workforce themselves with possibly a national subscription to provide the rest. The initial idea was agreed to 'readily' by NVT (1974: 10) who saw this as a means of disposing of assets. They were also interested in an end to the occupation which was obstructing the movement of completed motorcycles, spares and – probably more important – drawings and machine tools. After four weeks the negotiations broke down. Government and NVT plans still revolved around saving two plants, Small Heath and Wolverhampton, with the closure of Meriden. NVT wanted the release of resources in Meriden, blockaded by the occupation.

## Political changes

The UCS work-in and the occupation movement began to have an impact. The Heath government, which had entered office with a neo-liberal policy, was moved to make a 'U-turn'. A new Industry Act was introduced in 1972 allowing intervention to support industry in deprived areas or where it was considered in the national interest. Powers were given to the Secretary of State for Industry to award up to £5 million assistance to an individual enterprise; any assistance beyond this needed a vote in parliament. As well as the nationalization of Rolls Royce to avoid bankruptcy of this flagship company, government help was given to UCS to stage a survival plan. One of the yards was sold for the construction of oil rigs, and the government contributed grants worth £6 million. The remaining yards were re-organized, receiving £35 million in government aid – a sum considerably more than they had previously been refused.

The economic situation was deteriorating, with unemployment continuing to rise while inflation was moving into double figures. The government introduced pay restraint, holding down wages across the economy. The economy was hit by the oil crisis in 1973 and, at the same time, the miners threatened their second national strike in two years. Further emergency measures were introduced to save power, including a three-day working week. Finally, in 1974, Heath called an election around the issue of 'Who Governs Britain?' The obvious inference was that power was slipping towards organized labour.

On 4 March 1974 Labour took office as a minority government, with policies of establishing a National Enterprise Board to manage and extend public enterprise; the establishment of planning agreements agreed between management, unions and government for larger companies; and for extension of industrial democracy. The architect of the industrial policy was to be Tony Benn. Benn had played an active role within the IWC, as well as in the campaign around the UCS work-in, and sought a new model of state enterprise alongside greater involvement of workers in 'bottom-up' decision making (e.g. Benn, 1979). Benn became Secretary of State for Industry in the incoming Wilson government.

## The heyday of occupation

### The Benn cooperatives

In the limbo of the election period, as a means of freeing machines, spares, company records and 'the contents of the engineering department', NVT came to an agreement with the Meriden occupation. This would allow the prospective cooperative assets of between £2 and £7 million, from a shopping list compiled by the company, as long as evidence of their ability to pay was provided before the end of March (NVT, 1974). When Benn arrived at the Department of Industry this plan was on his desk. Previously the government assistance to the motorcycle industry had been directed at NVT itself but Benn now encouraged the Meriden workforce to formalize their plans for a workers' cooperative into an application to the Department of Industry for assistance under the 1972 Industry Act. The consequences of what had previously been an attempt at state intervention to rationalize the motorcycle industry around two factories, and the third's resistance to this solution, was then turned into an attempt at a rescue of all three plants.

Benn facilitated rapid assistance to the Meriden workforce. It set up as a separate entity so that it could qualify for £4.96 million aid – a figure strategically within Benn's independent authority as Secretary of State for Industry under the Conservatives 1972 Industry Bill. This was awarded separately from the assistance that NVT had already received under the previous government. This not only allowed the establishment of the cooperative but also allowed the release of the machine tools and plans the NVT had been waiting for. It also gave the NVT a ready buyer for the factory and excess plant. It also meant the creation of, essentially, a sub-contractor to produce the Triumph Bonneville motorcycle.

The Meriden and NVT experience had a profound effect on Benn's perspective within the Department of Industry. It seemed that, through the discovery of the workers' cooperative (reminiscent of the roots of Labour radicalism), he had resolved the paradox between extending 'socialization' of the economy with commitment to extending industrial democracy. The workers' cooperative, which the Meriden workers had proposed, seemed the answer; especially when similar plans were forwarded from Beaverbrook newspapers in Glasgow. This was to allow the establishment of a newspaper, *The Scottish Daily News*, which was run for a few months as a workers' cooperative. Other groups of workers approached Benn directly. The workers at Fisher Bendix, by then IPC, were again facing closure and sought assistance. Benn encouraged them to put forward their own business plan to support this and advised them to consider establishing a cooperative.

## Alternative plans

As well as the organization of production, debate emerged concerning the product itself, although again initially pragmatically. It was one thing to argue the social case for continuing employment – whether remaining in private ownership, as a workers' cooperative, or as a nationalized enterprise – but practical as well as ethical arguments were being raised by workers concerning the outcome of their labour. The continuation of printing at Briant Colour Printing and of leatherwork at the Fakenham work-ins gave the workers control over their product, although only as a short-term solution. The long-term future for the workers was not addressed.

Lucas was a large corporation, expanded through merger and takeover. Its operation ranged across automotive, electronic and aerospace industries (see CIS Anti-Report, n.d.). Workers at its diesel division, company name could be expanded to "CAV Ltd", staged a number of occupations resisting redundancy as an outcome of corporate rationalization. Lucas Aerospace was also proposing redundancies and plant closures following the bankruptcy of Rolls Royce over the RB211 engine for Boeing – for which Lucas was a supplier. The company reduced the workforce by around 19 per cent within six months of the announcement, while the level of production remained the same (CIS Anti-Report, n.d.; Lucas Aerospace Annual Survey cited in Wainwright and Elliott, 1982: 22).

While the redundancies at Lucas Aerospace impacted all the factories in the group, one in particular had been earmarked by management for closure. The plant in Willesden in North West London had been the company headquarters. By this stage shop stewards across the company were attempting to organize a combine committee across the 17 sites of Lucas Aerospace Division. However, they were as yet not in a position to organize around this closure which was left to the Willesden workforce alone. However, after a six-month struggle, including a short occupation, management were able to remove machinery and tear down the roof. The dispute, which was initially responsible for mobilizing the Lucas Aerospace Combine Shop Stewards' Committee (LACSSC), was a 13-week strike, again with an initial occupation, at their Burnley plant around the 1972 engineering dispute. After one week of trade union sanctions, management turned off the power to the plant and workers occupied. Within a few weeks the occupation was transformed into a strike, continuing for a further four weeks sustained by a hardship fund organized by the LACSSC.

With concern about these job losses, and how this might be alleviated by inclusion in government proposed nationalization of aerospace, the LACSSC met with Benn at the Department of Industry. He asked them to produce their own plans for preserving jobs (see Wainwright and Elliott, 1982). Lucas Aerospace, as a component supplier and not engaged in final assembly of aircraft, was not included in the nationalization plans. However, Benn suggested to the delegation of shop stewards meeting at his office to put forward their own plans for the future of Lucas Aerospace. Wainwright and Elliott (1982), in their study of the Lucas Plan, describe the meeting with Benn, which lasted for two and a half hours, as 'unprecedented' (83). Not only was the meeting criticized by the Secretary of States' own Senior Civil Servants but was also frowned on by the trade unions, who considered that all formal engagement with government should be with officials of the Confed or the affiliated unions rather than with shop stewards and unofficial bodies.

The critique of the UCS closure tended towards emphasizing the cost of closure (Murray, 1972), with the implication of large-scale redundancy outbalancing a rescue with the IWC promoting a 'social audit' (IWC, n.d.). At Lucas Aerospace, also partially within the arms industry, members of the Shop Stewards' Combine Committee (LASSC) carried out a detailed survey of the capacities and working practices across the company. Shop stewards at each of the aerospace plants were asked 'How could the plant be run by the workforce itself?' and if there were any 'socially useful products' they might manufacture (Wainwright and Elliott, 1982: 88–89). In this attempt at turning 'swords to ploughshares', they raised 150 proposed products. These included combined heat pumps and hydrogen fuel cells, both suggested in an early engagement with energy reduction alongside the production of kidney dialysis machines, which had been produced by the company, and a new design of artificial limb (Elliott, 1977; LACSSC, 1978). Not only did their plan list a range of 'socially useful products' they also articulated a challenge to capitalist production based around what Mike Cooley, their Chair later argued, drew on 'four major contradictions in industrial society' (1985: 19–20):

> First, there is the appalling gap which now exists between that which technology could provide for society, and that which it actually does provide ...

> The second contradiction is the tragic wastage our society makes in its most precious asset – that is the skill, integrity, energy, creativity and enthusiasm of its ordinary people ...

> The third contradiction is the myth that computerisation, automation and the use of robotic devices will automatically free human beings from soul destroying backbreaking tasks and leave them free to engage in creative work ... the reverse is the case.

> Fourth, there is the growing hostility of society at large to science and technology as at present practiced.

### Things fall apart

Benn was picking up on some of the IWC strategy. Workers were directed to put forward their own proposals on how to save their own industries. This was integral to a realization by these workers that the Minister favoured the cooperative form rather than 'old style' nationalization. In January 1975, Litton Industries announced its plans to close its Imperial Typewriter factories in Hull and Leicester. A plan was produced, principally authored by Tony Topham of the IWC who was also a local university tutor in trade union studies, arguing for support from Benn's Department (see IWC, 1975; TGWU, 1975). Benn addressed a lobby of workers from the Hull plant where he advised that they 'stay together'; this they took as advice to occupy if the plant was closed. When the Hull factory was closed on 20 February, a day earlier than announced, members of the workforce climbed the gate and started an occupation. A sign was erected outside the plant announcing 'Tony is with us'. However, by the following month Benn was to write to Tony Topham that:

> The whole official machine is 100% against you as you probably realise, and I am doing my best to prevent disastrous recommendations from going in so as to give you time to reorganise. It is going to be very hard, but I will do my very best.[2]

While Benn was instrumental in mobilizing action among groups of workers his openness to delegations, especially where these were from workforces staging what appeared to be militant industrial action, was isolating – if not demonizing – him elsewhere. Benn had been the initial architect of Labour's industrial policy but its formulation after the election was taken from him by the Prime Minister with the measures in the 1975 Industry Act diluted from the original (see Coventry, Liverpool, Newcastle and North Tyneside Trades Councils, 1982). However, the disputes in the government were largely masked by the referendum on European Common Market membership and, after this, Benn was moved from Industry to the Department of Energy.

Senior civil servants in Industry had also made official complaints against Benn because he used the direct route to workers and ignored Departmental advice against support for these projects. When the LACSSC produced their plan, which was to pioneer and symbolize 'socially useful production' (see LACSSC, 1978; Wainwright and Elliott, 1982), they found their path blocked by a bureaucratic web (see LACSSC, 1979, 1982). Trade union officials also objected to access being given to shop stewards and combines, both were considered unofficial bodies. From the political right Benn was increasingly demonized. The *Daily Telegraph* on 27 July 1974, commenting on the financing of the Meriden cooperative, argued that:

> Apart from the fact that such schemes seem in a general way an abuse of taxpayers' money, there are two grave, particular objections to them. One is that they must act as an encouragement to workers to think that unauthorised occupation of premises...is a sure ticket for Mr Benn's cornucopia. The other is that...Mr Benn has acted against the advice of the Industrial Development Advisory Board...For Mr Benn no doubt Socialist ideology overrides such considerations. It must be noted, however, that his ability to do

those things without going to Parliament is derived from the last Conservative Government's Industry Act.

(27 July 1974)

Such arguments, and particularly that the interventionism of the previous government could lead to such 'socialist' measures, helped mobilize the neo-liberal wing within the Conservative Party, further strengthened by the Labour government's approach to the International Monetary Fund (IMF) for a loan in 1976.

State assistance for the workers' cooperative in the short period Benn was at the Department of Industry was not only very limited but mostly went to recompense previous owners for what was already an obsolete plant. Hence while all three cooperatives were shortlived, there was an inevitability of their closure. The assistance still left them drastically undercapitalized and therefore unable to resolve problems, and left them unable to establish an independent existence through research and development. Cooperative structures were undermined by financial stringency as well as lack of research and development. The failure to invest in innovation, often the very cause of corporate problems which precipitated the crisis that led to worker takeover, and following established traditions in British manufacture meant that prototypes created by the workers tended to be rehashes of existing models. More importantly the cooperatives were encouraged to bring in management expertise – supposedly subordinate to the collectivity of the workers' cooperative – subverting social objectives through the reconstruction of corporate identity and enforcing economic stringencies. At Meriden, at least, this not only meant the establishment of a membership hierarchy but also redundancies to accommodate the frailties of markets for motorcycles in the USA.

## Towards Thatcherism

The move of Tony Benn from the Department of Industry might be seen as marking the end of the heyday of workplace occupation in Britain. With the exception of early 1972, which saw the engineering dispute, the period of late 1974 through till mid-1975 saw more occupations than any other. The period brought together workers facing closures and redundancies, the conditions which generate occupation, and the apparent possibility of support at the very centre of government. The three worker cooperatives, the Benn cooperatives, have become totemic of the period, and cooperative development became associated with economic policies, formulated by some UK local authorities, challenging the emergent neo-liberalism of the Thatcher government. The idea of socially useful production, associated with the LACSSC, is another important outcome from the period (Gold, 2004). The LACSSC proposals, including hybrid engines and alternative power sources, have a significant resonance with growing concern about the environment and appear, if anything, far more prophetic in the early 21st century than they did in the mid-1970s. More importantly they remain symbolic of what can be achieved by organized workers through their imagination and will to address social need, rather than the drive for accumulation. Perhaps also representing how such an initiative can be stifled by the frustration of the state, capital, as well as the trade unions.

The occupation was slow to disappear after its heyday in the mid-1970s. A number of significant occupations (at Meccano, Lee Jeans, Lawrence Scott and at the magazine *Time Out*) occurred towards the end of the 1970s. However, there was a noticeable decline. Even earlier in the 1970s only a small minority of workers facing closure or large-scale redundancy considered the tactic and even fewer deployed it. And this deployment, while maybe more often considered, was usually the relatively spontaneous action of a minority of the workforce involved. Far more commonly, when closure or redundancies are announced, the union sees its role not as mobilizing opposition but in negotiating the most advantageous redundancy terms. The breaking of the cash nexus, which gave a glimmer of the capacity and creativity in transforming their working life, succumbed to the process of re-commodification. The introduction of the 1975 Employment Protection Act introduced the formal requirement for employers to give 90 days' notice of redundancies and to consult with recognized trade unions over these redundancies this further dissipated any resistance as fracturing the collectivity of potential resistance from the redundant workforce.

New areas of occupation did open in the mid-1970s. One challenged cuts in the public sector and particularly hospital closure. These were used as bases for mobilizing campaigns beyond the immediate labour movement. The Labour government, faced with a sterling crisis, approached the IMF for a $3.9 billion loan in 1976. Conditional on the loan was a 20 per cent cut in budget deficit. Almost three years before the election of Thatcher's Conservative government Britain saw the initiation of the rolling back of the Keynesian Welfare State. Rationalization in the National Health Service (NHS) saw a move towards consolidation in larger units and the closure of smaller, specialist or local hospitals and some hospital wards. This often meant redeployment of staff rather than redundancy, but it still led to opposition. A number of occupations occurred to try to keep hospitals open. The first, at Elisabeth Garret Anderson, a specialist women's hospital in central London, the occupation lasted for more than two years. In some cases these involved continued care; however, in Hounslow, management staged a 'raid' to remove hospital patients, although occupation continued based around ex-staff and local supporters. Another area involved the adoption of flags of convenience by merchant vessels so as to reduce wages to crew. Dependent on the vessel for accommodation, the means of resistance to changes in conditions was for crew members to occupy.

## Some lessons

Gall (2009, 2010), in examining occupations in Britain in recent years, has reflected on what he sees as a more limited response after 2007 against the 1970s. There are relatively obvious differences in the periods, particularly in comparing the capacities and strategies of the labour movement. While, however, we can look at the political leadership of the unions and the officers who might mobilize action (Darlington, 2006), we need also look at the strategies adopted by capital as well as labour. While, on one side, there may be a move towards the establishment of an alternative to capitalism rooted in social need; from the other, there is an imperative to extend commodification.

We might see the foundation of the occupations in Britain in the 1970s as being rooted in the strong and confident workplace trade unionism that had developed within the full employment of the post-war consensus. Through the 1960s and 1970s we see signs of this organization being under threat, with, for example, the escalation of the engineering industry dispute in 1972 – caused by management's attempt to control shop stewards. By the early 1980s this was becoming a full assault. Signs were already evident that employers were becoming more willing to challenge and attempt legal action to evict workers, but in the early 1980s the legal framework for trade unions and employment relations in Britain was itself transformed, making any action more difficult. In a detailed study of an occupation of Caterpillar in Uddingston, Scotland, in 1987 – perhaps the last of this wave of actions in Britain – Woolfson and Foster (1988) noted that while the work-in at UCS had been dependent on such strong organization by politically active shop stewards, action at Caterpillar lacked these 'organizational advantages'. The motive for mobilizing the occupation was that workers at Caterpillar saw no alternative: workers had nothing to lose.

In the early occupations there was a sense that jobs might be maintained; that, whatever it was, there was a value in the creativity – be it in shipbuilding or manufacturing manual typewriters – that would be lost to the rationale of capital, and with it came the decline of tradition and community. This rationale had its last stand in the UK miners' strike in 1984–1985 which also symbolically represents the end of the organized and militant unionism that grew in the shadow of post-war affluence and full employment, essentially through the capacity to commodify grievances, but proved vulnerable to economic recession.

Most of the reflection on occupation and property initially revolved around rights to the sale of labour, that somehow employment vested property rights in the job similar to those of a shareholder. This was the very ethos that developed around redundancy pay. Its practice was to commodify jobs by putting a cash payment in place to buy out any job 'possession' by workers (Fryer, 1973, 1981). The very extension of market philosophy incorporated, through commodification, defused the capacity of workers to resist the prerogative of capital. In these circumstances the reaction of workers is likely fractured: between those who might keep their jobs and those that might be losing them; between different groups who might blame each other for economic failure; and between those who seek to resist and those willing or resigned to accept redundancy payment. Only a minority of closed workplaces, and other threat to jobs, prompted worker occupation in resistance and, when they did, it was through the active participation of a minority of the workforce.

The mid-1970s in the UK did seem to show a coincidence of strong workplace organization capable of organizing and maintaining work as well as drawing up plans for a future rooted in social imperatives rather than the profit motive. Briefly, this was also enhanced by support from senior government figures. However, the state apparatus soon marginalized this support, bending to the prerogatives of capital through the efforts of civil servants, government as well as trade union officials. The very process of the emergence of neo-liberalism in Britain swallowed not just the capacity to resist but also any alternative rationale to that of commodification and the market.

## Notes

1. A total of 264 occupations were found through a search of newspapers covering the period 1971–1981. The newspapers used for the whole period were: *The Financial Times*, *The Times*, *The Guardian*, *Labour Research*, *Socialist*

*Worker*. For specific periods and for particular occupations the local press (e.g. *Manchester Evening News* and *Hull Daily Mail*) were also used (see Tuckman, 1985 for details, list and methodology).
2. From Benn to Topham (17 March 1975), available at the Brynmore Jones Library DTO unclassified collection, donated by Tony Topham.

## References

Anderson, A. 1964, *Hungary 56*, Solidarity, London.

Anti-Report. 1972, *The General Electric Company Limited*, Counter Information Services, London.

Barratt Brown, M. 1968, *Opening the Books*, Institute for Workers' Control, Nottingham.

Barratt Brown, M., Coates, K. and Topham, T. 1975, 'Workers' Control Versus "Revolutionary" Theory', in *The Socialist Register 1975*, R. Milliband and J. Saville (eds), The Merlin Press, London, pp. 293–307.

Benn, T. 1979, 'Labours Industrial Programme', in *Arguments for Socialism*, C. Mullin (ed.), Penguin, Harmondsworth.

Bruce-Gardyne, J. 1974, *Whatever Happened to the Quite Revolution? The Story of a Brave Experiment in Government*, Charles Knight & Co Ltd, London.

Castoriadis, C. 1988, 'On the Content of Socialism II', in *Political and Social Writings*, D. Ames Curtis (ed.), University of Minnesota Press, Minneapolis, pp. 90–154.

Chadwick, G. 1970, 'The Big Flame – An Account of the Events at the Liverpool Factory of GEC-EE', in *Trade Union Register*, K. Coates, T. Topham and M. Barratt Brown (eds.), Merlin Press, London.

Chadwick, G. 1973, 'The Manchester Engineering Sit Ins 1972', in *Trade Union Register*, K. Coates, T. Topham and M. Barratt Brown (eds), Merlin, London.

CIS Anti-Report, n.d., *Where is Lucas Going?*, Anti-Report No 12, London.

Clarke, T. 1974, *Sit-in at Fisher-Bendix*, Institute for Workers' Control, Nottingham.

CM-71. 1971, Cabinet Minute, CAB-128-49, Index of Cabinet Conclusions, The National Archive. http://www.nationalarchives.gov.uk, accessed 29 June 2010.

Coates, K. 1968, *Can The Workers Run Industry?*, Sphere in association with the Institute for Workers' Control, London.

Coates, K. ed. 1976, *The New Worker Co-Operatives*, Spokesman Books, Nottingham.

Coates, K. 1981, *Work-ins, Sit-ins and Industrial Democracy*, Spokesman Books, Nottingham.

Cooley, M. 1985, 'After the Lucas Plan', in *Very Nice Work if You Can Get It*, Collective Design/Projects (ed.), Spokesman, Nottingham, pp. 19–26.

Coventry, Liverpool, Newcastle and North Tyneside Trades Councils. 1982, *State Intervention in Industry: A Workers Inquiry 1980*, Spokesman Books, Nottingham.

Crouch, C. 1977, *Class Conflict and the Industrial Relations Crisis*, Heinemann Educational Books, London.

Darlington, R. 2006, 'Agitator "Theory" of Strikes Re-Evaluated', *Labor History*, vol. 47, no. 4, pp. 485–509.

Darlington, R. and Lyddon, D. 2001, *Glorious Summer: Class Struggle in Britain, 1972*, Bookmarks, London.

Eccles, T. 1981, *Under New Management: The Story of Britains Largest Worker Co-Operative – Its Successes and Failures*, Pan Books, London.

EEF. 1972, Presidents Address, Engineering Employers Association Annual Report, 1971–72.

Elliott, D. 1977, *The Lucas Aerospace Workers' Campaign*, Young Fabian Pamphlet 46, London.

Fryer, R. H. 1973, 'Redundancy, Values and Public Policy', *Industrial Relations Journal*, vol. 4, no. 2, pp. 2–19.

Fryer, R. H. (Bob). 1981, 'State, Redundancy and the Law', in *Law, State and Society*, B. Fryer, A. Hunt, D. McBarnet and B. Moorehouse (eds), Croom Helm, London, pp. 136–159.

Gall, G. 2009, 'Agitate, Educate, Occupy! Examining the Potency of Occupations to Resist Redundancy', *Communist Review*, no. 55, Winter, pp. 5–11.

Gall, G. 2010, 'Resisting Recession and Redundancy: Contemporary Worker Occupation in Britain', *WorkingUSA*, vol. 13, no. 1, March, pp. 107–132.

Gamble, A. 1988, *The Free Economy and the Strong State: The Politics of Thatcherism*, Macmillan, Basingstoke and London.

Gamble, A. 2009, *The Spectre at the Feast: Capitalist Crisis and the Politics of Recession*, Palgrave Macmillan, Basingstoke.

Gold, M. 2004, 'Worker mobilization in the 1970s: Revisiting Work-ins, Cooperatives and Alternative Corporate Plans', *Historical Studies in Industrial Relations*, no. 18, pp. 65–106.

Gramsci, A. 1977, *Selections From the Political Writings (1910–1920)*, Lawrence & Wishart, London.

Hansard. 1968, House of Commons Debates, HMSO, London.

Hyman, R. 1974, 'Workers' Control and Revolutionary Theory', *Socialist Register*, vol. 11, no. 11, pp. 241–278.

Inside Story. 1973, 'How Red was Briants Colour?', *Inside Story*, no. 10, August.

IWC. 1969, *GEC-EE Workers' Takeover*, Institute for Workers' Control, Nottingham.

IWC. 1975, *Why Imperial Typewriters Must Not Close: A Preliminary Social Audit By the Union Action Committee*, Institute for Workers' Control, Nottingham.

IWC. n.d., *UCS: The Social Audit*, Institute for Workers' Control, Pamphlet Number 26, Nottingham.

LACSSC. 1978, *Lucas: An Alternative Plan*, Lucas Aerospace Shop Stewards' Combine Committee, Institute for Workers' Control, Nottingham.

LACSSC. 1979, *Democracy versus the Circumlocution Office*, IWC Pamphlet Number 65, Nottingham.

LACSSC. 1982, *Diary of Betrayal: A Detailed Account of the Combine's Efforts to Get the Alternative Plan Implemented*, Centre for Alternative Industrial and Technological Systems, London.

Lomax, B. ed. 1980, *Eyewitnesses in Hungary: The Soviet Invasion of 1956*, Spokesman, Nottingham.

Lomax, B. 1976, *Hungary 1956*, Allison & Busby, London.

Mason, P. 2008, *Live Working or Die Fighting: How the Working Class Went Global*, Vintage, London.

McGill, J. 1973, *Crisis on the Clyde*, Davis-Poynter, London.

Mills, A. 1974, 'Factory Work-ins', *New Society*, Thursday 22 August.

Murray, R. 1972, *UCS: The Anatomy of Bankruptcy*, Spokesman Books, Nottingham.

Newens, S. 1969, 'The GEC/AEI Takeover and the Fight against Redundancy at Harlow', in *Trade Union Register*, K. Coates, T. Topham and M. Barratt Brown (eds), Merlin Press, London.

NVT. 1974, *Meridian: Historical Summary 1972–1974*, Norton Villiers Triumph, Coventry.

Panitch, L. 1976, *Social Democracy & Industrial Militancy: The Labour Party, the Trade Unions and Income Policy 1945–1974*, Cambridge University Press, Cambridge.

Pannekoek, A. 2003, *Workers' Councils 1948*, Southern Advocate for Workers' Control, AK Press, Edinburgh, London & Oakland.

Schubert, J. 1970, 'Big Flame Flickers', *Anarchy*, vol. 10, no. 2, February, pp. 41–42.

Sherry, D. 2010, *Occupy! A Short History of Workers' Occupations*, Bookmarks, London.

Smith, B. 1981, *The History of the British Motorcycle Industry 1945–1975*, Centre for Urban and Regional Studies, University of Birmingham, Birmingham.

Solidarity. 1972, *Under New Management? The Fisher Bendix Occupation*, Solidarity Pamphlet Number 39, London.

Spriano, P. 1975, *The Occupation of Factories: Italy 1920*, Pluto Press, London.

TGWU. 1975, 'Threatened Closure of Imperial Typewriters, Hull: The Case for Government Aid to Maintain Production, and/or To Establish a Co-operative to Assume Ownership and Management of the Plant: A Preliminary Statement', Available at Brynmore Jones Library, University of Hull, DTO Unclassified Papers Donated by Tony Topham, Hull.

Topham, T. 1964, 'Shop Stewards and Workers' Control', *New Left Review*, no. 25, May/June, pp. 3–15.

Topham, T. ed. 1967, *Report of the 5th National Conference on Workers' Control and Industrial Democracy*, Centre for Socialist Education, Hull.

Tuckman, A. 1985, *Industrial Action and Hegemony: Workplace Occupation in Britain 1971 to 1981*, unpublished PhD thesis, University of Hull.

Wainwright, H. and Elliott, D. 1982, *The Lucas Plan: A New Trade Unionism in the Making?*, Allison & Busby, London.

Wajcman, J. 1983, *Women in Control: Dilemmas of a Workers' Co-Operative*, Open University Press, Milton Keynes.

Woolfson, C. and Foster, J. 1988, *Track Record: The Story of the Caterpillar Occupation*, Verso, London & New York.

# 3
# Going Underground: Workers' Ownership and Control at Tower Colliery

*Russell Smith, Len Arthur, Molly Scott Cato and Tom Keenoy*

## Introduction

This chapter addresses the nature and limits of an alternative model of work organization in a UK coal mine. It charts the history and progress of the Tower Colliery coal mine in South Wales as an historic form of industrial democracy – the worker-owned producer cooperative – across its 13-year existence as a productive mine under the ownership and direct control of its workers. It further explores the argument that workers' cooperatives are significantly different to typical work organizations, in that they are social movements, and that research into their experience can make a relevant contribution to the discourses of work and the sociology of social movements.

This analytical framework draws upon sociological traditions as synthesized in Archer's work (1996) on culture and Mouzelis' work (1995) on patterns of social interaction. Reference will be made to social movement concepts and social skills, as identified by Fligstein (2001). It will be argued that the changed democratic-based power relationship at Tower not only created a different social space but that the difference was such that it could be seen to amount to an alternative social movement – a mode of 'transgressive contention' (McAdam et al., 2001) – while at the same time surviving as a mainstream economic organization. We further propose a concept of 'deviant mainstreaming' as a possible way of capturing the generic social processes at the cooperative during its existence.

Methodologically, the research relied upon site observations; individual and group interviews at all 'levels' of the organization; published documents; the cooperative archives; and extensive and intensive local newspaper reportage.

The chapter details the establishment and development of the Tower cooperative. In analysing the 13-year history of Tower Colliery as a workers' cooperative, we identify and discuss a range of issues which have wider significance for the nature and limits of 'workers' control' in the cooperative form of organization. These include the nature of management authority; the extent to which the employment relationship is transformed; the complex role of the union in the cooperative; and the extent to which the Tower 'experience' can be viewed as a social movement that offered a viable alternative to conventional employee-relation approaches in the workplace.

## Tower Colliery: The historical context

From the beginning of the Industrial Revolution, the economy of South Wales was dominated by two major industries – coal mining, and iron and steel production (Massey, 1984; Cooke, 1985; Rutherford, 1988). Coal mining, for the most part, was concentrated in the valley communities of South Wales. While 'the geography and geology of the valleys were ideal for this form of employment' (Cato, 2004: 29), they offered few, if any, alternatives should coal mining fall into structural decline. Such decline did occur over the course of the 20th century, and for the valley communities this resulted in high levels of unemployment, as the displaced mining jobs could not be directly replaced.

Out of this decline, Tower Colliery eventually became the last deep mine in the South Wales coalfield. It was situated to the north of the coalfield, just outside Hirwaun, and just above the watershed of the rivers Neath and Cynon. It was in an area where the hard coal anthracite seams start. First opened in 1864 (with its name derived from a nearby folly built by the Hirwaun ironmasters, the Crawshays), it was threatened with closure in 1994, after over 100 years of coaling, along with other remaining working deep mines in South Wales.

In part, the dire consequences of closure in the context of regional economic decline help to account for the decision of the Tower Colliery workers to fight to preserve their jobs and incomes. Thus a campaign was started by the National Union of Mineworkers (NUM) lodge members at Tower to purchase the coal mine. This involved organizing an employee buyout bid in order to establish Tower Colliery as a workers' cooperative. Initially, through what turned out to be the charismatic leadership of a long-time union activist, Tyrone O'Sullivan, a small tight-knit executive group was elected by the Tower workforce, all of whom had committed an initial £1000 of their redundancy payment to the project in order to prepare the tender for the mine. This group was known as the Tower Employee Buyout (TEBO) team.

Notwithstanding the economic necessity for the bid described above, the organization of the employee buyout bid debated the political direction and control of industry, and the influence to be accorded to workers. Thus, while the buyout was contingent upon the pragmatism of economic necessity – as O'Sullivan, in an often cited quote from his TV interview on the day the TEBO bid was accepted, commented: 'We were ordinary men, we wanted jobs, we bought a pit' – the form of workers' control established at Tower can legitimately be seen as the legacy of nearly a century of experience with political and utopian ideologies and uncertain expectations. Historically, the nationalization of 'the commanding heights of the economy', under the 1945 Labour government, while a singular achievement, also represented a singular dilution of left-wing aspirations for workers' control and demands for state ownership which had dominated the labour movement's thinking from 1910 to 1921. South Wales was among the most active centres advocating the syndicalist model of workers' control of industry (Kendall, 1969).

In an earlier historical example of this tradition, in 1912, union activists created the Miners' Unofficial Reform Committee which published *The Miners' Next Step* (1912). This influential publication dismissed the objective of nationalization as irrelevant and repudiated both collective bargaining and conciliation: the sole concern of unionized miners should be direct control of their own industry. This concern for workers' control was further highlighted by the experience of the bitter dispute, and ultimate defeat, of the national miners' strike in 1984–1985 – meticulously planned by the UK Conservative government. This dispute, its unsatisfactory resolution and the recognition of the effects pit closures could have on communities became key factors in the determination of the Tower workers to fight against the closure.

Throughout most of 1994 the TEBO team prepared all aspects of the bid. By the time the bid was submitted the team had raised £1.93 million – with 239 miners each investing their £8000 redundancy pay to buy a share in Goitre Tower Anthracite Ltd, the holding company which then secured a £2 million loan from Barclays Bank. In November 1994 the Department of Trade and Industry (DTI) confirmed that the bid had been accepted and the colliery became the property of the workers from 1 January 1995. The historic and heroic struggle to buy the colliery and its attendant vicissitudes of fortune has been well told as a French feature film released in February 2000 titled *'Charbons Ardents'* (*'Burning Coal'*) and through an opera – *'Tower: the opera'* written by the late, celebrated Welsh composer, Alun Hoddinott.

At its inception as a cooperative, Tower employed around 230 people; coal production averaged 500,000 tonnes per year over the 13 years that Tower Colliery was owned by its employees. In April 1994 the former owners, British Coal, claimed the pit was uneconomic, yet the cooperative turned in regular surpluses of around £4 million per year on taking ownership.

## Theorizing social movements

Historically, workers' cooperatives have been part of the 'repertoires of contention' within working class movements (Tilly, 1995; Traugott, 1995). They are firmly recognized in the classics of UK social history (Thompson, 1968), and they have experienced cycles of research 'interest and attention since their first appearance in the 1820s. One cycle of interest declined in the early 1990s (Mellor et al., 1988; Bayat, 1991; Prychitko, 1991), another started in recent years (Gates, 1999; Pendleton, 2001). Despite this history of interest, workers' producer cooperatives and other forms of cooperative mutual organization have received little attention within work- and employment-related literature. Possible reasons for this neglect include: the numbers of both producer cooperatives and cooperative employees are comparatively small and do not 'fit' easily with discourses of industrial relations, management or human resource management (HRM). Moreover, much of the literature suggests cooperatives are relatively easily incorporated within the mainstream and are – or have become – little different to more conventional work organizations. Because of their historic political 'failure', cooperatives are not easily seen as a 'new' social movement and, more generally within the sociology of social movements, they are rarely seen as being part of a movement cycle amenable to mobilization techniques which can take advantage of political opportunities to 'transform consciousness'.

Nonetheless, a more sensitive approach to the 'social experience' of cooperative production shows that such workers' cooperatives are not only characterized by a distinctive labour process but can be regarded as elements of a social movement offering a viable alternative to conventional employment relations. Research into their experience can make a relevant political and practical contribution to the sociology of work and social movements. Cooperative production as a social movement shares with the trade unions the contradiction that they can be both socially contentious and emancipatory, while serving to support and re-affirm the dominance of the main features of capitalist production. Hyman (1989: 232) argues that workers' organizations 'which are defined and constituted through struggle tend also to contain and inhibit such struggle'.

Narratives of social movement studies offer two broad conceptual frameworks to help analyse this contradiction. More recently, these have been supplemented by some attempted syntheses (Buechler, 1999; Della Porta and Diani, 1999; Crossley, 2002). First, resource mobilization theories – largely of American origin – tend to stress the importance of understanding the methods of collective organization that underpin waves of mobilization and challenge dominant power and legitimacy. These frameworks have a clear relevance to an understanding of the trade union movement that tends to be characterized by cycles of activity and have been drawn upon most noticeably by Kelly (1988, 1998) and Hyman (1989). However, there is a key problem with their relevance to organizations less characterized by cycles, such as cooperatives. As cooperatives are rarely the outcome of a period of 'collective mobilization' it is very difficult to see them as challenging existing forms of domination. 'Abeyance' is one way of understanding a social movement that is not on an upswing of mobilization (Bagguley, 2002), but this effectively means it is 'ticking over' and not challenging. In effect, the resource mobilization framework condemns workers' cooperatives to a permanent condition of incorporation or degeneration (Mellor et al., 1988). One of the reasons for the lack of recognition of the role of workers' cooperatives as a social movement has been the privileging of forms of contention through waves of mobilization by this framework.

By contrast, new social movement theory places more analytical stress on the forms of movement development that serve to contend through challenging the dominant forms of legitimation (Della Porta and Diani, 1999; Crossley, 2002). This approach enables recognition of social action and practice that is characterized by incrementally establishing alternative social space within the existing order, rather than directly confronting that order through mobilization. This framework tends to privilege a voluntaristic approach and opens up a greater variety of social movements for analysis: there is a greater acceptance of what actors do in practice and an intention to understand and explain such movements in their own terms. Although the term 'new' is still used to distinguish this approach, there is a general acceptance that such challenging of the dominant forms of legitimation – through the creation of alternative cultural and social space – is not actually historically new, but the term is retained to distinguish it from resource mobilization theory. The possibility of a space of permanent resistance underpins the analysis. As Williams (1973) expressed:

> no mode of production, and therefore no dominant society or order of society, and therefore no dominant culture, in reality exhausts human practice, human energy, human intention.

Such 'alternative' social practices do not wait for the next wave of mobilization but constantly open up the possibility of alternative social and cultural space. The mere act of social interaction and the construction of an 'alternative' discourse is a creative act having the potential to challenge the existing order. Similarities can be seen with Habermas's (1981) notion of 'lifeworld' developed by the new social movement theorist Melucci (1995).

More recently a *rapprochement* between these frameworks has opened up a more inclusive understanding of social movements with a wider range of analytical possibilities. As Buechler (1999: 211) suggests:

> Thus, from their inception, social movements have a dual focus. Reflecting the political, they have always involved some form of challenge to prevailing forms of authority. Reflecting the cultural, they have operated as symbolic laboratories in which reflexive actors pose questions of meaning, purpose, identity, and change. When social movement theory recognizes this inevitable duality in social movements, it will once again be on a productive path.

Such frameworks provide a method for understanding workers' cooperatives as social movements that create an alternative and potentially emancipated space. However, in the narrative of both frameworks and the synthesis quoted above, the notion of a dynamic social process over time is central. This is perhaps more visible with the emphasis on cycles in resource mobilization theory. But change over time is also central to understanding in new social movement theories, such as the extent to which they are able to retain their alternative identity as a 'symbolic laboratory' and thus mount a challenge. Social movements that create alternative space also have to cope with the paradox of the extent to which they challenge but re-affirm and apparently emancipate while simultaneously incorporating. Clearly, new social movement theory and more recent syntheses seem to offer a more relevant approach to an understanding of movements that do not appear to be cyclical. In the absence of a readily identifiable cycle, they suggest a way of clearly identifying the extent of their difference, the extent of its 'alternativeness' and the extent of their challenge. It is easier to plot an upwards and downwards cycle of mobilization than to unpack the more qualitative description of the emancipated space of a workers' cooperative; an essential prerequisite to understanding whether their trajectory is towards emancipation or incorporation, or even whether such terms have any meaning for the actors.

Research at Tower raised these tensions empirically, and this analysis of the cooperative space draws generally upon the approach of new social movement theory and the more recent synthesis, to offer an evaluation of the cooperative. The analysis is also informed by the work of Margaret Archer (1996) and Nicos Mouzelis (1995), who provide a framework rooted in the tradition of sociological theory that approaches agency and structure as being explicable through social interaction and the power resources available to the actors. The power resources take institutional and legitimating forms in Bourdieu's sense of economic, cultural, political and social capital (Mouzelis, 1995; Crossley, 2002). Concentration of these resources sustains hierarchies of macro and micro actors, but these resources are also capable of re-distribution and re-definition through processes of social interaction. Archer and Mouzelis share the same basic framework assumption as Williams (1973). This chapter therefore presents an analysis of how the advent of cooperative ownership transformed the interactive social space of the labour process by redistributing power and authority to the employees – the micro actors.

It is argued that the democratic base of cooperative power relations not only created a qualitatively different social space but that the difference was of such an order that it could be seen as an alternative social movement. In short, while taking action to survive as a mainstream economic organization, the Tower experience can simultaneously be seen as a mode of 'transgressive contention' (McAdam et al., 2001). In order to account for this seeming paradox, the concept of 'deviant mainstreaming' is developed as a possible way of capturing the transformative social processes which appear to characterize cooperative production.

## Tower Colliery: A social movement?

It is suggested that the pragmatic conceptual framework proposed by Mouzelis (1995) helps to provide a method for understanding the extent of the difference of the Tower cooperative experience. Drawing upon David Lockwood's distinction between 'system integration and social integration', Mouzelis proposes the importance of recognizing the voluntaristic 'interactive-situational dimension' of social space, or as he expresses it: 'moving from a virtual order of rules to an actual order of actions and interactions' (77). Analytically, he insists that acknowledgement of: 'the distinction between langue and parole, between the paradigmatic and the syntagmatic, between the virtual and the actual, is fundamental' (137).

Empirically, any interactive social space can be seen to have three compatible, but analytically and logically distinct, dimensions of social action: 'positional', drawing upon the logic of social roles in institutional settings (e.g. the legal authority of management); 'dispositional', drawing upon the logic of habitus (e.g. the historical significance of union membership); and 'interactive-situational', drawing upon the voluntaristic recognition that actors can reproduce or change the other two dimensions in interactive practice (e.g. the observable change in the miners' behaviour in crises). In hierarchical social spaces, where interaction is dominated by positional and dispositional dimensions, macro actors will have a preponderance of economic, social, cultural and political capital or power resources. For these actors, access to power enables domination through their control of positional and dispositional interaction. Power enables macro actors to have a choice over change or reproduction within these dimensions. For meso and micro actors within such a hierarchy the positional and dispositional dimensions appear external and paradigmatic, because they have little control over shaping these dimensions. The opportunities of micro actors to influence the form and outcome of social reproduction are confined to the dimension of interactive-situational interaction. Essentially, a macro actor's detail is a micro actor's world.

As suggested above, there is always a part of interaction (more usually interactive-situational and dispositional) that is not fully integrated and provides space for alternative – even oppositional – discourses. The power of macro actors can be challenged by collective action and their legitimacy can be undermined by their actions that are contradictory, amount to a misuse of power or contravene dispositional authority and experience. Under British Coal, the employment relationship can be seen to have been characterized as a macro-micro hierarchy with meso actors such as shift captains and NUM officials.

The extent of the change in the interactive social space within the Tower cooperative can be appreciated within this framework. The macro actors were now the board and not British Coal. Four of the six members of the board were NUM members. Two members of the board were subject to re-election by the worker-owners every year. Political and social capital was now derived bottom up instead of top down. Economic capital was still constrained by the market and technical/managerial role, but the distribution and use of revenue changed markedly and was open to continuous debate. Cultural capital and some political capital still resided with the mine manager, but became more subject to negotiation and debate. Using Mouzelis's framework, it can be seen that the British Coal hierarchical form had gone and, although the board retained a degree of control over economic capital, it was forced to continuously negotiate its political, social and cultural capital to achieve legitimacy. From this, it is suggested that the interactive social space of the cooperative became dominated by the 'interactive-situational' dimension, with that of role and position much reduced.

This was a qualitative change of some significance, which was reflected in the changed sense of 'habitus' among the cooperators (i.e. the dispositional dimension of social interaction). The cooperative existed for 13 years and though the traditions and experience of mine work, South Wales Mining and the NUM remained strong, there were indications of an emergent additional view. For instance one respondent, at the time the NUM Lodge Secretary at Tower, suggested:

> I would say they're [the miners] more relaxed now ... because everybody is a part owner ... [w]hen you come to work you're a worker – you're only a shareholder at the shareholders meetings – every so often. Some people can't switch that off. They think 'Oh, I'm a shareholder, I've gotta have a say in how it's all done'; and I think the managers have taken that on board. They still fall back into their 'British Coal' ways now and again coz a manager is a manager at the end of the day and they been brought up under British Coal. I think it was a bigger change for them than us. They were there and we were here and now things are more 'even' – not so much them and us now. There was a dividing line then and that was it. But I would say that line has been crossed both ways – we gone that way, they've come this way. We still don't see eye to eye every day but at the end of the day – we have our arguments – the manager might decide. 'Well

I want to do it this way'; that's where the union's, well, more of a peacemaker because you've got the men saying they want to do it this way and the manager saying he wants to do it that way – I'm in the middle, well most of the time – and we come to some sort of compromise ... [w]e don't have to go on strike for it like we did with British Coal.

This quote also suggests a further feature of the interaction that emerged from the widespread participation in the process of debate. The fact of being both a worker and an owner could not just be ignored; it was a constant feature of discourse within the colliery. This might suggest that a form of partnership or an 'alternative' psychological contract emerged from the experience of Tower. However, we suggest that the concept of 'social skill' is more consistent with a sociological analysis. Drawing upon the work of symbolic interactionalists, Fligstein (2001) suggests a useful definition:

The idea of social skill is that actors have to motivate others to cooperate. The ability to engage others in collective action is a social skill that proves pivotal to the construction and reproduction of local social orders.

This, we argue, is more relevant to the work at Tower. It seemed that the increased role of the voluntaristic interactive dimension of 'interactive-situational' was not just an outcome of the re-distribution of power in the cooperative, but also the ongoing outcome of the actors' improved ability to engage in discourse and negotiation, re-enforcing their move away from being mere micro actors.

## Workers' control and market competition

In terms of workers' control and market competition, the first point to make is that the managing board of Tower were involved in what Putnam (1988) calls a two-level game. At one level, they were serving the interests of their constituents – the employee/shareholders – while at another level they were operating commercially in what was rapidly becoming a globalized energy market. This meant walking an often fine line between meeting the cooperative members' expectations while simultaneously ensuring operational effectiveness through securing and retaining market share in a competitive context. While the nature of the colliery's product (anthracite) helped alleviate some of these pressures, commercial vigilance was a constant requirement. Thus, involvement in this two-level game gave rise to interesting tensions and contradictions for the managing board and the employee shareholders in the areas of participation, work organization and decision-making.

Perhaps the most significant tension can be best described as the 'strategic tension' between prioritizing the objectives of business success, as opposed to cooperative and social objectives. The financial and technical trajectory and supporting culture were based upon the desire for Tower to survive as a successful business and, in this respect, it succeeded in expanding production and securing its market position. However, Tower had been established to save jobs, the mine and the way of life it sustained, and, to some extent, to provide a broad example to others. These wider social objectives could be achieved only if the mine successfully secured its economic boundaries. Over the 13 years, the combination of these two ideas gave priority to the financial and technical strategic arguments and ceded some political power away from the worker-owners into the hands of 'technocrats', such as the mine manager, accountants and marketers. This trajectory had its own internal tensions as its very success placed an emphasis on those who provided the technical knowledge to sustain the strategy. Thus the technocrats' expertise and success were used to justify them continuing to hold leading roles within the board.

Nonetheless, the legitimacy of these technocrats could only be sustained through the broader democratic process and, from time to time, this placed an emphasis on a wider basis of representation. Throughout its lifetime the cooperative managed to maintain a reasonable balance of professional and lay representatives, and a degree of parity between the social and democratic strategy alongside the successful financial and business strategy. In part, this is one reason for staying with the structure and working practices that existed before the buyout and with the attempt to sustain the difference between owner and employee. This strategy continued to be successful in terms of employment, production and general profitability over the lifetime of the mine. In short, ideological convictions were always informed by what we term a 'principled realism' honed in the historic experience of South Wales trade unionism.

While purists might sniff at the resort to such pragmatism, its astute deployment over Tower's 13-year existence permitted the cooperators to sustain democratic ownership; to control, maintain, develop and promote an alternative and successful form of corporate enterprise; and to develop a distinctive idea about the role and status of employee-owners. More prosaically, in terms of demonstrating 'home-grown' managerial skills, they displayed both managerial ingenuity and a practical adequacy when dealing with internal and external stake-holders. While unresolved tensions persisted throughout the Tower 'experience' these never proved unmanageable. In the context of glob-alizing neo-liberalism, which has prevailed and dominated both public policy and private practice over the last 30 years, this is considered as no small achievement.

Indeed, this strategic tension – maintenance of democratic organiza-tion and control *vis-à-vis* organizational effectiveness in 'the market' remained a critical focus of self-management for the worker-owners throughout the lifetime of the cooperative.

## Work organization at Tower Colliery

The surface appearance of authority-control structures at Tower was more familiar than might be expected. As indicated previously, legis-lation and company law prescribed the remit and responsibilities of the board; more exceptionally, the coal industry is probably almost unique in British industry in that there is a legal requirement that its managers must possess specified qualifications before being licensed to practice operational management. Such constraints meant that, *prima facie*, little appeared to have changed when the miners returned to work following the buyout. There were new 'bosses' (owners) but colliery management, work organization, work roles and operational practices were virtually identical to the situation under British Coal. Except that, well, everything *was* different. Sociologically, it was possible to iden-tify four mutually implicated, and sometimes competing, sources of effective authority.

*Charismatic authority.* The driving force behind the buyout, Tyrone O'Sullivan, sometime Chairman of the Board, Personnel Officer and the NUM Lodge Chairman is possessed of that elusive quality described by Weber as 'charisma'. He is an exceptional speaker and negotiator and people followed him for who he was. While sometimes the subject of aggressive criticism, it seems undoubted that his remarkable leader-ship skills and key historical role secured him an institutionalized role as the figurehead of Tower. That said, his position by no means went unquestioned (O'Sullivan et al., 2001).

*Employee authority.* Ownership of Tower was vested in the employee-shareholders, each of whom had one share and one vote. As sharehold-ers, they elected members of the board, who had to stand for re-election on a two-year rotating cycle. It is important to recognize that the Tower board was a significant break with the past and indicative of a very clear shift to bottom-up democracy and accountability, but the continued use of traditional terms such as 'directors' and 'board' obscured the complete break with the past in terms of ownership and control of economic capital. British Coal had had a UK-wide board that owned and controlled at that level. Similarly, mine management at Tower was accountable to a South Wales office based in Cardiff and then ultimately to British Coal. Managers were just that, and were not ultimately responsible for the economic capital of Tower. The TEBO broke this link. The land, mineral assets and capital were legally vested in the cooperatively owned company, which became the employer. Ownership now defined the geographic, economic and social boundaries of the space of the cooperative. Control was now in the hands of the on-site Tower board – all of whom were working employee-owner directors. The forms of power once so distant were now in the hands of the board and owners: in a very real sense 'the buck stopped' with them. Board members and managers were responsible for decisions and their consequences; the possibility of blaming distant bureaucracy became a luxury of the past. Ownership and control being vested in the Tower board fundamentally underpinned the interactive significance of the democratic process: who became a board member and the decisions taken by the board now really mattered in the context of Tower's survival. Collective ownership, control and democratic accountability became the source of a different social space, enabling a redistribution of economic, political, social and cultural capital resources.

For instance, elections in 1999 and 2001 resulted in defeat for two of the founding board members; this indicated not only a commitment to the authority of 'primitive democracy' (Webb and Webb, 1897) but also that no member of the board was safe. In addition, the directors, who were all working directors, had to account for their actions at the company annual general meetings (AGMs), which were never innocuous affairs. While it would be dangerous to generalize, it seemed that a continual tension existed between the politicized vision of the majority (including nearly all the board members) – who prioritized the value and achievement of worker-ownership and direct control over their work-lives – and a significant minority among the shareholders with a more instrumental approach to the objects of cooperative enterprise whose primary concern was to privilege the wage–labour exchange.

*Legal authority.* Unqualified formal management authority was legally vested in the colliery manager (who was not a board member) and his team of mining experts. This authority was unqualified because, in the strongly regulated mining industry in the UK, the mine could not have operated without his assent and hence his authority was tacitly accepted by the worker-owners. Indeed, for the most part his authority, which derived also from his technical knowledge and experience as well as his legal standing, was uncontested. Insofar as other managers represented his views, they too enjoyed strong 'line authority', although this was never as unqualified or unconditional. Nonetheless, this legal context, augmented by technical knowledge and experience, is a persuasive explanation for the apparently privileged position that surrounded some managerial functions and particularly that of colliery manager. It also begins to suggest some entirely defensible reasons for the apparent distance between the ideals of worker democracy and the realities of managing complex and dangerous industrial production processes. In other words, some of the management functions and instructions were mandatory and could be neither removed nor altered through the processes of democratic debate and discussion. However, in terms of wider arguments about the necessity of all members of a cooperative having an equal voice in matters of management policy and practice, our view is that this particular characteristic of mining significantly reduced the potential issues which might have generated possible conflict during the history of the Tower cooperative.

*Union authority.* The source of this authority was rooted in the historic working-class culture that typifies valley communities in South Wales. Everyone working at Tower was a trade union member; the majority belonging to the NUM. While it might seem that insistence on union membership was counter-intuitive both practically and symbolically, union membership was the bedrock of social solidarity, without which the whole enterprise would have been impossible. Its importance in terms of work organization must not be undervalued. Indeed it is accurate to say that the local NUM lodge, as the instigator and organizer of the cooperative, was the *only* authority. In this respect, it can be said that the cooperative was founded on the ideals of politicized unionism.

Nonetheless, although still key actors, the unions' authority appeared to be marginalized. Institutionally, they continued to signify and directly represent the publicly proclaimed (but ambiguous) distinction drawn between the 'member-as-employee' and the 'member-as-shareholder'. There were annual negotiations over terms and conditions but, while all enjoyed high wages and excellent welfare benefits, collective bargaining appeared to have lost its former edge. However, the continued presence of unions clarified and maintained the continuing sectional conflicts over distribution, defined here as the 'revenue tension'. As a cooperative and during a period of relatively stable coal prices, Tower increased the surplus available for distribution through an absolute growth in output. However, coal mines, by definition, are declining assets and without new investment capital it was inevitable that productivity would plateau (2000) and then subsequently decline as the pit reached the end of its operational life. Nevertheless, the increased revenue experienced enabled wages, benefits and dividends to rise and kept at bay the issue of absolute distributional shares. However, distributional and cost control issues were debated beyond the confines of the board meetings and remained a major source of tension. All members were acutely aware that the pit had a limited life and this in itself fuelled much of the debate about any proposed new investments – including those necessary to prolong the working life of the mine – or business initiatives.

Secondly, in terms of work organization, the age-old structural tension between 'bureaucracy and democracy' remained a persistent, if entirely predictable, phenomenon. Managing organizational tensions from above and below was the source of a range of debates. Both of these established patterns of social relations came under pressure and an ongoing tension developed between the established bureaucratic and technical systems and the inevitable democratic pressures from the power that the employees enjoyed as the co-owners of the cooperative. Despite an outwardly deceptive appearance of a strict top-down hierarchy of almost machine-like appearance, it is a fact that the daily uncertainties of coal mining as a productive process require constant shared decision-making at all levels.

More generally, the contradictions and tensions that emerged in the work organization of Tower were immanent and continuous. Insofar as it is possible to generalize, workers' attitudes and working practices continued to resonate deeply with what might be called the 'anarcho-socialist' tradition in which the achievement of nationalization was regarded as a very poor substitute for workers' control. Unionized workers now owned the enterprise but with what contrived deference South Wales miners could muster, in the interests of the 'collective' (a construct which, for Tower miners, was grounded in unreflective belief in the values of union membership) – on most occasions – they diligently abided by managerial *dictat*.

Beyond the founders and trade-union activists, the majority of employees were less directly involved in daily decision-making, although this lesser involvement should not be interpreted as disinterest. From its inception as a cooperative, Tower tried 'to encourage an open-door policy so that all the information we can possibly give gets down to the ground floor as well' (Cato, 2004: 188, quoting from an interview with one of the TEBO team).

Nonetheless, from interviews, observations and surveys undertaken, many employees indicated some disenchantment with the way the cooperative was being run. This disenchantment particularly related to a claimed lack of information, an alleged lack of contact with the board and a continuation of British Coal management attitudes. Such tensions came to a head in an astonishing 48-hour unofficial strike which was the result of a group of underground workers being disciplined for 'belt-riding', a not uncommon breach of health and safety regulations. Old habits die hard but, at the heart of this event was the issue of whether or not managers backed by statutory authority could exercise management control in a non-democratic and directive manner.

Practically, the matter was quickly settled in favour of the 'management'. But it led to a wider debate about the question as to how the worker-owners should tackle such issues and other disputes over managerial authority – was it as employees or as shareholders? Ultimately, the matter was resolved in favour of the *dictum* that once a member came through the gates s/he became an employee but the whole affair was a vivid reminder of the complex of organizational ambiguities which characterize any attempt to exercise workers' control through cooperative ownership, management and organization. This said, few worker-owners, if any, could now draw the lines between 'them' and 'us' with the same clarity or genuine conviction that they could have done before the buyout.

## Politics at Tower Colliery

Within Tower, a number of trends and tensions were identified concerning the operation of the mine as a worker-owned cooperative. Of course, in all these analyses, ambiguity was ever present and alternative interpretations possible. However, and importantly, these tensions were invariably the subject of internal debate. Before describing these tensions it is also important to place Tower within its own historical and political context, in order to provide a direct link to wider debates.

Firstly, political support from the neo-liberal Conservative government of the day[1] was essential to allow the TEBO bid to go forward. In addition, the TEBO team garnered immense sympathy from both trade unions and the population of South Wales. Contrary to the apparent political support coming from the government, the establishment of the cooperative was regarded as a defiant challenge to pit closures and a final defence of the coalfields ravaged by the same Conservative government. This general political support continued under the Labour government and was subsequently reinforced by the policy of political devolution which saw the creation of the National Assembly for Wales.

Secondly, during the last 10 years of British Coal ownership of Tower – presumably on the managerial principle of putting all the dangerous elements in an isolated location – many NUM activists had been transferred to the colliery, joining an already very active NUM lodge. Such individuals joined the Chair and the Secretary of the Tower Lodge, who shared a long history of rank-and-file and more general political activism throughout South Wales. Unsurprisingly, most of these activists were supporters of and workers for the TEBO team and they became founder directors of the Tower cooperative. The Lodge Secretary (O'Sullivan) became a board member and was briefly the personnel officer; he also served as Chair of the Management Board and was a tireless 'propagandist' for the cooperative. The Lodge Chair (Glyn Roberts) retained his position for three years before becoming the Personnel Officer.

During this period, O'Sullivan, the Chair of the Management Board, when accused of 'losing touch' with the underground worker-owners shifted his office alongside the pithead baths and had the connecting door sawn in half. This was simultaneously a graphic and symbolic indication of his determination to stay in touch with his fellow worker-owners.

To some degree, what we are calling 'the politics of Tower', is a worker-owner issue that permeated daily operations and intimately informed the way power was exercised across the working relationships between managers, supervisors and the workforce.

With respect to events at Tower, what is remarkable is not that this issue caused problems but that it was negotiated with such remarkable skill that it caused so few problems. Indeed, on occasion, the worker-owners' deep-rooted instinctive distrust of all things 'managerial' belied their behaviour.

This point is best exemplified by the cooperatives' response to a series of production problems over its 13 years of operation that would probably have shut the pit in the days of British Coal. In 1998, the face collapsed and buried the cutting machinery. The whole mine revolved around this piece of equipment (which would have cost about £1 million to replace). The engineers and colliers devised methods to dig the machinery out, repair it and restart coaling. Later (2002), methane gas under pressure came into the face from old workings – an extremely dangerous event which shut down face operations for over three months. Again, novel means were devised to resolve the problem. It involved the surreptitious purchase of four miles of domestic plastic waste pipe from building stockists around the country to channel the gas out of the pit (secrecy was necessary to stop prices being raised against them). Tower managed to start coaling again, just before the coal stocks were depleted and customers went elsewhere. Although the engineering ingenuity and attitudinal commitment only lasted during the course of these 'emergency' events, they were collectively owned experiences that were often referred to in our discussions and interviews. Individuals were clearly aware that their collective ownership of these problems had made it possible for the Tower cooperative to overcome problems that would probably have defeated British Coal.

More widely, with respect to understanding the political processes in a cooperative organizational form reliant upon some system of direct democracy, it highlights the analytical significance (and practical importance) of the need to continually renegotiate and redefine the relationship between the employment contract and being a shareholder.

## The nature and limits of change at Tower Colliery

During its 13 years as a cooperative, Tower Colliery could be considered both an economic and a social success. Internally, the organization and management were emancipatory and empowering to the workers and this permitted them, collectively, to reassert some degree of control over their economic and social space. Consequently, over the same period, where coal prices were stable and the global market contracting, Tower increased its sales and output, diversified its activities, created additional jobs, invested with a view to the longer term and distributed part of its increased surplus to support local community initiatives. Furthermore, the continued existence of Tower ensured that capital was effectively anchored in the local community. In addition, Tower's activities contributed to the economic security and wellbeing of the local community. However, despite the emancipatory nature of the democracy at Tower, there were found to be some fundamental constraints and limits.

In the first instance, 'work organization' at Tower was very traditional and varied little during the cooperative years from how the mine was organized under British Coal. In one sense this was hardly surprising as deep mining operates under an extensive legislative regime with certain layers of mine management being a statutory requirement. The mine itself was semi-automated and thus there was an element of techno-logical determinism influencing work organization. Research findings indicate that while there had been a fundamental change in the owner-ship of Tower, the tangible effect of this on daily work-relations between workers and managers was less visible. Everything *had* changed but as one underground shift-captain observed at the time 'We're all supposed to be on the same side now, but management is still management.' In part, what underlies this comment is the fact that operational work organization did not, and could not, change to any great extent due to the strict legislative criteria.

Indeed, the *fundamental* change in the labour process was reflected more in the *context* of work relations than the specific *content* of the labour process. As one individual commented:

> Someone once said to me its like working at a holiday camp for adults, working at Tower! Some people think it is, but you know, you still got middle management and senior management there. It's more relaxed though. Under British Coal you was working for a company and that company wanted X amount of coal and they put pressure on you to get that coal. With Tower, although we got to get certain production, there's not that much pressure on people, even though we know if we don't produce it, Tower could close. People are more 'laid back'.

Tower also established a training scheme for any potential board mem-bers and offered facilities to allow workers to progress into the more 'professional' jobs, such as financial management. However, it would be wrong to see the extant work tasks (i.e. mining coal) as somehow unrewarding. Given the intrinsic dangers of mining, virtually all roles carried a significant responsibility for safety and there were, in fact, very few unskilled jobs at Tower. The level of discretion that this engendered within the more 'owned' environment of Tower enabled groups of work-ers to develop their own domains within the workplace. In this sense, workers' control of the labour process increased when Tower operated as a cooperative.

This point can also be made about more traditional workplaces, but within the democratic context of Tower, it allowed workers to operate with a greater autonomy and gave all the appearances of providing a platform for enhanced political and democratic participation. At the very least, the 'voice' of the workers was always listened to and could not be ignored.

Another issue explored was the extent to which the democracy of the cooperative led to an enhanced role for coalface workers. Under the previous (British Coal) regime, shift captains played an important representative role; and this role continued. Nonetheless the impression created was that worker-owners' relations between the shift-captains and operational management softened and, although a 'them and us' attitude continued to prevail, there was far greater willingness to accommodate each other's perspectives and values than had been the case under the British Coal regime. Differential interests became more muted; control issues more diffuse and mutual interests became enhanced. Historic specificity was important here, as 150 years of institutionalized mistrust could not (and did not) evaporate overnight despite the establishment of the workers' cooperative.

Modern mining may look like a production line but close up considerable variation takes place. At Tower, this required the winning over of the active participation of the workers, who were the possessors of the specialized skills and knowledge needed, and this meant that they enjoyed considerable work discretion. While the mine remained open these skills were in demand and were not easily substituted. This was enhanced in the situation of Tower as the only deep mine in South Wales, and Tower was heavily reliant on this special category of workers. Added to these circumstances was the new dimension of the employees also being owners.

It is perhaps surprising that these tensions did not create more problems than they appear to have done. A possible explanation is the very active debates that took place across a wide range of issues and circumstances. Most of these could be considered 'informal', and beyond what was required by production requirements and the line between employee and owner. However, such debates, although they could be viewed as tangential to the purpose in hand, were in essence the social processes that 'managed' the tensions between the bureaucratic/technical systems and the reality of the democracy. Therefore it was helpful, in the long run, to legitimize these debates, to accept that maintaining the hard line between employee and owner wasn't always possible and that such discussions are an essential feature of a cooperative. It did make managing work even more political (and probably more difficult than had been the case under British Coal) and required a different approach to managing than that required by more traditional mining practices.

This supports the idea that such initiatives can act as a counter to the globalizing pressures inherent to the contemporary economic system. Nonetheless, despite 13 years of operation as a successful cooperative, it is evident that tensions persisted in the organizational structure and relationships at Tower. This was despite the fact that lasting improvements were made in the wider socio-economic milieu – including substantial improvements in organizational relationships, workplace democracy and control, workers' wellbeing, employee rewards, social performance and productivity.

In terms of employment, mining remains a male-dominated industry and Tower was in an area where a large-scale loss of full-time male jobs had occurred. The regeneration of the colliery as a cooperative therefore offered some degree of amelioration to this trend in that it actually expanded the number of full-time male jobs during a period in which such jobs had been shrinking locally. More importantly, in terms of the skill mix, Tower had the full range of job categories found in a working deep mine. In addition to the mix of often highly skilled surface and underground workers, it involved extensive use of information and communications technology (ICT) in controlling and monitoring the mining process. The information technology (IT) control room was typically staffed by ex-face workers who had been re-trained for this 'white collar' work. In contrast, the few women employed at Tower were almost exclusively employed in the offices and canteen but were full members of the cooperative and benefited equally from any pay increases and improvements in the terms and conditions of employment.

Since we were dealing with just one mine, it is not possible to generalize for the whole Welsh economy in terms of 'widespread' employment creation. However, within the local Hirwaun and Aberdare area, the impact was very significant. After the buyout, the mine continued for 13 years and the employment and other opportunities it created can be viewed as a singular medium- to long-term achievement. If the lessons of Tower's survival are applicable in other contexts, the positive implications for employment are clear.

Furthermore, over the period of its operation as a cooperative, Tower was able to achieve employment advantages better than under British Coal and in comparison with 'traditional' privatized production. A sick-pay scheme that provided for 6 months on full pay (under British Coal only Statutory Sick Pay was available) serves as an indicative example of this, as well as the highest average wage rates for face workers in the UK (Cato, 2004).

Maintaining democratic organization and control, and ensuring organizational effectiveness in 'the market' remained probably the critical managerial activity throughout the life of the cooperative. Indeed, the absolute limit to the democracy at Tower was the strategic tension between prioritizing the objective of business success as opposed to cooperative and social objectives. The financial and technical trajectory and supporting culture was based upon the desire for Tower to survive as a successful business. The formation of the cooperative was a means of saving jobs, the mine and the way of life it sustained, as well as providing a broad example to others. Ultimately however, these wider social objectives could only be achieved if the mine survived economically. The combination of these two ideas tended to give priority to the financial and technical strategic arguments, at least in the short to medium term. In part, this explains the reason for staying with the structure and working practices that existed before the buyout, and with the attempt to sustain the difference between owner and employee. This strategy was successful in terms of employment, production, general profitability and in achieving an improved market position for Tower.

Nonetheless, it can be argued that this short- to medium-term accommodation of the cooperative and social objectives with business success led to the decision not to invest in the sinking of the required new shaft for continued coaling, and hence the decision to close the pit. In this sense it is argued that, ultimately, the realities of the all-pervasive 'market system' compromised the ideals and values of the workers' cooperative at Tower.

Of course, it can always be argued that a worker-controlled enterprise, operating within a capitalist society in a neo-capitalist manner, is far from ideal. But such a view fails to appreciate the practical achievements and the ideological challenge that the Tower experience demonstrates. At the level of social practice, the choices facing the Tower cooperators were long-term unemployment or investing their meagre redundancy payments in a collective enterprise. In choosing the latter course of action they not only preserved jobs, work, income and their own sense of themselves as powerful social actors but – in the process – created the biggest local employer in the area which sustained the local economy during an extremely difficult period. Also, at the level of ideological challenge, it is easy to forget that the intentions of the Conservative government had been to promote employee share-ownership and expand the scope of the neo-liberal privatization project which, if met, would have furthered the managerialist capitalist agenda. Against all expectation, what the Tower cooperators proceeded to enact was a highly productive organization operating through direct democracy which, at least for a time, put in place an enterprise grounded in the community which fed profits back to serve the collective social interests of the locality. The cooperative thus created a stream of 'public profit' which – through what we might call 'the cooperative economic multiplier' – facilitated economic prosperity without worker exploitation.

## Conclusions: Deviant mainstreaming

> Few things are harder to put up with than the annoyance of a good example.
>
> (Mark Twain Puddn'head Wilson, 1894)

Tower Colliery was such an example. It was a place of work where the majority still had to go underground. The workers were the owners, but they also had a life outside of work and didn't hang around at the end of their shift. From the outside, the colliery gave little appearance of moving from British Coal ownership and a look at the annual reports will give few clues to the radical change that had taken place; revenue, markets and profits were, and remained, all important. Consequently, it would appear, *prima facie*, that the charge of incorporation and degeneration (Mellor et al., 1988) that is historically used against such 'islands of socialism' could yet again be confirmed.

However, a closer inspection reveals outcomes, social relationships and discourses that were radically different from the days of British Coal. These differences were not just internal, but were also evident in external activities such as marketing. Central to these differences was the form of bottom-up ownership and control. The redistribution of power enabled radical changes to take place in the use of the value created in the production process, and indicated a qualitative shift towards equality in work and social relationships, in discourse and in decision-making. A community was created that challenged the institutions and their legitimating that had existed in the days of British Coal, and it is argued that a 'symbolic laboratory' had been created as suggested by Buechler (1999) that had emancipatory qualities.

Insofar as it operated successfully in the market – producing, selling and financing its activities – the Tower cooperative colliery affirmed its appearance as a business like any other in private ownership. However, the way it was owned and controlled was not only different, but serves as an example of an alternative way of working and sharing the benefits of work. However, the fundamental question is in what way could it be said that the alternative features of the Tower cooperative were an emancipatory challenge to the dominant mode of capitalist production and is it possible to say that Tower was in 'transgressive contention' (McAdam et al., 2001)?

We suggest three possible answers. Firstly, Tower was (and still is) an inspiration for others to emulate. It may not have been – in Crossley's (1999) terms an entire 'working utopia' – but it was a potent practical symbol that an alternative can work and survive. Many of the Tower activists and founders continue to be directly involved in advising other cooperative organizations, credit unions and local community regeneration schemes. It also inspired a range of social economy and community activity throughout South Wales. As Crossley himself (1999) suggests, it was inspiring and rejuvenating to visit Tower and talk to the worker-owners.

Secondly, the trajectory of Tower was not towards degeneration of its ideals and purpose, if anything it suggested that new 'social skills' were developed by the worker-owners, pointing towards ongoing and well embedded social change. Clearly market pressures and coal contracts dominated the cooperative's survival, but the experience did not become a simple contingent translation of market forces inevitably leading to degeneration. These forces were actively contended and counteracted over its 13 years, and within Tower there was constant discourse over the tension between the need to have technical and managerial expertise on the board and two of the six board members being subject to election every year.

Thirdly, Tower challenged the legitimacy of the dominant mode of top-down capitalist organization. Tower's very success within the market – but with an alternative form of ownership and control – is a fundamental challenge to the authority of the discourse that supports companies dominated by a small number of private owners. This, in turn, can be linked with current ideological fashions of entrepreneurship, leadership, and top-down governance and managerialism. Tower defied these powerful concepts and legitimating assumptions and in this way deviated from them.

Moreover, Tower's very success challenges the practical usefulness of such terms. Tower acted as a deviant, having the appearance of the mainstream while at the same time serving to challenge and undermine the mainstream. This is what makes cooperative production a successful challenge: in expressing the value of 'self-reliance', it appeared to conform to the mainstream but, simultaneously, challenged it in a way that was difficult to frame or label – far less demonize – as an opposition movement. It therefore became an alternative way of seeing the tension between affirming and challenging.

The assumption that without revolutionary change in the context, the inevitable cycle will be towards degeneration and incorporation, and that social movements not mobilizing are in 'abeyance', is challenged. What is suggested here is that surviving – and even thriving – while retaining alternative practices and discourses is in itself a challenge that is difficult to ignore. Cooperative survival does not depend wholly on a negotiated compromise with the more powerful. Indeed, the emancipatory ownership and control practices pose an ongoing but fundamental challenge of the dominant mode of managerial thinking and practice. It is therefore suggested that the notion of 'deviant mainstreaming' captures this tension and the ironic quality summed up so well in the quote from Mark Twain above.

Tower Colliery finally closed as a working mine on 25 January 2008, some 15 years after British Coal had decided that it was 'too expensive to run'. As the NUM Lodge Chairman Dai Davies said at the ceremony to mark the day:

> The Government hasn't closed us, British Coal hasn't closed us, we have made our own decision. We got to the end with our pride and dignity intact. It's a victory for the miners.

## Note

1. The Conservative government viewed the employee buyout as another means of spreading share ownership among the working classes. Politically and ideologically, they considered it an extension of their privatization policy, which had already sold off many other nationalized industries. The putative new owners, of course, held different views.

## References

Archer, M. S. (1996) *Culture and Agency: The Place of Culture in Social Theory.* Cambridge University Press. Cambridge.

Bagguley, P. (2002) 'Contemporary British Feminism: A social movement in abeyance?', *Social Movement Studies*, 1 (2), pp. 169–185.

Bayat, A. (1991) *Work, Politics and Power: An International Perspective on Workers' Control and Self-Management.* Zed Books. London.

Buechler, S. M. (1999) *Social Movements in Advanced Capitalism: The Political Economy and Cultural Construction of Social Activism.* Oxford University Press. Oxford.

Cato, M. S. (2004) *The Pit and the Pendulum: A Cooperative Future for Work in the South Wales Valleys*. University of Wales Press. Cardiff.

Cooke, P. (1985) 'Class practices as regional markers'. In Gregory, D. and Urry, J. (Eds.), *Social Relations and Spatial Structures*. Macmillan. London.

Crossley, N. (1999) 'Working utopias and social movements: An investigation using case study materials from radical mental health movements in Britain', *Sociology*, 33 (4), p. 809.

Crossley, N. (2002) *Making Sense of Social Movements*. Open University Press. Buckingham.

Della Porta, D. and Diani, M. (1999) *Social Movements, an Introduction*. Blackwell Publishing. Oxford.

Fligstein, N. (2001) *Social Skills and the Theory of Fields*. University of California. Berkeley.

Gates, J. R. (1999) *The Ownership Solution: Toward a Shared Capitalism for the Twenty-First Century*. Penguin. London.

Habermas, J. (1981) 'New social movements', *Telos*, 49, pp. 33–37.

Hyman, R. (1989) *Strikes* (4th Edition). Macmillan Press. Basingstoke & London.

Kelly, J. (1988) *Trade Unions and Socialist Politics*. Verso. London.

Kelly, J. (1998) *Rethinking Industrial Relations, Mobilization, Collectivism and Long Waves*. Routledge. London.

Kendall, W. (1969) *The Revolutionary Movement in Britain 1900–21: The Origins of British Communism*. Weidenfeld and Nicholson. London.

Massey, D. (1984) *Spatial Divisions of Labour: Social Structures and the Geography of Production*. Macmillan. London.

McAdam, D., Tarrow, S. and Tilly, C. (2001) *Dynamics of Contention*. Cambridge University Press. Cambridge.

Mellor, M., Hannah, J. and Stirling, J. (1988) *Worker Co-Operatives in Theory and Practice*. Open University Press. Milton Keynes.

Melucci, A. (1995) 'The process of collective identity'. In Johnston, H. and Klndermans, B. (Eds.), *Social Movements and Culture*. University of Minnesota Press. Minneapolis.

Mouzelis, N. (1995) *Sociological Theory: What Went Wrong?* Routledge. London.

O'Sullivan, T., Eve, J. and Edworthy, A. (2001) *Tower of Strength: The Story of Tyrone O'sullivan and Tower Colliery*. Mainstream Publishing. Edinburgh.

Pendleton, A. (2001) *Employee Ownership, Participation and Governance: A Study of ESOPs in the UK*. Routledge. London.

Prychitko, D. L. (1991) *Marxism and Workers' Self Management*. Greenwood Press. Westport CT.

Putnam, R. D. (1988) 'Diplomacy and domestic politics: The logic of two-level games', *International Organization*, 42 (3), pp. 427–460.

Rutherford, T. (1988) 'Industrial restructuring, local labour markets and social change: The transformation of South Wales', *Contemporary Wales*, 4, pp. 9–44.

Tilly, C. (1995) 'Contentious repertoires in great Britain, 1758–1834'. In Traugott, M. (Ed.), *Repertoires and Cycles of Contention*. Duke University Press. Durham, NC.

Thompson, E. P. (1968) *The Making of the English Working Class*. Pelican. Harmondsworth.

Traugott, M. (Ed.) (1995) *Repertoires and Cycles of Contention*. Duke University Press. Durham, NC.

Twain, M. (2009 [1894]) *Pudd'nhead Wilson and Those Extraordinary Twins*. Barnes and Noble. Lyndhurst, NJ. Classics Series.

Unofficial Reform Committee. (1912) *The Miners' Next Step: Being a Suggested Scheme for the Reorganisation of the Federation*. South Wales Miners Federation. Tonypandy.

Webb, B. and Webb, S. (1897) *Industrial Democracy*. Trade Unionists of the United Kingdom. London.

Williams, R. (1973) 'Base and superstructure in marxist cultural theory', *New Left Review*, November–December, (82), pp. 3–16.

# 4
# Workers' Participation in a Globalized Market: Reflections on and from Mondragon

*Joseba Azkarraga Etxagibel, George Cheney and Ainara Udaondo*

## Introduction

The Mondragon Cooperative Experience (MCE) is a general but recognized term that refers to the totality of contexts surrounding the Mondragon cooperatives in the Basque Country, Spain. The centrepiece of that movement and institution is the Mondragon Corporation (hereafter called simply Mondragon) – a large, diverse conglomerate of cooperatives federated into a cooperative group. There are 120 cooperatives in total, the majority of which are medium sized, representing four sectors: finance (banking and insurance); industry (including automotive, machine tools, appliances and electronics); distribution; and knowledge (including primary, secondary and tertiary education, plus 12 technical schools). Mondragon is currently the largest private firm in the Basque Country, in terms of both employees and sales, and the seventh largest private firm in Spain. The headquarters of the group, and indeed the seat of cooperative movement in the Basque Country, is the small city of Mondragón (in Spanish) or Arrasate in Euskara, the Basque language.

Another reason why it is appropriate to refer to the MCE is because it has taken on a mythical status in some circles, especially in commentaries over alternative economic and organizational forms (see, e.g., Whyte and Whyte, 1991). Curiously, or perhaps not so surprisingly, Mondragon is described by some commentators as a utopia, by others as a sell-out of democratic ideals (compare, e.g., Morrison, 1991; Kasmir,

1996). In reality, neither version of the experience can be sustained argumentatively, although both narratives hold certain elements of truth (Cheney, 1999, 2002). A more balanced view sees the MCE as a genuine, though inevitably limited, attempt at realizing a long-term business venture with profound social and political, as well as economic values, in mind. On a more practical level, such a commitment implicates sophisticated models of management, highly participative techniques, transparent communication (in all directions), enhanced coordination and cohesion, and with attention to collective as well as individual goals (Azkarraga, 2007).

A few more historical details are required here. Fagor, the first cooperative in the Mondragon system, was established in 1956, producing small lamps and heating devices. That brand name now applies to many other products and represents a large industrial group within the corporation. However, the cooperative ideal and model in the area developed over a period of 15 years before Fagor opened its doors – a period characterized by social upheaval, poverty, widespread disease, dictatorship, and political and cultural oppression. General Francisco Franco's fascist regime oppressed Catalonia and the Basque Country because of their support for the democratic socialistic government and the legally established Second Spanish Republic. These regions were two of the most industrialized areas of Spain – the first parts of modern Spain to become industrialized in the mid-19th century. However, while the period under Franco's rule was marked by significant industrialization elsewhere, there was a significant economic drain on the Basque Country and Catalonia in terms of taxation. Not surprisingly, there was less state-sponsored attention to development in those regions.

In the town of Mondragón/Arrasate, the large industrial firm Unión Cerrajera (UC) – a typically hierarchic and bureaucratic capitalist firm – played an enormous economic role. It was from this company that the Basque parish priest, José María Arizmendiarrieta, recruited five young engineers to work on his vision of a practical, but transformative, economic model for the Mondragón valley. Following 15 years of discussions, planning and education, they opened the first industrial cooperative in 1956 (for a detailed account see Azkarraga, 2010).

This group of engineers proposed democratic reforms within the traditionally hierarchical capitalist industry, including the sharing of some of the equity of the firm by employees, but these ideas were rejected by top management at UC. This moment marked the origin of the cooperative movement in the Mondragón valley. The kernel idea was to guarantee dignity through participation in decision making for all employees, and by extension in the larger economic system.

The key dimensions of Mondragon's emergent cooperativism from the early 1940s can be outlined as follows. In explicit terms, the origins of Mondragon concerned three important questions on the conduct of business: ownership; direction or authority; and the distribution of profit. In turn, all three questions have their bearing on actual participation. In more specific terms, the principles of Mondragon sought to enact a strong blend of economic and 'political' or decisional ownership for all workers, putting real and sustained power in their hands. Even more dramatically, the cooperatives began with a vision that included contributions to the community, to the common development of the area and to social justice. This represented the external commitment of the cooperatives. Ultimately, the Mondragon vision placed a premium on self-management that would apply not only to the internal workings of the firm but also to the larger society in which the cooperatives operated and were sustained (e.g. Azkarraga, 2007). The objective of Arizmendiarrieta and other founders was one of a thoroughly participative society, building on Basque traditions of governance, drawing upon local knowledge regarding the mechanism of participation at group, firm and community levels, and yet utilizing relevant forms of knowledge and examples from other parts of the world.

During their first two decades (1956–1976), the cooperatives experienced tremendous business growth, ironically benefiting from certain tax laws that favoured cooperatives because of Franco's commitment to Catholic agricultural cooperatives in the south of Spain, and because there was a reasonably open market for industrial production within Spain due to its relative international isolation.

After the end of Franco's regime in 1975, and the sanctioning of the new democratic constitution in 1978, the 1980s witnessed an expansion and transformation of the MCE, as the Basque cooperatives faced the effects of Spain joining the European Economic Community in 1986. The 1990s – especially 1992 in Europe – featured significant market globalization. The cooperatives had to adapt to a wider competitive market, particularly for industrial and household products, and they chose to import some managerial regimes from other parts of the world (see Cheney, 1999, 2006). Today, the Mondragon cooperatives are fully engaged in the global market. In fact, Mondragon today represents the largest system of work-owned and managed businesses in the world.

The great diversity of the Mondragon cooperatives – with respect to size, economic activity, location and vitality of 'social organs' or councils – makes it exceedingly difficult to generalize about the entire system. Nevertheless, responses to recent globalization processes and pressures at the end of the 20th century and the beginning of the 21st century have meant substantial, visible changes for the Mondragon cooperatives. In terms of structure and reach, the Mondragon cooperatives gradually extended production and sales to a variety of countries and continents – often through strategic acquisitions, in addition to pursuing numerous business partnerships with other different types of business players, and the establishment of commercial delegations and industrial plants (often acquired) in numerous countries around the world, including in the Americas. Moreover, there are now non-cooperative enterprises at the heart of the group, which has increased the number of non-owning employees/members, as well as the number of temporary workers (Errasti et al., 2003). The overall organizational fragmentation and geographical dispersion led to an increase in complexity and scale, which in turn has diminished what might be called authentic democratic decision-making processes. (For relevant reviews see Cheney, 2006; Azkarraga, 2007; Williams, 2007; Altuna, 2008; Sarasua, 2010.)

Because of the cultural flows between the cooperatives and their larger social-political-economic contexts, the cooperatives' organizational cultures have certainly become more individualistic, more consumerist, and generally more utilitarian (see Azkarraga, 2007, 2010). These shifts in social attitudes, largely associated with the process of globalization, have created profound changes in local practices, on multiple levels (Cheney, 1999, 2002). Especially, Cheney found, over the course of the 1990s, a major part of this shift was embodied in the master symbol of 'customer service' – both inside and outside the cooperatives. That is, as members of the community saw themselves less as citizens and more as consumers, the cooperatives themselves imported managerial regimes that privileged constant orientation towards the customer/client. In a very real sense, then, the developments of consumerism, careerism and bureaucratization in the emergence of a large managerial superstructure co-occurred.

All of these trends are important for understanding the internal functioning of the cooperatives as well as their larger social, political, economic and environmental contexts. Perhaps the first, and most important, principle of the Mondragon cooperatives – though not always explicit in MCE documents – has always been business success in the market. From a broader social standpoint, it is this financial success that makes it possible to carry out the project of societal transformation supported by the cooperative movement (if we may call it that, at least loosely), understood as a collection of social as well as economic commitments and processes (the generation of employment, the equitable distribution of wealth, the return of some surplus to the larger community, with all of this being created through private/communitarian firms that are democratic and participative).

In this sense, the cooperative movement of Mondragon has been necessarily pragmatic, alert to the powerful and dynamic demands of the market (Azkarraga, 2007). At the same time, the cooperatives are committed to maintaining their social system and cooperative identity, in an increasingly globalized economy. A key theoretical as well as practical question is how to reinvigorate and perhaps transform participation in a way that recognizes the internal and external changes which have occurred, yet takes the best of local and global knowledge to bring employee decision making and commitment again to the forefront of everyday business practices. Indeed, under the pressure as well as the perception of global competition, this question has been considered at various points for two decades and is receiving more focused and concrete attention today, following a process of self-reflection on the cooperatives values opened at Mondragon in 2005. Taking workers' participation seriously in Mondragon involves both deep ideological commitments, tracing back to the origins of the cooperatives, and strategic competitive advantages derived from enhanced employee involvement. This chapter thus presents an analysis of these issues as well as practical initiatives related to this. Understanding the course of these developments is crucial not only for updating the long-standing case but also in making useful applications to the vitality and potential of cooperatives in other parts of the world.

## The foundations for a renewed approach to participation and decision making at Mondragon

In this regard, it is important to distinguish between participation and democracy, considering their areas of distinction and overlap. To be sure, both are contested terms, with long and multiple histories (Cheney et al., 2011). Moreover, each term inevitably carries with it certain ideational and ideological content, to some extent shaped or framed by different viewpoints. The two terms may be used to create a four-cell grid, meaning that specific cases may be classified or examined heuristically in terms of being high or low on each dimension. For example, an organization may be highly participative in terms of the activities of its members, yet not very democratic in terms of its capacity to influence major decisions or with respect to ownership. This was one of the reasons why Dahl (1985) wrote *A Preface to Economic Democracy*. He recognized the limits of many models of decision making and participation, and argued strongly in his later career that authentic democracy required both tangible economic sharing as well as actively used channels of democratic governance. As we discuss below, it is entirely appropriate to consider the Mondragon system by the measure of this two-pronged treatment of democracy, particularly insofar as the system itself is explicitly grounded in both. There is obviously much more to be said for developing such a meta-analysis of employee participation and democratic organization, but we do not have the space to perform that here and we direct the reader to Parker et al. (in press).

The Mondragon cooperatives have been criticized regularly for not carrying forth a strong commitment to democracy, in terms of their representational system and work processes. For two decades, critiques of Mondragon's system have been advanced, principally from the point of view that democracy was, ultimately, of limited scope, deteriorating or simply overcome by managerialist, bureaucratic and market-oriented concerns (e.g. Kasmir, 1996). Most such critiques have certain traction; growth, professionalism and consumerism have all taken their toll on direct participation. However, a number of critiques have been advanced without deep or long-term knowledge of the functioning of the system, let alone the diversity of opinions and practices within the corporate and cooperative reach of Mondragon. Moreover, as Cheney (1999, 2002) described, the tensions within the system over social values remained dynamic and unresolved, even as Mondragon was globalizing in several regards. These critical analysis critiques should be considered not only with respect to sweeping assessments of the system as a whole but in terms of particular sectors and individual cooperatives. Moreover, as we discuss in this chapter, the vitality of the 'social organs' or councils, in addition to the depth and breadth of training in participative forms of work and decision making, are key to evaluations of democracy in the cooperatives. Recent discussions, initiatives and planning by Mondragon offer hope for the revival of some of the democratic practices that had declined, especially since the late 1980s.

Fortunately, from our perspective, in 2005 the cooperatives set in motion a process of self-reflection and debate entitled 'Reflection on the Meaning and Future Directions of the Cooperative Experience' (hereafter referred to as Reflections on the Future of the Cooperative Experience, or simply RFCE). This unprecedented project for Mondragon included reflections by cooperative members about themselves, the past, the present and the future of the Mondragon cooperative movement, considering in particular barriers to and mechanisms for enhancing horizontal control, and genuine participation in decision making by members. The cooperatives therefore paused to look at themselves critically – to understand themselves not so much in a self-affirming way, but to consider how to take decision making and participation beyond immediate business needs and concerns. This process of reflection, which was initiated before the Great Recession of 2007 onwards, was led by the cooperative group's Department of Social Management, in close collaboration with Mondragon University (specifically, LANKI, the Institute of Cooperative Research).

This institutional, broad-based reflection process was a landmark event in the MCE's history, for two reasons: *quantitatively*, in that all the social bodies from practically all the cooperatives took part; and *qualitatively*, by inviting ideas that transcended the business challenges immediately on the table. The fact that this process began before the 2007 global recession is also extremely important. Overall, this was, and is, a debate about ideas – probing the major topics of decision making and participation, cooperative education, and interaction between cooperative employee participation and socio-political participation in the wider community. In Pateman's vision (Pateman, 1970), which indeed parallels that of many leaders at Mondragon, past and present, the interdependence between community, national and economic participation, and the creation of opportunities for direct democracy are considered as vital.

We now turn to summarize that process of debate, focusing on the results that implicate decision making and participation, extending to social transformation.

### Outline of the process of systematic reflection

This process of reflection (RFCE) originated with a core concern that was expressed plainly at the Mondragon Cooperative Congress in May 2003.

Frequently we hear complaints about the absence of cooperative debate in the heart of the Corporation and of the presence of an increasingly pragmatic perspective that is distant from the cooperative principles that we approved in the I Congress. There has been a movement towards conventional commercialism, and towards topics that are not aligned with our authentic identities as cooperators. On the other hand, it is clear that the balance between our principles and values and the economic treatment of the capital and work that was approved in 1987 and 1991 has not been usefully updated ... The German theologian Juan Bautista Metz noted that in present day Europe it is not religion that transforms the bourgeois society; rather, it is more the bourgeois society that reduces and detracts from the best part of the Christian religion. Could something like this be happening to us with respect to our principles? ... Are we moving away from the original purpose of cooperative experience, which was to model a more cooperative and caring type of person? Are we forgetting the great force of the education, to nourish the values sustaining our cooperativism? We therefore ask if now is the time for a real debate about these issues.

> (Permanent Commission of Mondragón, 2003,
> unpublished report, n.p.)

Thus, many attendees expressed a desire to reflect on the meaning and direction of the cooperative experience. Some charged that there was a lack of debate over cooperativism within the group and a corresponding need for empirical analysis of the extent and limits of participation today.

The first step taken to address these concerns and complaints was a series of meetings with all the presidents (the democratically elected, highest representatives) of the Mondragon cooperatives. These meetings produced the following set of observations. First, there has been a loss of explicitly cooperative identity; that sense has diminished as the corporation has grown and has been especially felt since Mondragon has become truly global in its holdings. Second, it is necessary to update or renew cooperativism (as a broad set of commitments, including equality, solidarity and participation) and cooperative identity (as a value-based brand) to make it more attractive, especially to younger generations. This recognition first became apparent in the late 1980s, but it has begun to be addressed by younger leaders in the cooperatives in the past decade. Third, people are deemed to be the main asset of the cooperative model, and participation needs to be supported at all levels of

the organization. There is a broad acknowledgement that active participation beyond the sphere of one's job has diminished over the decades
in the cooperatives, and both an historical review and a contemporary
approach are needed to reinvigorate democracy within the cooperatives.
Fourth, social transformation, in the sense of support for community
projects beyond the scope of the cooperatives themselves, should be
pursued more vigorously towards a more thoroughly democratic society.
Thus, in an important way, the entire set of concerns speaks of issues of
participation.

The first set of findings from the cooperative presidents were placed
within the context of research on the MCE, carried out since 2001 by
LANKI, the Institute of Cooperative Research. The findings converged
on this imperative: the need to return to a shared feeling of belonging by worker-owners as well as active debate, in order to revitalize
participation and the involvement of all cooperative members, especially considering specific avenues and parameters for decision making.
With this goal uppermost in mind, a wide-ranging process of reflection and debate was opened to everyone in the various bodies (or
organs) of the Mondragon cooperatives (i.e. governing councils, social
councils and management councils).[1] After the presidents' reports were
offered, a larger cooperative debate was opened up, inviting contributions by all the members of all the 'organs' or councils of all the
individual cooperatives. In total, there were 134 sessions involving more
than 1300 *socios* or members (worker-owners) from the cooperatives.
The reflection process took place between 2005 and 2006; it was final-
ized with a report submitted and approved by the 10th Cooperative
Congress on 30 May 2007. Since then the recommendations of the
report have been established and prioritized, guiding the lines of action
of Mondragon.

For the deployment of the RFCE a diverse working group was established, consisting of members of the Mondragon group's standing committee (20 members, who played the role of facilitators in the meetings)
and researchers from the LANKI Institute (8 members, who also carried
out the role of facilitators, were in charge of the technical aspects of the
process: that is, following up on the sessions, gathering and systemizing
information, analysing the results and preparing the final diagnosis).
See Table 4.1 for details of the bodies, the number of meetings and the
number of participants.

The debating sessions were conducted at the sites of the cooperatives. It was the cooperatives themselves who decided how to articulate
the debate in their bodies. The meetings lasted about three hours and

*Table 4.1*   Numbers of bodies, meetings and participants in the RFCE

| Body | Number of meetings | Number of participants |
|---|---|---|
| SC (social council) | 38 | 407 |
| GC (governing council) | 19 | 164 |
| MC (management council) | 21 | 200 |
| GC-MC | 30 | 319 |
| GC-SC | 6 | 57 |
| GC-SC-MC | 18 | 197 |
| Standing committee | 1 | 16 |
| General council | 1 | 13 |
| Total | 134 | 1.373 |

adhered to the following format. They began by offering a context for the process of reflection and outlining steps to be taken. Then, there was a presentation for each of the subject areas, followed by debate. Each of the topics was discussed along the lines of two questions:

(1) 'Where are we?' (diagnosis);
(2) 'In what direction could we and would we like to go?' (projection).

The methodology for gathering information consisted of grouping the contributions of participants in each block and sharing them with the group. Using the material obtained in each of the meetings/debates, the technical team drew up a report or minutes. In order to validate the information gathered, each report was sent back to, and checked with, the cooperatives in which this method had been used.

Based on these minutes, an extensive diagnosis was conducted of the concerns and proposals put forward in each of the areas debated. In a detailed report, the LANKI Institute presented a quantitative and qualitative analysis of data gleaned from the RFCE. The content analysis of contributions to the reflection process was multi-phasic, both qualitative and quantitative. Thematic or topical clusters were generated from the verbatim minutes of discussion-and-debate sessions, although the precise degree of support for a particular idea was not strictly indicated or weighted. We do not have the space to detail the methodology or the data analysis here; however, we can point the reader to the technique called Metaplan, which was selected for this project by the Department of Human Resources at Mondragon: http://en.wikipedia.org/wiki/Metaplan.

The three major sections of the report, and indeed the entire process, were: participation and cooperation; cooperative education; and social transformation. From the start of this process of reflection, it was widely understood that the revival of the cooperative movement needed to take into account three main dimensions: democratic participation, in as direct a form as possible, as an essential feature internally (the *intramural* dimension); education, an instrument and the foundation stone of the cooperative movement, the basis for conscious participation and preparation for decision making; and commitment and social responsibility to the society and its betterment (the *extramural* dimension).

These three pillars have historically supported the MCE. Based on these foundations, the cooperatives have maintained a strong focus on job creation and equitable distribution of the wealth generated by the cooperatives. In the end, the MCE is an experience which aims to introduce democratic practices to the business world; in short, the creation of participative companies in which decision-making processes are regulated by democratic logic (an imperfect experience, but broadly relevant in the world of business and organizational democracy). These were the three main areas highlighted by a joint report of the cooperative presidents requiring reflection, discussion and action.

The central theme of the RFCE report, and indeed the MCE, is the question of participation, through both direct and representative democratic practices, and the sustenance of a broader cooperative culture. In this sense, participation within the Mondragon cooperatives – both at the level of the individual cooperative or in the MCE as a whole – can be considered in terms of Bernstein's (1976) three primary dimensions of participation in decision making: *the degree or extent of control* employees exercise over specific decisions; *the issues* (both type and range) over which control is exercised in a given case or in more general practice; and *the organizational level* at which control is exercised (i.e. in terms of containment at certain lower levels of the organization versus extending upwards). In a very real sense, the process of self-reflection at MCE entailed reconsideration of all of these, especially because of the support by top management for a wide discussion and debate about the very nature of democracy in the cooperatives, a re-evaluation and potentially a reinvention of practices that had been called for by some interests within the system. Moreover, while certain aspects of the RFCE process could be read as top-down, the fact was the process itself was quite open-ended. Bernstein's well-articulated and empirically based model reminds analysts of participation and decision making to clarify the locus of their observations. It also reminds practitioners to keep in mind all three important dimensions – as indeed should be done as the policy and practical implications of the reflection process described here become evident. Moreover, while Bernstein's model is focused on the internal dynamics of a firm or organization, the principles and their relevant indicators may be extrapolated to other levels of participation, such as the wider community.

The RFCE was, in itself, an extensive process of participation and decision making, and that is why we relate the structure, phases and conclusions of it in some detail. The principal conclusions from the RFCE, set out below, were approved by the group's maximum decision-making body (the 10th Cooperative Congress) in 2007; the lines of action, which have guided Mondragon in these areas since that date, were established and prioritized.

## Conclusions from and implications of the RFCE

### Reconsidering participation and cooperation

The tension between social and economic goals – broadly speaking – is well understood, not only with respect to the MCE but also in many other contexts. The dynamics of large organizations, of bureaucratization and of corporate capitalism and marketization can militate against sustained attention to individual dignity and community wellbeing. In the very origins of Mondragon, and embedded in its dual structure of leadership and governance, is just this tension. What we are calling a more 'political' orientation towards participation is the elevation of social goals and individual agency through the mechanisms of the councils. What might be called the 'technostrucure', on the other hand, is oriented towards more immediate goals of profitability, service to the client or customer, and market share.

At a more concrete level, the tension is manifest in the debate over the incorporation of new *socios*, or worker-owners into the system from outside the Basque Country and even Spain. This is not an easy matter to resolve because of the way cooperative identity and local identity mix or conflict, especially where the 'Basqueness' of Mondragon is concerned. But, apart from the local-cosmopolitan tension, there is concern over how best to extend cooperativism, even in organizational and business contexts, where it has little or no history, or perhaps a different sensibility. All this is being debated at the same time as the feeling of loss of the sense of being cooperative at the heart of the system.

Internal factors have played roles in the horizons of possibilities and limitations of participation in the cooperatives. In this respect, five tendencies have been identified by both participants in, and observers of, the MCE, all bearing mention here. First, the deterioration of informal, non-technical communication within the cooperatives; second, the relative inattention to more philosophical, political and social education (or 'formation') for *socios* or worker-owners; third, the ossification of some channels of communication such that they no longer function with great degrees of spontaneity and authenticity; fourth, the presentation of decisions as *fait accompli* rather than as the results of processes in which there is a certain degree of involvement by *socios*; and fifth, the inevitable – that is, in terms of the problems outlined above – decline in job satisfaction, especially in the sense of identification with cooperativism. These issues form a backdrop of concern and instigation for the RFCE process and outcomes.

In most of the meetings related to RFCE, the theme of participation received the greatest attention. Of course, the question of participation has greater immediacy than the other two discussion areas, cooperative education and social transformation: it is linked to the day-to-day working experience of each cooperative member and everyday life of the cooperative as a whole. As we have already introduced and discuss further below, participation applies perhaps most importantly to the functions, structures and performances of the organs or councils.

Two key areas were flagged for attention: first, what do we want to preserve and maintain? Second, what should we alter and improve?

Four core areas for preservation and maintenance stood out:

(1) democratic organization;
(2) participation at work;
(3) participation as a value in itself; and
(4) cooperation between cooperatives (or what is known at Mondragon as 'intercooperation').

The classic organizational structure of Mondragon cooperatives – especially in terms of the dual structure (representation and management), one-person-one-vote in the general assembly, and roles of the various decision-making bodies – were the features most often marked for 'conservation' and strengthening.

Participants discussed various levels and senses of participation and desired changes. First, they looked to enhance the personal connection to cooperativism. Many contributions focused on this level of cooperative functioning. A motivational deficit, a notable passivity among the members, was frequently observed. A great deal was said about the need to develop a feeling of belonging, especially in terms of interaction in day-to-day work processes.

Second, they sought to improve intracooperative institutional participation. We have already said that the contributions about 'what to conserve' were clearly in favour of maintaining the cooperative system in its classic sense: featuring political-institutional participation, or cooperative democracy. Within this call for improving institutional participation, one concern became clear: the need to improve the operations of both the governing councils and the social councils, especially in terms of communication between them. There was also an insistence on involving members more than just members of organs at a particular time.

Third, they sought to promote participation at work (organizational area). There were numerous calls for improvement in terms of participation at work. The majority of participants were clearly in favour of re-organizing work, such as: preferences for a less hierarchical organization of work, an organization based on autonomous work teams, and the need for cooperative members to draw up their own designs for management/participation/organization. That is to say, in addition to paying attention to the structures and processes that are strictly speaking democratic, the cooperatives are expected to introduce forms of participation and extend the margins of decision making in how work is carried out on a daily basis. This means a concerted effort to move beyond the legacy of Tayloristic elements in work design and towards a greater emphasis on horizontal control with a wider purview for decision making at the level of the work group or team.

Fourth, they sought to improve intercooperative institutional participation (cooperation between cooperatives). The importance of institutional participation does not end with intracooperative participation (inside the cooperative); cooperation between different cooperatives was also seen as something begging improvement. In this way, intercooperation was discussed not only in the strictly financial senses by which cooperatives support one another during challenging economic times but also in terms of regular networking and shared information.

A comprehensive approach to participation is therefore a concern; in other words, steps need to be taken to improve participation in all its dimensions: interpersonal, institutional and organizational. In fact, the different dimensions are very much interrelated (García, 2006). Organizational democracy requires a strengthening of the structures that make it possible, improvement of the decision-making processes within those structures, and the building, on a daily basis, of relations and interactions inherent to a democratic culture (Cheney et al., 1998).

The process resulted in calls for the enhancement of participation at the interpersonal level (personal and attitude levels), improvement in participation at work (what we call here the organizational level) and improvement in the democratic dimension of the cooperatives (at the widest institutional level). There was a very high assessment of the cooperative organization as a system that aims to incorporate democratic logic in decision making, of the cooperative movement as a driving force for democracy in the business world; accordingly, there was a call to improve participation on a complete institutional basis.

Faced with the emerging opinion of many that the cooperative movement is not so much about a legal-corporate framework but rather about a climate, a culture and an experience, and therefore, the focus is on improving participation and involvement at work (Cheney, 1997; Azkarraga, 2007; Altuna, 2008), the contributions to the process indicated that there is no desire to play down the legal-corporate-institutional side of the cooperative movement (directly democratic structures, 'one person one vote').

In the MCE there has nearly always existed a tension between reliance of local knowledge, especially about democratic practice, and the importation of management systems from an increasingly globalized market (Cheney, 1999, 2002; García, 2006; Azkarraga, 2007; Altuna, 2008). This tension is natural and to an extent inescapable; however, it must be revisited periodically and confronted creatively.

In relation to 'organizational improvement' participants expressed the need to strengthen the horizontal dimension of work organization. They highlighted the need for individual cooperatives, to some extent, to develop their own management models based on their values and experiences. In fact, this opinion was in line with some work already under way at the corporate level, as revealed in interviews by members of the LANKI Institute with cooperative presidents.

At the same time, participants felt that a management style based on cooperative values should be aimed at improving the quality of relations and communication in the daily life of the cooperatives.

In terms of 'strengthening democracy', there was a clear call for improving the democratic life of the cooperatives, for greater participation by a wider segment of the membership and for enhancement of institutional participation. In deeper terms, this requires two specific structural considerations. First, what should be done with the development of participation programmes in non-cooperative enterprises that are acquired or created abroad? Clearly research is required, not only on the complex mixes of labour, capital and management in a variety of other countries but also on the cultural contexts in which those various enterprises are situated. Further, some types of training in participation are implicated, even for non-cooperative firms.

Second, within existing cooperatives, there is a need to probe the specific aspects of participation, both facilitated and sometimes obstructed by governing bodies, depending on their particular composition, vitality, performance. The sheer variability in the strength of the social councils, across individual cooperatives, shows the difficulty of maintaining consistent and energetic participation by members and also of the possibilities for contemporary experiments in new techniques of participation. Ultimately, as is well known in the literature on participation and democratic theory, it is the group level that is a key to energizing and realizing democracy (Seashore, 1954).

### Renewing the commitment to and engaging in a multi-dimensional approach to education

One of the most widely understood conclusions about the MCE is that cooperative education has been central to the cooperatives' success and yet allowed to decline in importance over the past two decades (Azkarraga, 2007, 2010). In fact, it is difficult for there to be deliberate, self-reflective participation and a democratic decision-making process without ensuring that individual members are properly prepared. 'No experience that aims to come up with something different to what there is can maintain its identity over time if does not constantly nourish its own view of things, its course, and the way it sees and understands itself' (2007: 37).

The participants concluded that training has focused on the functions of the governing bodies, and that no work has been done on the area of social and ideological reflection. Many participants noted that there is no training pertaining to today's socio-economic challenges and the attendant implications for the cooperative movement.

The majority of participants in the RFCE thought that day-to-day work and institutional participation have always been important areas in terms of education – the most important in many cases. The size of the cooperative, or any designated unit within it, is an important factor for shared learning. Thus, the sheer scale of the cooperatives today creates a significant hurdle to this kind of cooperative experience. Three basic areas were identified:

(1) education in participation and decision making in governing bodies (organs or councils);
(2) education via day-to-day work, relying chiefly on personal contact; and
(3) education through wider organizational channels of information and institutional debates.

The management councils and the governing councils were also reproached for not having promoted cooperative education from their position of responsibility, given that the transmission of the cooperative spirit is understood to be one of their functions.

Participants called for a new phase in education/training to ensure that people and institutions are more aware of the professed cooperative values. The decisions that set an institution's course must be in line with their cooperative nature and, therefore, there was an express call for officials (institutional and executive) to ensure that their personal behaviour and institutional decisions were in keeping with the way cooperatives are, and how they do things.

Intensive training for the governing councils and social councils was therefore deemed essential to promote the cooperative identity. Participants in the RFCE noted the asymmetry between the institutional and executive branches, that is, an imbalance caused by the greater weight and the power of the executive (general manager) compared to the democratically elected bodies (governing councils). There was, therefore, a call for more training for institutional posts to achieve a more cooperative and participative organization. Managers and management councils were urged to revive social values alongside their more accustomed concern for the bottom line.

In summary, a new phase of education and training should fortify a feeling of belonging, to strengthen personal commitment to the cooperative and to deepen cooperative identity.

Six groups were identified as possible recipients of this new training: management councils; governing councils; social councils; managers and team leaders; new members; and, finally, the whole cooperative as a group.

Another important conclusion concerns the outline of specific forms of cooperative training, for which five types were identified for attention. The articulation of these approaches is especially important from the standpoint of revitalizing participation.

(1) *Dialogical and participative training.* This refers to a perspective on the worker-member as an active co-participant in the knowledge and practices of the educative process, in contrast with a top-down conception and style of education.

(2) *Ideological training*, placing the cooperatives in contemporary economic, political and social contexts, gives meaning and direction for work from within a common framework of cooperativism. Such educational experience may be considered as a crucial complement to technical and job-specific training.

(3) *Dynamic training* that brings the participants together and helps them to get to know each other can open interpersonal channels of communication towards relations based on equality and respect, as well as receptivity to constructive criticism.

(4) *Action training*, with a vocation for transformation, can enlarge the sense of the cooperatives' goals by encouraging members to be alert to means of improving the cooperative's role in society, as well as its performance along standard lines of assessment.

(5) *Training which is cyclical and on-going*, integrated in the company's normal processes, can serve as a continuous feedback loop for the organizations. Above all, the ongoing and reflexive nature of cooperative training is underscored.

These conclusions of the RFCE have led Mondragon to innovate and develop a comprehensive and forward-looking cooperative education strategy, the key points of which are explained in the next section.

## Extending the culture and network of participation and decision making beyond the organization

The RFCE explicitly addressed the wider social commitment beyond the cooperatives, treating identifiable community needs and opportunities for extending the circles of participation beyond the cooperatives.

This refers to the broad set of goals under the heading of 'social transformation'.

If we analyse the cooperatives' record of social commitment, beyond their being an agent for economic development and job creation, we find that they have encouraged the promotion of education and technical training, also been supportive of Basque culture and offered support for many different types of community initiative.

It is well known that the social and economic environment has changed. Today, ethical and social changes have to be rethought. A reading is required of the social reality and its challenges, based on cooperative values and vision. The cooperative experience has distinguished itself at creating self-management processes, 'cooperativizing' different spaces and areas, and extending the idea of citizen self-government and community leadership (Azurmendi, 1988; Azkarraga, 2007; Sarasua, 2010). How can this transformation work be continued today? In other words, how can a truly wide vision of participation and responsibility for decision making be stimulated and take hold? (see Pateman, 1970).

The fact of having set up a successful cooperative network was considered to be a contribution in itself: cooperation between cooperatives, the creation of umbrella organizations, having demonstrated the viability of the cooperative enterprise, having embodied cooperative values in society. This led to work on disseminating the cooperative experience in the region, nation and larger world.

This third arena of discussion on social transformation was aimed at identifying current social needs as 'possible areas of action', and invited people to contemplate unexplored avenues. As a result, the contributions already being made, which are now core elements (for example, job creation, support for education centres), were not frequently mentioned in the contributions. Education was commonly characterized throughout the reflection process as the starting point for social transformation. Yet, as we have already noted, non-technical, specifically cooperative education has been seen as lacking in the past two decades or more.

There is a second set of themes that we could call emergent, and these are related not only to the broad cooperative social commitment of the cooperatives but also to the participation of individual members in community-related programmes. These concerns consistently surfaced in discussions: support for the normalization of the Basque language in the cooperatives, and support for Mundukide, a non-governmental organization established by cooperative members to pursue cooperation with solidarity-economy projects in the developing world.

The spheres of activity most commonly highlighted for the larger community surrounding the cooperatives were: housing, needs of senior citizens, environment/ecology, the integration of immigrants and the reconciliation of work and family life. The reflection process revealed three distinct but overlapping orientations towards such work: charity and community service; socio-cultural transformation; and global social justice.

In more specific terms, there were numerous calls for a rethinking of the cooperatives' social funds. The suggestion was to prioritize the funds, overcome the tendency to fragment with unconnected support and focus actions by reflecting on common purposes. It could be an important idea when it comes to designing future policies.

At the same time, there was an expressed interest in creating alliances, collaborations or links with social movements and bodies working for social transformation (e.g. movements related to land-agriculture-nature, insertion of the underprivileged, the cultural sphere, emerging movements like ethical banking and fair trade). It is a second idea for seeing actions for social transformation.

The third idea to be highlighted is, without doubt, the one that was mentioned most. This was how to act in these areas, and the suggestion was to promote cooperative projects in social areas (to extend the cooperative formula to the social field).

## Programmes established as a result of the RFCE

This section summarizes the main courses of action that were taken after the approval at the 10th Cooperative Congress (2007) of the conclusions from the RFCE. Below we sketch new policies based on the three main areas of the reflection process: participation in decision making; education and socialization; and social transformation. Here we focus on participation and its implications for enhanced ownership of and contributions to decision making.

In the arena of participation and decision making, the self-diagnosis pointed to the need for approaches to be taken along the following lines: the field of motivation and cooperative behaviour; the institutional sphere and its dynamics (cooperative democracy); and the organizational field (work models tending towards horizontality and the engaged, proactive participation of all members of the cooperative).

Since 2007 different proposals have been articulated, designed to tackle the problems shown in the RFCE. The primary objectives have been to re-examine the corporate management model in the light of cooperative principles and values to fortify cooperative culture. Moreover, in 2010 continuing with the areas for improvement detected in the RFCE, the group's standing committee decided to continue with the lines of work started and also to pursue proposals in another area: institutional participation.

Below we offer a brief summary of each of the lines of work which, with more or less progress made, are currently under way at the cooperative group level.

First, the cooperative group has been looking towards a new management model. A central controversy at Mondragon for two decades has been how best to reconcile a familiar and globally dominant corporate management model, and its accompanying and often 'value-free' technostructure, with cooperative principles. In June 2007, Mondragon's general council approved an in-depth review of the corporate management model and the accustomed means of self-assessment. From that moment, and in keeping with the lines of action established after the RFCE, a great deal of work has been done, yet specific outcomes await still further work under the auspices of the corporation.

Second, much more than over the past two decades, the cooperatives are preparing to restructure and reinvigorate participation at the institutional level. This speaks to the basic democratic organization and character of the cooperatives. The diagnosis associated with the RFCE was clear in this regard: although the cooperatives remain an important reference point in economic democracy, they are in need of innovation as far as formal mechanisms and channels of participation are concerned.

This problem has been addressed from two standpoints:

(1) by designing better uses of existing channels of participation, within cooperatives as a whole and especially in their principal organs; and
(2) through developing new approaches to cooperative democracy.

When we speak of institutional dynamics of organizational democracy, and consistent with conceptions and practices well established in the Mondragon cooperatives, we include: the roles and functions of each council within a cooperative, the profile of cooperative leadership, the relations between the key organs or councils, the joint charge for the executive council and the management council in the construction of a cooperative culture; and of course, the constant improvement of communication channels and media. Further development of the project, along all of these lines, will be seen by 2013.

With respect to education, as a result of the reflection process, an updated, wide-ranging and standing Cooperative Education Model was established. The decision was taken to open up cooperative training to all levels of the organization (including governing councils, social councils, management councils, executive officials, and the rank and file), and specific programmes were designed (lasting between 8 and 16 hours) for each of these groups. The content and methodology proposed aimed to meet the need to promote reflection and participative debate about the social and identity dimensions of the cooperative.

In addition to these programmes, an Expert Course in Cooperative Development was designed at the Mondragon University (LANKI Institute), lasting 250 hours. The purposes of this training initiative are twofold: to provide the elements necessary for reflection on and promotion of the cooperative movement from a social and ideological viewpoint; and to offer the basic skills to train people who will work on the process of disseminating the cooperative idea at the heart of their organizations.

In the area of social transformation (in the wider field of social commitment, the extension of the cooperative idea and community participation), the White Paper approved at the Congress included the following lines of action:

(1)  to maintain links with institutional partners in the development of projects of social transformation;
(2)  to carry out sector-based analyses to establish targets for 'cooperativization' in the larger community;
(3)  to analyse the alternatives models for effectively and efficiently managing the cooperatives' social funds; and
(4)  to promote the cooperativization of new areas of society, and in so doing to develop policies for sustainability and social responsibility within them.

In this regard, a new institutional tool was created – in the form of a foundation – in order to meet the concern expressed in the RFCE about the slowdown in the cooperativization of new economic and social areas. To help achieve this strategy the two big cooperative supraorganizations in the Basque Country came together: Mondragon itself

and the Basque Cooperatives Confederation (the confederation represents the cooperative movement as a whole in the Basque Country,
beyond the MCE).

The heart of this approach is to identify and analyse the areas with the
greatest opportunity for cooperative development and then to earmark
funds for those sectors.

In addition to the establishment of this foundation, in 2008 a proposal emerged for social transformation and community development
in and for the Alto Deba, a Basque administrative division (the area
where the cooperative experience was born). This was not an official
effort by Mondragon, but a project promoted by the convergence of different socio-economic and popular groups in the area: presidents of the
Fagor group in a personal capacity, change agents from Mondragon University (LANKI Institute), the Arizmendi cooperative school and other
social agents in the area.

The Mondragón valley – and, to an extent, the Basque Country as well – has unparalleled community structures based on self-
organization. Within this context, there is high density and diversity of
cooperatives, in the sectors of production, consumption, finance, education and research. These are interesting starting points for putting
together an innovative strategy and reinvigorating the cooperative
experience: to move towards a more cooperative person in a more self-
organized and self-managed society at all levels (Azkarraga, 2010, 2011;
Sarasua, 2010).

Following on directly from the systematic process of reflection, the
association Bagara was created in 2010, involving industrial and educational cooperatives, some leaders in the cooperative movement, and
officials in other organizations across the area. The purpose of Bagara is
to design a proposal for *integrated* community development, including
issues of responsible consumption, culture, civic education of youth,
immigration. This project harks back to Mondragon's origins and the
wider vision of community engagement and community participation;
it also represents a direct response to the challenges of globalization
for the Basque society. Bagara offers one means of enacting, and later
testing, ideas of social transformation.

## Conclusions

The entire matter of participation at Mondragon, now as before,
involves a complex of economic and social factors. The expansion of
the system in the past two decades has included an increase in the

proportion of non-salaried and non-owning members. For this reason, one of the most important recent developments in the cooperatives has been raising the question of broadened opportunities for participation in foreign but heretofore non-cooperative plants owned by the corporation. How this internationalization of cooperativism and participation is conducted, and what it means for the identity – as well as vitality – of the cooperatives will be critically important to follow in forthcoming research investigations.

To be sure, the need to respond, sometimes urgently, to changes in the market and the economy as a whole, are at odds with more deliberate, careful and multilayered processes of reflection and participation. Nevertheless, there is a growing recognition by some younger leaders in the cooperatives of the need to preserve and fortify means of participation at the group, firm, intercooperative, and by extension, community levels. Of course, as we indicated earlier, each individual cooperative has its own history, culture and uses of participation. Thus, the question of participation, in many ways, comes down to the performance and vitality of the councils, and especially the strengthening of the governing councils so they can function as a true counterweight to the technocracy, as manifest in the management councils.

Returning to the wider level of participation at Mondragon, we would say that self-reflection and self-criticism are essential to the strength, sustenance and periodic revitalization of democratic practices. In fact, the years 2008–2011 have been marked by more intense debates within the cooperatives than have been seen for many years; this level of activity is provoked by both the economic crisis and the process of reflection. The fact that the RFCE was not an empty exercise, or simply an excuse for the implementation from above of a new managerial regime, is evident from its early outcomes.

We look forward to following the new experiments outlined above, to consider especially the interrelations of participation, decision making, commitment and identity on all levels of analysis relevant to the Mondragon cooperatives. Importantly, the MCE is being revised, even at the time of economic crisis. As Cheney (2009) found, there is a searching reconsideration of cooperative identity that perhaps could not have been predicted – certainly not expected – in the late 1990s or early 2000s. To be sure, part of the self-examination is linked to bottom-line concerns, such as the 'translation' of cooperative identity into a value-added advantage for the cooperatives. But, at the same time, there is a desire commonly expressed from the top leadership – as well as the rank and file membership – to return to the core values of equality, solidarity and participation. Especially encouraging is the talk of capitalizing on 'local knowledge' of democratic structures and processes. This, in turn, relates significantly to the matter of cultural identity for the Basques and especially to the widely held commitment to self-determination which applies to both work and politics. What precisely this will mean in the coming years, in terms of participation and decision making within and between the cooperatives, remains to be seen. In considering the possibilities for realizing Pateman's (1970) wide vision of participation in terms of social transformation and Bernstein's (1976) concrete model of decision making, the Mondragon cooperatives and associated organizations still offer one of the most important laboratories for observation and experimentation.

## Note

1. Each cooperative's governance is structured around several key councils. First, there is the general assembly: this is the cooperative's supreme body, in which maximum sovereignty resides. It consists of all the members of the cooperative. Next is the governing council: this is the cooperative's representative, governing and management body elected by the general assembly; it is responsible for governing and representing the company before the general assembly and society. The management council is the executive body which manages the cooperative; it is the management team, consisting of the managing director (chosen by the governing council) and members of management. The social council is the permanent participative body for members in administering the cooperative; it has an advisory, consultative and social communication role; members are elected by work areas and ratified at the general assembly; its main functions are labour advice, information, negotiation and to some extent social control.

   There are another three bodies at the cooperative group (or intercooperative) level. The standing committee is the body at the cooperative group level equivalent to a cooperative's governing council. Its principal function is to carry out policies and agreements adopted by a plenary session of the congress; the business performance of the group; and management of the presidency of the general council. The general council is the body (at the cooperative group level) equivalent to a cooperative's management council, which has the following functions: to draw up and apply corporate strategies and targets; and to coordinate the policies of the different divisions and cooperatives. The cooperative congress is the general assembly of all the Mondragon cooperatives, made up of 650 representatives from all the group's cooperatives.

## References

Altuna, L. (Coord.) (2008). *La Experiencia Cooperativa De Mondragon: Una Síntesis General*. Eskoriatza, Gipuzkoa: LANKI – Mondragon Unibertsitatea.

Azkarraga, J. (2007). *Mondragon ante la globalización: la cultura cooperativa vasca ante el cambio de época.* Eskoriatza, Gipuzkoa, Cuadernos de LANKI, no 2, Mondragon Unibertsitatea.

Azkarraga, J. (2010). *Educación, Sociedad y Transformación Cooperativa.* Aretxabaleta, Gipuzkoa: Gizabidea Fundazioa – Mondragon Unibertsitatea.

Azkarraga, J. (2011). "La cooperativa Mondragon y la nueva forma de gestión económica", *El Ciudadano*, noviembre de 2011 (http://www.elciudadano.cl/2011/11/01/43395).

Azurmendi, J. (1988). *El Hombre Cooperativo.* Aretxabaleta, Gipuzkoa: Otalora.

Bernstein, P. (1976). Necessary elements for effective worker participation in decision making. *Journal of Economic Issues*, vol. 10, 490–522.

Cheney, G. (1995). Democracy in the workplace: Theory and practice from the perspective of communication. *Journal of Applied Communication Research*, vol. 23, 167–200.

Cheney, G. (1997). The many meanings of "solidarity": Negotiation of values in a worker-cooperative complex under pressure. In B. D. Sypher (Ed.), *Case Studies in Organizational Communication: 2* (pp. 68–83). New York: Guilford.

Cheney, G. (1999 [2002]). *Values at Work: Employee Participation Meets Market Pressure at Mondragón.* Ithaca, NY: Cornell University Press.

Cheney, G. (2006). Democracy at work within the market: Reconsidering the potential. In V. Smith (Ed.), *Research in the Sociology of Work, Vol. 16: Worker Participation: Current Research and Future Trends* (pp. 179–203). Oxford: Elsevier.

Cheney, G. (2009). *Las Cooperativas Ante La Crisis Económica Mundial: Responsabilidades Y Oportunidades En El Mercado Global Futuro.* Mondragón/Arrasate, Gipuzkoa: Gizabidea.

Cheney, G., Christensen, L. T., Zorn, T. E. Jr. and Ganesh, S. (2011). *Organizational Communication in an Age of Globalization: Issues, Reflections, Practices, 2nd ed.* Prospect Heights, IL: Waveland Press.

Cheney, G., Straub, J., Speirs-Glebe, L., Stohl, C., De Gooyer, D. Jr., Whalen, S., Garvin-Doxas, K. and Carlone, D. (1998). Democracy, participation, and communication at work: A multidisciplinary review. In M. E. Roloff (Ed.), *Communication Yearbook 21.* Thousand Oaks, CA: Sage.

Dahl, R. (1985). *A Preface to Economic Democracy.* Berkeley: University of California Press.

Errasti, A.M., Heras, I., Bakaikoa, B. and Elgoibar, P. (2003). The internationalization of cooperatives: The case of MCC, *Annals of Public and Cooperative Economics*, vol. 74, no. 4, pp. 553–584.

García, O. (2006). *La participación en la empresa. Perspectiva histórica, perspectiva crítica y perspectiva cooperativa.* Eskoriatza: LANKI – Mondragon Unibertsitatea.

Kasmir, S. (1996). *The Myth of Mondragón.* Albany: State University of New York Press.

Morrison, R. (1991). *We Build the Road as We Travel.* Philadelphia, PA: New Society Publishers.

Parker, M., Cheney, G., Fournier, V. and Land, C. (in press). *The Routledge Handbook of Alternative Organization.* London: Routledge.

Pateman, C. (1970). *Participation and Democratic Theory.* Cambridge, UK: Cambridge University Press.

Permanent Commission of Mondragón, 2003, unpublished report, n.p.

Sarasua, J. (2010). *Mondragon en un nuevo siglo. Síntesis reflexiva de la experiencia cooperativa*. Cuadernos de LANKI, no 3, Mondragon Unibertsitatea.

Seashore, S. (1954). *Group Cohesiveness in the Industrial Work Group*. Ann Arbor: Institute for Social Research, The University of Michigan.

Whyte, W. F. and Whyte, K. K. (1991). *Making Mondragón, 2nd ed.* Ithaca, NY: Cornell University Press.

Williams, R. C. (2007). *The Cooperative Movement: Globalization from Below*. Aldershot, UK: Ashgate.

# 5
# Democracy and Solidarity: A Study of Venezuelan Cooperatives

*Camila Piñeiro Harnecker*

## Introduction

The social transformation process currently taking place in Venezuela is radical: it has declared overall human development as its main goal, and it recognizes that people's experience of democratic practices is crucial to attain such a goal. These ideas appear in the Venezuelan Constitution (Article 62), as well as in the discourse of government officials and institutions. They are reflected – although not without contradictions and shortcomings (with regard to cooperatives see Piñeiro, 2009) – in state policies that promote participatory democracy, not just in the political sphere but also in economic, cultural and educational realms.

Since the approval of a new constitution by 70 per cent of the Venezuelan electorate in a 1999 referendum and the passing of a package of 49 laws in December 2001, public administration has been decentralized, and diverse spaces have been opened for direct participation of all citizens from the local to the national level. Workers have been called to create workers' councils in the enterprise where they are hired, and to create their own democratic enterprises.

Indeed, the number of Venezuelan co-managed and especially self-managed enterprises such as cooperatives, the most common form of workplace democracy[1] internationally, has increased sharply. From less than 1000 cooperatives in 1998, there are now between 30,000 and 74,000 estimated in operation in the country (García Müller, 2007; Tovar, 2007; Baute, 2009).

This exponential rise in the number of cooperatives in Venezuela is largely the result of public policies put forward by the Chávez administration. In September 2001, the Special Law of Cooperative Associations was passed, facilitating the creation of cooperatives, emphasizing the obligation of the state to protect them, and extending their tax-exempt status. Growth accelerated in 2003, primarily as the result of direct promotion by state agencies and the implementation of training and employment programmes. From 2004 to 2006, the Vuelvan Caras[2] (now Ché Guevara) programme promoted the creation of nearly 15,000 cooperatives. Other policies promoting cooperatives involved the creation of financial institutions that lend at preferential terms to cooperatives, and the passing of presidential decrees demanding that enterprises contracting with the state have priority contract-bidding mechanisms for cooperatives (Piñeiro, 2005).

After some idle private enterprises were finally nationalized in 2005, cooperatives were created by workers from those enterprises, who co-managed them with state representatives. Under the co-management model used at that time, the state would own 51 per cent of the enterprise stocks and the cooperative 49 per cent. The cooperative would manage the enterprise, and only those decisions related to production levels, investments and strategies needed to be approved by the corresponding ministry. More recently, nationalized enterprises have not been organized under this co-management model that turned workers more into stockowners than collective managers of social wealth. Now, the state keeps the ownership of all enterprise stocks, and workers are organized in workers' councils that – at least on paper – democratically manage them under guidelines set by the corresponding ministry. Government officials have encouraged workers in state and private enterprises to create workers' councils as tools to increase their participation in management.

Since 2007, in addition to workers' councils in large enterprises, other forms of workplace democracy have been promoted instead of conventional cooperatives (i.e. those of collective legal property) for small and medium enterprises. Reflecting the need for more coordination with social interests, even in small or medium enterprises that produce basic or strategic goods, 'communal' and 'socialist' enterprises are being prioritized.

Communal enterprises are, in general, spontaneously created and controlled by the communities organized in communal councils.[3] Communal councils – in many cases with financial support from state institutions – set up economic units for the production of basic goods and services (e.g. food, production materials, transportation, landscaping) and choose community members to work in and manage them. Although their legal form might be that of a cooperative, these enterprises are managed in close coordination with communal councils. President Chávez and other government officials have encouraged communal councils to create enterprises of communal property and democratically manage them (Chávez: *Aló Presidente* # 280).

Socialist enterprises are set up by state institutions and then transferred to the communities to be democratically managed by them. These firms are characterized by state legal property and are more directly controlled by the state. Unlike before, when conventional cooperatives were seen as the 'one-size-fits-all' solution, instead of promoting the organization of participants of public professional training programmes into cooperatives only, they are now encouraged to join the more than 200 'socialist enterprises' that the Plan for the Social and Economic Development of the Nation 2007–2013 (Plan para el Desarrollo Económico y Social de la Nación) expects to set up. At the end of 2009, 70–80 were in operation, mostly in the production of processed food and construction materials. The idea is that workers in these enterprises are chosen by communal councils, and state-assigned technicians and managers prepare workers to assume full control. But I have not been able to verify whether these enterprises are really being democratically managed, or to what extent state representatives are truly working to transfer management to workers and their communities.

In 2009, Venezuela's National Superintendence of Cooperatives' (Superintendencia Nacional de Cooperativas – SUNACOOP) former president, Juan Carlos Baute, emphasized that in Venezuela 'cooperatives are not going to disappear because cooperativism is a leading movement of the revolution, [...] but they do need to be transformed from the capitalist cooperative model to a socialist one'. SUNACOOP is advancing the idea that cooperatives ought to be created by communal councils so they become 'communal cooperatives' (Baute, 2009). In any case, these new types of enterprise promoted by the Venezuelan government are still characterized – at least in theory – by workplace democracy (democratically managed by workers), although now with institutionalized mechanisms for social orientation and control.

With the emphasis on communal and socialist enterprises, Venezuelan officials recognize that, in order for an enterprise to really satisfy social needs, it is not enough for workers to organize their production under democratic, egalitarian and solidaristic principles (the philosophy that defines cooperatives and workplace democracy), and not even enough if they are also members of the surrounding communities. Similarly, even if enterprises are also offered incentives to commit themselves to being socially responsible, as occurred with the policies behind the concept of 'social production enterprises' promoted between 2005 and 2007, they are only going to do so if those policies are effectively enforced by those social groups affected by their operation, and to the degree that their market position is not jeopardized.

Thus, it is acknowledged that for an enterprise to be socialist or of social property, and thus to be oriented towards the satisfaction of social needs, it has to be controlled by those communities. The modification of Article 115 of the 1999 Constitution regarding property rights, and the examples of enterprises that could be of 'indirect' and 'direct' social property (on one hand, the national oil company Petróleos de Venezuela S.A. [PDVSA] and on the other hand, 'a factory created by the state and then transferred to a community') put forward by Chávez on 15 August 2007 suggest that the control of an enterprise by a community or the entire Venezuelan society is not reduced to conventional property titles of its means of production.[4] Whether an enterprise's assets are legally owned by a working collective, or by a local, regional or national state institution, what makes its property 'social' is whether its administration or management is controlled by society, especially by those communities more directly affected by its activities.[5] Social control could be achieved in different ways, not necessarily through direct intervention of social interests representatives in enterprise management, although in some cases it might be necessary. It is important to note that to be under such control is not understood as subordination or to be irreconcilable with levels of autonomy required by any effective enterprise.

What motivated my study of Venezuelan cooperatives was precisely whether members of those democratic workplaces could internalize social interests. At the time when I conducted fieldwork more intensively, between early June and late August 2006, Venezuelan public officials argued that cooperatives would spontaneously orient their economic activities towards the needs of the local communities because they were formed by persons from those communities. They assumed that the democratic practice of these types of workplace, guided by a public discourse of solidarity, would be enough to promote a cooperative's potential for social responsibility. The main question I tried to answer was how workers in cooperatives – or any other type of democratically managed enterprise – could go beyond their collective interests and see the interests of surrounding or farther away communities as their own?

Using different qualitative and quantitative research methods,[6] I studied 12 workers' cooperatives and three civil associations, self-described as cooperatives, located in Caracas (Venezuela's capital), Mérida and Lara. Five of the cooperatives in my sample were created as part of the Vuelvan Caras programme. Due to the short time available for research, and to make my sample more easily comparable, I focused on non-agricultural production cooperatives. The newest of the cooperatives I studied was then one-and-a-half years old and the oldest was founded 22 years ago. The size of their memberships varied from 5 to 160 members. The organizations studied were involved in food production (four), construction (three), textile production (three), footwear (one), ironworks (one) and handcraft wool production (one). Because of their similar origins and circumstances to other cooperatives in the sample, I decided to include two tourism service cooperatives. My sample was strategically chosen by looking for the widest possible range of workplace democracy levels; it is thus not representative of the vast population of cooperatives or other democratic workplaces that existed in Venezuela then, much less today.[7]

## Workplace democracy and solidarity

The focus of my study of Venezuelan cooperatives has been to empirically analyse not only whether there is a relation between levels of workplace democracy and the development of workers solidarity, but mostly the main dynamics that could explain such a relationship.

Drawing on Manson (1982), and Espinosa and Zimbalist (1978), I developed a conceptualization of workplace democracy with the following dimensions: extension, mode, scope, equality of information, elimination of division of labour, collective monitoring, workers' power, workers' motivation, workers' comprehension skills, workers' communication skills. I was not interested in precision but on general estimates that could serve to problematize my inferences. The measure of workplace democracy I used is the average of assessments of these ten indicators (Piñeiro, 2007: 30–34).

As I mentioned before, my aim was to look not only at cooperative workers' solidarity among themselves (which I defined as 'collective consciousness') but also towards other communities (which I defined as 'social consciousness'), and how it might occur. The conceptualization of a workers' collective consciousness is my own doing, and considers: their awareness of the interests and problems of other co-workers;

willingness to contribute resources towards their solution; and materialization of this disposition into statements and/or actions. I measured collective consciousness by the average of assessments of these three indicators (Piñeiro, 2007: 35–37). Similarly, the conceptualization of workers' social consciousness towards a community has the same three dimensions of analysis, but in relation to the communities in question, rather than to other co-workers (2008: 311).

In previous publications, the results of my study were presented with regard to the direct relationship between workplace democracy and collective consciousness (2007), as well as – although less axiomatic – workplace democracy and social consciousness (2008). In both cases, the effects on those relationships of other factors or conditions beyond workplace democracy were also analysed. I found that to the extent that cooperatives were truly democratic, their members tended to develop their collective consciousness and also – especially in the presence of facilitating external conditions – their social consciousness.

My study identifies the main dynamics inherent to the democratic practice and other external conditions that explain how the development of cooperative members' solidarity takes place. I found that individuals' participation as equals in democratic decision making produces psychological effects that drive them to internalize or adopt the interests of others in that community; that is, to develop their collective consciousness or 'group solidarity'. This expansion of their self-interests to include broader, collective concerns is mainly a result of individuals' *moral self-transformation* (greater self-confidence and feelings of control over their lives) and the *sense of community* that emerges among them (i.e. belonging, trust, equality of rights and responsibilities); both products of their experience with a genuinely democratic practice and both mutually reinforcing (2007: 35–37).

With regard to social consciousness, I found that, although workplace democracy in itself is not sufficient to promote cooperative members' social consciousness or 'broader solidarity', it can facilitate such a process. I identified two similar dynamics that could explain how workers in democratically managed enterprises are encouraged to internalize the interests of other communities beyond their workplaces: workers' *adoption of solidaristic values* (a superior stage of their moral self-transformation) and the *proximity* between workers and members of those communities (mainly due to shared experiences or social interaction that leads them to feel part of that wider community).

The occurrence of these two conditions is independent of the reach of workplace democracy in the enterprises, but they can come to influence and be reinforced by democratic decision-making processes (Piñeiro, 2008: 318–322).

In this chapter, I investigate how these relations occur by delving into those aspects of workplace democracy in the cooperatives that I consider to be crucial for producing these four dynamics that promote the development of workers' solidarity. The main aspects internal to the democratic management of cooperatives that I identify are: the substantive character of their democratic practice; their emphasis on deliberation; and their attention to creating an environment of true equality of rights, duties and social status among members. I also expand on the main external factors that seem to advance the development of cooperative members' collective and social consciousness: their exposure to a solidaristic ideology; their democratic participation in other spaces; and cooperatives' avoidance of market logic. I conclude by highlighting that democratic practice cannot be limited to some spaces but needs to be ever expanded and perfected if we are to consolidate democratic workplaces and propel them to exercise their solidarity more broadly.

## Key aspects of workplace democracy acting upon solidarity development

### Substantive participation in decision making

Although with varied success and commitment of their elected 'coordinators' (as cooperative presidents, directors or managers, are called), the Venezuelan cooperatives that I studied, both newer (created during the Chávez government) and older, placed key attention on establishing democratic procedures for decision making. More importantly, they were aware that formal participation is not sufficient, that substantive or qualitative aspects must be taken into consideration so that those formal procedures are used effectively, and to prevent formality from limiting or discouraging workers' participation.

The cooperative members I interviewed knew that they were not just in any conventional enterprise, but one that was meant to be managed democratically by them through elected coordinators accountable to them, general assemblies, and other formal and informal spaces that were available to discuss problems and make decisions. Even in those cases where the edifice and machinery were not the legal property of the collective of workers, they considered themselves 'owners' because they felt that they had real control over the decision-making process.

To highlight the difference between *formal* and *substantive* participation, Espinosa and Zimbalist define 'formal participation' in regard to the existence and design of participatory bodies and procedures, while 'content participation' refers to the topics discussed and workers' influence on final decisions (1978: 60). For Pateman, the difference is that in 'partial participation' workers can only influence the decision, while under 'full participation' workers have control over the decision-making process (1970: 71). The substantive character of participation for Pateman depends fundamentally on the non-hierarchical nature of the organizational structure, as well as on the extent to which workers discipline themselves rather than when it's done by an external management (Pateman, 1970: 59). As we will see below, this is related to workers' social status equality.

Although some formal bodies and procedures can facilitate substantive participation, they are not enough. Espinosa and Zimbalist assert that without its substantive component, 'participation will not be dynamic and self-sustaining' (1978: 181). To the degree that participation is only formal or partial results in apathy, thus negatively affecting workers' involvement in decision making and their performance in the production process (Espinosa and Zimbalist, 1978: 97, 106; Bayat, 1993: 111–112, 126). Pateman argues that only full participation produces the psychological and educative effects she praises in workplace democracy (1970: 73–74).

In other words, for democratic management to have the desired effects on the development of workers' human abilities and attitudes, they ought to truly experience real control over their enterprise's decision-making processes, as a collective and through democratic means, participating in substantive decision making directly or indirectly through representatives and procedures approved by them. Once workers are called to take part in decision making, to limit their participation to some issues or to exclude the most defining ones has an inhibiting effect on participation.

Venezuelan cooperative law promotes the substantive dimension of participation because it mandates that the assembly of all members has the final decision-making power over all topics (Articles 21, 26). The scope of workers' decision making must include all subjects; some being directly discussed by the assembly, others by the coordinators, whose proposals must then be submitted to the assembly. To ensure that the most important decisions (e.g. distribution of income, credit requests, inclusion or exclusion of members, election of coordinators, application of sanctions to members, changes of rules) are being made democratically, SUNACOOP has demanded that a report of the corresponding general assembly is submitted, showing that the quorum and voting rules set by the cooperatives were respected. Although the law only requires cooperatives to hold general assemblies once a year, most cooperatives meet weekly or monthly.

Unlike many of these organizations in other countries, the majority of the Venezuelan cooperatives I studied differentiated little between managers and other workers. This was perhaps because of their generally small size and, even in larger ones, management positions were shared by a group of workers and most were rotated. Also, decisions related to new clients, new providers and changes to contracts were made in assembly or in consultation with the affected work teams. For participation to be substantive and not just only really exerted by those in management positions or who are better prepared, it is crucial to create a sense of equality among all members, as will be analysed below.

## Deliberation

Another significant feature throughout the cooperatives I studied was their keenness to debate all important decisions in general assemblies and to reach a consensus before voting, that is, their preference for deliberation. Cooperative members and public officials engaged in the promotion of cooperatives valued deliberation as key to the construction of common interests shared by the collective. A member of a cooperative explained: 'We meet every week, even if it seems like there is nothing to talk about, because it is important to communicate; and assemblies serve to inform and to reach agreement on decisions.' For Elías Jaua Milano, former Minister of Popular Economy, democratic deliberation 'is necessary to dissipate the contradictions between those defending their particular interests and putting them before the general interest' (2005: 26–27).

Several cooperative members explained that the deliberative character of the democratic practice within their workplaces had – on some occasions where the reasons behind other positions were made evident after thorough debate – provoked them to voluntarily adjust or abandon initial positions. For the same reasons, deliberation had led some to adopt decisions adopted by a majority that they hadn't been part of. In addition to making decisions more transparent to all, open debate facilitates the assimilation of complex or unfamiliar information by members.

Moreover, the deliberation of options before making decisions facilitates the construction of common interests, because it helps to eliminate the most individualistic proposals. Theorists of deliberative democracy argue that, as a result of the 'moderating' and 'moralizing' effects of deliberation, participants assume a 'public role', excluding choices that are perceived as 'narrowly self-regarding' and 'repugnant to the moral beliefs of their society' (Miller, 2003: 183, 189). In other words, deliberation within the workplace allows universal rules of reciprocity and morality to bring workers' preferences closer to those of other co-workers and even to those of other communities.

Like theorists of participatory or deliberative democracy and social capital, second-generation theorists of collective action reject the liberal assumption that human preferences are static, and defend the idea of a 'collective structuration of preferences' (Bowles and Gintis, 1986). They argue that preferences are socially constructed through practice and that institutions can be designed so they promote 'the formation of individual wills and group solidarity' (1986: 21–22). For them, it is only through everyday practice, and especially through genuinely democratic decision making, that individuals develop their capacities and attitudes, helping to shape their preferences closer to principles of cooperation and solidarity.

Thus, a democratic practice that privileges deliberation, rather than time-saving voting procedures, is more effective in shaping individuals' preferences, so the likely initial contradiction between their individual and collective interests is diminished. Devine (1988: 189) refers to this result of democratic deliberation and decision making in relation to the model of democratic planning that he puts forward: 'while conflicts of interest are not whished away, the process incorporates a transformatory dynamics in which particular interests are viewed in relation to one another and are integrated into a socially constructed general interest at each level of decision-making'.

### Equality of rights, duties and social status

As mentioned before, for the democratic practice to be substantive, there must be a sense of equality that allows and motivates all cooperative members to participate in decision making as subjects with equal opportunities and similar capacities to shape the outcomes. If workers do not feel as equals, it is likely that they will not be motivated to actively participate, and they will uncritically follow the positions of those who appear to be of a higher social status.

In the cooperatives I studied, as in most genuine cooperatives, the equality of voting rights is straightforward: it is 'one person, one vote'. No matter how much financial or material resources or time a cooperative member has put into a cooperative, all workers have an equal right to vote. Giving up one's vote to another member is not permitted.

For Pateman, in addition to workers' equality in their formal right to influence the decision-making process, other substantive aspects, such as equality of access to information, are also key (1970: 69, 107). For workers to be able to participate as equals it is crucial that all directors and managers comply with their duty of transparency and provide relevant information in a comprehensive manner. Without information, decision making is just a theatrical and ineffective exercise.

Despite its importance, equality in access to information was one of the most significant deficiencies among the cooperatives I studied. Although this limitation, in most cases, was not intentional because information was not even properly recorded, it still produced the same effects. Insufficient bookkeeping and few established mechanisms to present information effectively significantly limited members' access to crucial data (Piñeiro, 2007: 31).

Moreover, based on the idea that equal rights do not guarantee equal opportunities and abilities to exercise those rights, the 'division of labour' (i.e. the separation and distribution of work tasks and roles among workers and the resulting relations among them) must be transformed so that workers are able to develop those capacities required for participation and have similar conditions for exercising them (Bayat, 1993). The most important component of the division of labour is its 'social' component (not technical, indispensable to reach necessary levels of specialization), which determines the social status of workers, indicating that some are higher up in their social recognition while others are considered to be less 'valuable'. The higher levels in this social hierarchy generally correspond with positions of management, directors or technical experts. This is why Pateman (1970: 72) argues that managers should be elected by workers for short and non-renewable terms, made accountable to them, and, if the enterprise's size permits direct participation, then management should be assumed by all the workers collectively.

In many of the cooperatives I studied, there was a strong sense of equality in social status, in part because their organizational structure was significantly horizontal and inclusive. Although by law, all Venezuelan cooperatives must have a president, a secretary, a treasurer, a controller and a responsible for education, they generally have additional stand-in persons for each position. In small cooperatives, most members have some responsibility. In larger cooperatives, the number of directive positions is increased, and responsibilities are shared between multiple individuals, thus augmenting the percentage of members with roles of authority. These positions, by statute, have a maximum tenure of three years and only one re-election is permitted, but they tend to be rotated after the first term (Piñeiro, 2007: 32–33). The sense of equality that these organizational arrangements promoted was evidenced in the following statements: 'Power is in the general assembly, in the majority, even if the president doesn't agree'; 'This cooperative is mine, here we are all owners, and we are all the same'; 'We are all accomplishing something together, without bosses; and there is no better pay than working collectively as equals'; 'We will all have the opportunity to learn how to do those [executive] roles, because we should all be equal.'

Progress in the elimination of the social division of labour requires more than a horizontal organizational structure. It is necessary to establish changes to the organization of work to prevent the least desirable and creative tasks being concentrated in the same workers, thus diminishing their social status; and the inverse situations. Job rotation and job enlargement techniques can be used for this purpose to reduce the social division of labour, without renouncing to desirable technical division of labour or specialization. Devine (1988: 168–170) also differentiates between social (or status) and functional (or technical) divisions of labour, and argues that it is only necessary to eliminate the first through the rotation and redistribution of job tasks. In addition, Albert and Hahnel (1991: 18–21) propose 'job enlargement' to create more 'balanced-task jobs' that equalize the levels of empowerment and desirability of different job tasks.

In most cooperatives in my sample, job tasks were enlarged to include the least desirable activities, such as cleaning and security, and rotating them among the membership. In new cooperatives, there is stronger emphasis on the importance of equality, and the recognition that 'everyone should have the opportunity to learn everything', so it is more common that members change production tasks periodically. In one of the Vuelvan Caras cooperatives in my sample, members have insistently demanded that coordinators dedicate some time every day to production. They argued that they want to feel equal, and that coordinators can distance themselves from the others if they do not experience the reality of the shop floor.

This emphasis by members of Vuelvan Caras cooperatives on the need to transform the relations of production in order to eliminate the social division of labour can be tracked to the influence of Carlos Lanz,[8] one of the main contributors to the materials used by the Vuelvan Caras programme. He argues that division of labour, and especially the separation between manual and intellectual tasks, is one of the contradictions of capitalism that was not solved by historical attempts at building socialism; this contradiction must be solved in the socialism of the 21st century (2005).

Another element that promoted higher levels of workplace democracy and solidarity in the cooperatives I studied was that workers had not only equal rights but also equal duties. Among the substantive dimensions of workplace democracy analysed, I included the extent to which cooperatives had established mechanisms for collective – rather than external – monitoring. This helps to ensure members' equal responsibilities, and thus the sense of equality among them. Collective monitoring is crucial to evaluate individual and collective performance in order to prevent some members from shirking their duty to actively participate both in decision making and production activities. Necessary corrections can be made to discourage and to penalize freeriding. In fact, Ostrom (1990) identifies the presence of collective monitoring, along with gradual and consistent sanctioning, as an important characteristic of egalitarian institutions that are successful in solving this problem of collective action.

However, this important component of the democratic experience, which could have a very positive impact on the internal dynamics of the cooperatives I studied, was practically absent. Mechanisms for collective monitoring were not that common, especially in the newer ones. Most cooperatives had very informal and infrequent spaces where members could only partly evaluate the performance of their organization. Only one of the oldest cooperatives holds weekly assemblies where each member explains their progress in accomplishing tasks that were delegated to them in previous meetings. A newer cooperative had recently formalized similar collective monitoring mechanisms. Consequently, the absence of collective monitoring in the cooperatives I studied was also a source of disparity and conflict among members, which limited both their workplace democracy and their members' collective consciousness (Piñeiro, 2007: 33–34).

## Main external conditions acting upon solidarity development

### Democratic participation in other spaces

In addition to internal factors related to the functioning of workplace democracy, there are obviously factors or conditions that are external to the democratic practice within cooperatives and act upon the development of members' solidarity. My research results suggest that the most important positive external factor in the development of cooperative members' solidarity is their democratic practice in spaces other than their workplaces.

Theorists of participatory democracy (e.g. Pateman, 1970; Manson, 1982) argue that participation in the workplace can spill over into more participation in other political spheres. They explain that democratic skills and attitudes obtained through participation in enterprise management can be 'transferred' to other spheres. When workers feel more prepared to participate effectively, they are more willing to do so in other democratic processes (Pateman, 1970: 51–52). Indeed, Smith (1985) has noted a pronounced positive correlation between participating in internal workplace decision making and in community political affairs. Vanek states that a less conflictive and more democratic work environment 'will be necessarily reflected in human attitudes and human relations throughout and outside the economic world because the men will carry their attitudes from one world to the other' (1971: 28).

In the same way, when cooperative members participate in other democratic spaces, their democratic skills and attitudes are developed further, and the quality of their participation in all spaces is advanced. Coinciding with this idea that participatory skills and attitudes can be transferred from one space to another, I found in the cooperatives I studied that the quality of workplace democracy and of workers' collective consciousness is strongly tied to the levels of workers' participation in political and social organizations in their communities (Piñeiro, 2007: 35, 39). This participation in community organizations increases cooperatives' internal democracy, and it also contributes – by augmenting awareness, sensitivity and empathy of problems in those communities – to raise the levels of social consciousness or solidarity (2008: 330).

*Exposure to a solidaristic ethics*

If the democratic practice in workplaces occurs under the predominance of an egoistic logic, it is very improbable that workers are going to go beyond their collective interests and internalize those of other social groups. It is even an important risk to the health of workplace democracy: an individualistic ideology, moral framework or ethics makes our individual interests appear incompatible with those of others. Whereas, when cooperative members are exposed to a solidaristic ethics, and adopt it to some degree, their democratic practice is likely to be consolidated, and their moral self-transformation can reach higher levels.

The Chávez government has attempted to ideologically undermine the egoistic ethics that predominates in Venezuelan society. This moral framework has resulted from its long exposure to a liberal representative democracy and market economy that has consistently exalted selfish, rent-seeking and consumerist behaviours – especially entrenched after neo-liberal economic policies were put in place in the late 1980s. Indeed, the main objective of the current transformation process from its inception has been to turn Venezuela into a more inclusive, humane and solidaristic society; articulated since 2006 into a socialist project. Venezuela's new Constitution recognizes the importance of making solidarity a dominating principle of that society (Articles 299, 70, 135 and 274).

Policy makers have paid special attention to promoting 'social responsibility' and 'commitment to the community' as important values among cooperatives (Cooperative Law, Articles 3 and 4), and have conditioned access to credit on compliance with social clauses (Piñeiro, 2008: 314–316). After I conducted research, the Moral y Luces (Morality and Enlightenment) programme began in January 2007, seeking to advance socialist values of equality and solidarity through debates about social problems in schools, workplaces, libraries and all social institutions interested in doing so.

Therefore, Venezuelan cooperatives have been exposed to a strong public discourse advanced by governmental institutions and social organizations that seek to motivate them to produce not just for the benefit of its members, but also for the satisfaction of local community needs and those of the entire nation. Former Minister of Popular Economy Elías Jaua Milano stated that the cooperatives' main challenge is to give their production a 'social orientation', to satisfy 'social needs' over capital accumulation and individual benefits (MINEP, 2005: 17).

Indeed, when asked about their willingness to contribute to a national fund to help other communities, one cooperative member affirmatively stated: 'That is socialism; the idea is to share so we can all be equals' (19 July 2006 interview). 'One is always going to need money, but under socialism the idea is to share it, is not to become wealthy but to satisfy our needs; and now that is easier because we do not have to worry about education and health' (27 July 2006 interview). Showing the influence of Chávez's frequent and pedagogical speeches, another member said: 'we are all Venezuelans and the most needy also have rights: and, as my president says, we should help one another' (10 August 2006 interview).

This continued and apparently somewhat effective exposure to a solidaristic ideology of the cooperatives in my sample appears to facilitate the realization of one of the two dynamics that I hypothesize can enable workers in democratic enterprises to expand their solidarity outside the boundaries of their organizations. By drawing attention to the interconnectedness of all humans, an ethics of solidarity encourages them to see other communities as part of an extended community or human family, even if there is not as much proximity. Theorists of deliberation – as mentioned before – have suggested how the embracing of such a solidaristic ethics could lead participants of democratic processes to self-control their egoistic inclinations further, because the values that moderate deliberation are more demanding.

However, even heavy exposure to calls for solidarity is no guarantee that cooperatives will behave accordingly. In fact, I did not find a connection between workers' alleged adoption of solidaristic ideas and their social consciousness towards surrounding local communities. It was only significantly tied to their social consciousness at the national level. Although apparently contradictory, there was generally less inclination among the cooperatives I studied to contribute to their more proximate communities than to other ones further away. This could be because, while their adopted solidaristic ethics does not distinguish between nearby and further away communities, a closer, quotidian co-existence can have negative consequences on the relationship between cooperatives and neighbouring communities. Even more so if there are no mechanisms for coordination between them that could allow conflicts to be solved and their emergence to be prevented (Piñeiro, 2008: 328–329).

## Avoidance of market logic

Regardless of the degree to which cooperative members are exposed to a solidaristic ethics or even claim that have adopted it, in general, they will not act accordingly to those values if they see objective contradictions between satisfying their individual or collective needs and those of other communities due to how economic and social relations are organized. Evidently, the institutional context in which enterprises and workers find themselves determines, to a great degree, the levels of workplace democracy and solidarity that they perceive as possible and even desirable. Like institutional economists such as Bowles, Gintis, Hahnel and Devine, Karl's (1997: 10–12) 'structured contingency' approach to the structuration of choice argues that the range of options that an agent has is the result of the institutional framework that surrounds him/her, which creates 'a structure of incentives', rewarding some forms of behaviour and penalizing others.

Although some Venezuelan policy makers are aware of the egoistic or anti-social logic of market relations,[9] and their incompatibility with the goal of creating a more humane and solidaristic society, most cooperatives obtain their inputs and distribute their products through market relations. The Ministry of Communal Economy (MINEC, formerly MINEP) had anticipated that cooperatives and other enterprises in the social economy would set up their own exchange and distribution networks to avoid intermediaries and the 'rules of the market' (Jaua Milano, 2005: 27–28). But there are very few such cases, and most have been directly promoted by MINEC.[10]

A significant number of Venezuelan cooperatives avoid markets; only partly through contracts with state institutions that secure some of their inputs and buyers for some of their products. However, the cooperatives' reliance on contracts decided by undemocratic state institutions creates a dependency on bureaucracies that are far from efficient, transparent and reliable – and more dangerous – that can corrupt them by favouring those private enterprises that offer the highest commissions. Although the Chávez government has recently taken some measures to increase distribution spaces that are non-market-based and controlled by communities, the only significant non-market-based exchange system that exists is a state-run food distribution national network set up by the Venezuelan oil company PDVSA, which suffers from great deficiencies (most perishable products cannot be sold) and inefficiencies.[11]

Moreover, institutions for planning or coordination between cooperatives and communities were almost inexistent in Venezuela at the time of this study. They are still very rare, and where they do exist, cooperative members who participate generally do not act as representatives of their enterprises but as local residents. Although communal councils are mandated by law to coordinate all organizations in a community, including cooperatives, this was not yet a common practice.

There is also very little, and limited, coordination among cooperatives – something that could help them at least partially avoid market relations. Despite some successful and long-established experiences of cooperative integration bodies (second or third degree cooperatives) in Venezuela, as well as the effort by SUNACOOP to promote the creation of regional cooperative councils, the great majority of Venezuela's new cooperatives are dangerously isolated from one another (Piñeiro, 2009: 850–851). Without coordination with other enterprises and those communities that are or can potentially be their clients, cooperatives are left to the 'will' of the markets.

To be expected, some of the cooperatives I studied were behaving like capitalist enterprises – seeking to maximize their net revenue (i.e. their narrow individual and collective benefits) without consideration of the ways that they could help alleviate the needs of their surrounding communities by supplying goods and accepting new members. There was a generalized belief among members, and even policy makers, that cooperatives have to choose between consolidating their economic situation and being 'socially responsible'. Consequently, they see social responsibility as a cost that undermines their market position and that they cannot afford (Piñeiro, 2008: 334–335, 2009: 855–856). The profit-maximization logic inherent to market relations as well as the instability and unpredictability of market competition force economic agents to constantly attempt to secure a better market position that facilitates their survival. 'We can help the communities but only once the cooperative is doing well, and only a little because we have to save to prepare for any problems in the future', said one cooperative worker.

Exposure to the market logic of profit-maximization not only severely limits the potential of democratic enterprises for social responsibility or social solidarity, but it also impacts the internal organization of cooperatives. In fact, the only economically successful cooperative among the older (pre-Chavez government) ones in my sample had degenerated into a capitalist enterprise, where founding members make all the important decisions, regularly hire employees and receive much greater incomes for working much less. There are also several new cooperatives that are functioning undemocratically because coordinators, under the pressure of taking advantage of market opportunities, exclude the rest of the members from important decisions. In fact, the general coordinators of a few new cooperatives in my sample were experiencing reprobation and mistrust from other members, because during negotiations for contracts, fearing lost sales opportunities, they had decided to agree on terms different to those that had been discussed in assemblies (Piñeiro, 2007: 34, 2009: 854). Certainly, if coordinators had employed a more participatory leadership style, those situations could have had less negative repercussions; but still requirements for expedite decision-making over unexpected situations could not have been avoided.

It seems probable that if the cooperatives I studied had operated more under market relations, this weakening of the cooperatives' democratic practice could have been worse. An indication of this, although not a proof, might be the fact that the two most successful cooperatives (not including the older one that had degenerated into a capitalist enterprise) both are new and, so far, have the advantage of having secured their inputs and having found 'niche markets' for their products where they face very little competition (Piñeiro, 2009: 852).

## Democratic coordination to consolidate workplace democracy and solidarity

Democratic coordination or planning can serve to diminish the effect of market relations, and also to advance participation in other spaces and the adoption of a solidaristic ethics. To the extent that cooperatives participate in such institutional arrangements, they can take advantage of the positive spillover effects of these external conditions, and they can diminish the corruptive effects that operation in a market economy has over their organizational and ethical principles.

There is ample theoretical and practical evidence (Yugoslav self-management, the MONDRAGON cooperatives, to name the most well known examples) that the dynamics of market exchange weaken the democratic character of worker-managed enterprises, and not just the Venezuelan cooperatives that I studied. In order to react rapidly to market changes and not to compromise their market position, enterprises must concentrate their decision making in the hands of managers (Espinosa and Zimbalist, 1978: 26, 182; Atzeni and Ghigliani, 2007: 659–665). In this competitive environment, specialized and autonomous management becomes crucial for the success of the enterprise. As a result, shop floor workers' control and monitoring of managers are diluted (Bayat, 1993: 179). Indeed, Hahnel (2005: 354) argues that although the MONDRAGON cooperatives maintain a representative democratic process, 'de facto power has become increasingly centralized in the hands of technocratic business managers who manage the cooperatives' money'. The separation between managers and shop-floor workers has been also identified as one of the main reasons that lead to the failure of Yugoslav self-management.

Under market competition, differentiated material incentives become necessary to attract management and administrative personnel, and to prevent them from free-riding on their less monitored responsibilities. In the MONDRAGON cooperatives, the earnings of top managers were initially restricted to three times that of the lower pay, but it was increased to six times in the 1990s (Dow, 2003: 60, 63). Cheney (2002) argues that MONDRAGON – among other changes that may evidence the loosening of cooperative values – has moved to prioritize 'efficiency', defined in a narrow non-social sense, by introducing technologies that disempower workers. Therefore, there are strong pressures to also discard the principle of equality of income and, more importantly, social status.

The operation of cooperatives in a market system greatly limits workers' democratic practice and their solidarity. Indeed, Comisso (1979: 31–34) states that solidarity towards society 'will hardly last very long under the pressures of the competitive market' because neither equality nor autonomy (i.e. the faculty to make decisions independently) can be sustained. Contrarily to the liberal assertion that markets bring greater autonomy to individuals and enterprises, Comisso argues that market forces create 'the enterprise's new dependence on its market position for its income' (110). Thus, because workers require certain stability or autonomy from their circumstances to exert their solidarity, market dynamics also undermine the potential for social responsibility of democratic workplaces.

In short, a system of exchange that is atomistic and individualistic undermines democracy and solidarity. Because it reproduces narrowly self-interested and alienated people by not allowing them – due to its bilateral and thus undemocratic character – to take into consideration the interests of others affected by their decisions (Piñeiro, 2008: 333–334, 2009: 855–856). This is why it is necessary to democratize not only the relationships within workplaces but also exchange relations among economic actors, as essential components of those social relations of production that mark the functioning of a society (Marx and Engels, 1848; Engels, 1876–1878).

Market relations, as we know them, should not be assumed as natural and inevitable: it is possible to strip them from their hegemonic role and subdue them to social interests articulated through democratic planning. Other exchange relations that are also horizontal, decentralized and allow for individual choice, *and* – unlike even heavily regulated markets – make options compatible with social interests, can be established. Devine (1988) and Hahnel (2005), among others, have put forward very different models of 'negotiated coordination' and 'participatory planning', respectively, that would both allow producers and consumers, while enjoying the benefits of horizontal exchange relations, to democratically construct social interests along with those affected by their activities, and reflect them in pricing and other conditions of production and exchange.

From these and other models of democratic planning or socialized market, we can extract ideas to design institutions for the coordination of economic activity, starting with local communities. The objective wouldn't be to prohibit horizontal exchange relations, but to create the conditions so that they internalize social interests articulated in those spaces for negotiation, coordination and planning.

Such institutions would promote economic exchange relations that internalize democratically constructed social interests from the outset. They would create an institutional environment that facilitates their implementation by establishing a system of positive and negative incentives that rewards socially responsible behaviour and penalizes irresponsibility. Instead of promoting anti-social performance, as market exchange generally does, resources would be allocated according to the ratio of the social benefits and costs – democratically identified and valued – that they deliver. Therefore, democratic planning would allow the known limits of market regulation (mostly ex-post negative incentives) to be overcome and truly 'socialized' horizontal relations to be established that facilitate and motivate economic actors to internalize social interests (Piñeiro, 2008: 322–324, 336, 2009: 857–858).

## Conclusions

In the Venezuelan cooperatives studied, members do not believe that for people to develop their solidarity they first need to be able to satisfy their material needs: they are attempting to do both simultaneously. In other words, contrary to those self-described 'non-utopian', 'realistic' or 'pragmatic' socialist thinkers (e.g. Xiaoping, 1984; Nove, 1992), the Venezuelan road to socialism defends that a society does not need to achieve a high level of development of 'production forces' (generally wrongly understood as technology) in order to effectively promote social consciousness; although it does makes it easier. In Venezuela, there is an attempt to organize production, and society in general – although still distant from being materialized – so that individual interests are aligned as much as possible with collective (within work and living communities) and social interests (towards other communities, and larger communities such as nations and the global 'human family'). Thus, creating positive incentives for productivity and conditions for the exercise and growth of workers' solidarity.

The empirical evidence presented here confirms that participation in democratic decision making, and in enterprises in particular, plays a paramount role in the development of solidarity. Participatory democracy is key to promote this and other attitudes as well as skills crucial to human development.

But for the democratic practice to have these effects, it cannot be just formal and limited, but one that is substantial, deliberative and egalitarian. It has to allow people to truly take part, as equals, in decision-making processes where they interact with the interests of others, and thus consciously construct or become aware of their shared interests. Among the cooperatives I studied, those with the highest levels of workplace democracy and solidarity have not limited themselves to simply introducing formal procedures of participation. With varied levels of success, they encourage as many workers as possible to actively participate in all important decisions, in an egalitarian environment given by a true equality of rights, duties and social status, and decisions are debated until as much consensus as possible can be reached.

In addition to the democratic practice within cooperatives, the experiences of individual workers and of the working collectives outside the boundaries of their organizations also have a great impact on the extent to which those cooperatives can successfully establish workplace democracy and solidarity is developed. The cooperatives I studied show that democratic practice in one space is consolidated when members take part in democratic decision making in other spaces, and is undermined when experiences in other spaces advance a logic and practice of atomization and selfishness. In parallel, cooperatives, inevitably inserted in the Venezuelan and international market, cannot operate through market relations without exposing themselves to the effects of the logic of profit maximization that defines market exchange and drives competition.

To diminish their exposure to this logic, and to more effectively and sustainably promote the development of solidarity, the two main dynamics that I identify as promoting social consciousness (proximity and solidaristic ethics) ought to be part of workers' democratic experiences themselves and not depend on external factors. That is, for social consciousness to develop more fully and stably, spaces of democratic planning or coordination among workplaces and communities need to be established. Just as workplace democracy encourages members to internalize the interests of co-workers, democratic planning is necessary to drive them to take on the needs of other communities as their own.

Since workers' solidarity towards others is developed fundamentally through participation in decision making with those others, a sustained and effective development of workers' social consciousness mandates expanding the democratic practice to institutions for democratic planning or coordination among producers, consumers and communities affected by their activities, at all levels of society. Such an expansion of the democratic practice is necessary to create the kind of environment that workers' collectives require both to consolidate the ethical and organizational values that define workplace democracy and to materialize their potential for broader, social solidarity.

## Notes

1. By 'workplace democracy' I refer to different models of democratic management of enterprises by workers. Its formal conceptualization is presented below.
2. Literally 'about-face', Vuelvan Caras is a programme managed by the Ministry of Communal Economy that trains Venezuelans from the most marginalized sectors, encourages them to create cooperatives and assists them in the process by providing financial, technical and advisory support.
3. In April 2006, the Law of Communal Councils (Consejos Comunales) was passed by the National Assembly defining the general principles of a form of community self-government which is expected to be the local base of the truly democratic state that should characterize Venezuela's socialism (Burbach and Piñeiro, 2007: 184–190).
4. Cahan (1994) analyses the 'dual' character of the concept of property used by Marx. The one essential for Marx's analysis of history was the concept of property as 'a pattern of control and extraction of surplus' that explains 'a non-legal, socioeconomic phenomenon on practice'.
5. While legal ownership and control of decision making have historically coincided, they can be separated (Ellerman, 1990: 209; Dow, 2003: 107–108). Legal ownership can indeed secure control. But, the point is not really who is the legal proprietor of the means of production but who controls them.
6. Research methods and quantitative data can be obtained by contacting the author at camila.pineiro.harnecker@gmail.com.
7. Since I was not concerned with assessing levels of workplace democracy, collective or social consciousness in all Venezuelan cooperatives, I was not interested in finding a representative sample of Venezuelan worker-managed enterprises, but one that serves to understand whether there is a relationship between them, and how it occurs.

8. Carlos Lanz was President of the Corporación Venezolana de Guayana, one of the major state corporations with the most advanced experience in co-management, that of Aluminio del Caroni, S.A (ALCASA) (Harnecker, 2005).

9. It is important to clarify that I understand market relations are not just any kind of horizontal exchange relation, but those where prices and other exchange decisions are made bilaterally between the seller and the buyer – at least in theory – and each part seeks to maximize their individual benefit without consideration of the social interest. It is possible to establish horizontal relations that are non-market or 'socialized'.

10. As MINEP's former Commercialization Vice-minister Rita Peña expressed (25 August 2006 interview) a pilot experience of a 'social production exchange center' (*centro de intercambio socio-productivo*) was scheduled to begin in Sanare, Lara, in October 2006, where cooperatives were expected to take their production and sell it jointly to buyers. Two *truekes* or local barter systems were born in 2007 (*El Universal*, 14 August and 12 October 2007), and there are now at least 10 in Venezuela.

11. In 2006, an estimated 40–47 per cent of the population (around 10.7–12.5 million people) bought subsidized food through the Mercal programme, at discounts averaging 41–44 per cent (Datanalisis, 2006).

# References

Albert, Michael and Robin Hahnel. 1991. *Looking Forward: Participatory Economics for the Twenty First Century*. Princeton, N.J.: Princeton University Press.

Atzeni, Maurizio and Pablo Ghigliani. 2007. "Labour process and decision-making in factories under workers self-management: Empirical evidence from Argentina." *Work, Employment & Society*, Vol. 21, No. 4, pp. 653–671.

Baute, Juan Carlos. 2009. "Las cooperativas no desaparecerán." *Últimas Noticias*, April 7, 2010. http://www.aporrea.org/poderpopular/n136615.html.

Bayat, Assef. 1993. *Work, Politics and Power: An International Perspective on Workers' Control and Self-Management*. New York: Monthly Review Press.

Bowles, Samuel and Herbert Gintis. 1986. *Democracy and Capitalism: Property, Community, and the Contradictions of Modern Social Thought*. New York: Basic Books.

Burbach, Roger and Camila Piñeiro. 2007. "Venezuela's Participatory Socialism." *Socialism and Democracy*, Vol. 21, No. 3, November, pp. 181–200.

Cahan, Jean Axelrad. (1994) "The Concept of Property in Marx's Theory of History: A Defense of the Autonomy of the Socioeconomic Base." *Science and Society*, 58:4, pp. 392–414.

Cheney, George. 2002. *Values at Work: Employee Participation Meets Market Pressure at Mondragon*. New York: Cornell University Press.

Comisso, Ellen T. 1979. *Workers' Control Under Plan and Market*. New Haven, CT: Yale University Press.

Datanalisis. 2006. *Mercal: lugar más visitado para comprar alimentos*. May. http://www.datanalisis.com.ve/detalle.asp?id=265.

Deng, Xiaoping. 1984. "Building Socialism with a specifically Chinese character." in *The People's Daily*, June 30.

Devine, Pat. 1988. *Democracy and Economic Planning*. Cambridge, M.A.: Polity Press.

Dow, Gregory. 2003. *Governing the Firm*. Cambridge, U.K.; New York: Cambridge University Press.

Ellerman, David P. (1990) *The Democratic Worker-Owned Firm: A New Model for the East and West*. London, Boston: Unwin Hyman.

Engels, Frederic. 1876–1878. "Del socialismo utópico al socialismo al científico." Capítulo 2. *Marxists Internet Archive*. http://www.marxists.org/espanol/m-e/1880s/dsusc/2.htm.

Espinosa, Juan Guillermo and Andrew Zimbalist. 1978. *Economic Democracy: Workers' Participation in Chilean Industry 1970–1973*. New York: Academic Press.

García Müller, Alberto. 2007. "The big challenges of Venezuelan cooperativism today." *Venezuelanalysis*, 7 August 2007. http://www.venezuelanalysis.com/articles.php?artno=2109.

Hahnel, Robin. 2005. *Economic Justice and Democracy: From Competition to Cooperation*. New York: Routledge.

Harnecker, Marta. 2005. "Co-management advances in ALCASA: Aluminum workers in Venezuela choose their managers and increase production." *Venezuelanalysis.com*, 28 March. http://www.venezuelanalysis.com/articles.php?artno=1407.

Jaua Milano, Elias. 2005. *Nuevo Modelo Socio-Productivo Y Desarrollo Endógeno*. Caracas: Ministerio para la Economía Popular.

Karl, Ferry Lynn. 1997. *The Paradox of Plenty*. Berkeley: University of California Press.

Lanz, Carlos. 2005. *Dossier para la Crítica de la División Social del Trabajo*. July. http://www.aporrea.org/ideologia/a17683.html.

Manson, Ronald M. 1982. *Participatory and Workplace Democracy*. Carbondale: Southern Illinois University Press.

Marx, Karl and Frederic Engels. 1848. "El manifiesto comunista." *Marxists Internet Archive*. http://www.marxists.org/espanol/m-e/1840s/48-manif.htm.

Miller, David. 2003. "Deliberative democracy and social choice." In *Debating Deliberative Democracy*. James S. Fishkin and Meter Laslett (Eds.). Malden, M.A.: Blackwell, pp. 182–199.

MINEP. 2005. *Cooperativismo Revolucionario: Eje De Formación Sociopolítica*. Caracas: INCE.

Nove, Alec. 1992. *The Economics of Feasible Socialism, Revisited*. London: Routledge.

Ostrom, Elinor. 1990. *Governing the Commons: The Evolution of Institutions for Collective Action*. Cambridge, U.K.; New York: Cambridge University Press.

Pateman, Carole. 1970. *Participation and Democratic Theory*. Cambridge, U.K.: Cambridge University Press.

Piñeiro, Camila. 2005. "The new cooperative movement in Venezuela's Bolivarian process." *Venezuelanalysis.com*, 17 December.

Piñeiro, Camila. 2007. "Workplace democracy and collective consciousness: An empirical study of Venezuelan cooperatives." *Monthly Review*, Vol. 59, No. 6, November, pp. 27–40.

Piñeiro, Camila. 2008. "Workplace democracy and social consciousness: A study of Venezuelan cooperatives." *Science & Society*, Vol. 73, No. 3, July, pp. 309–339.

Piñeiro, Camila. 2009. 'Main challenges for cooperatives in Venezuela.' *Critical Sociology*, Vol. 35, No. 6, November, pp. 841–862.

Smith, Stephen C. 1985. 'Political behavior as an economic externality: Econometric evidence on the relationship between ownership and decision making participation in U.S. firms and participation in community affairs.' *Advances in the Economic Analysis of Participatory and Labor-Managed Firms*, Vol. 1, pp. 123–136.

Tovar, Ernesto J. 2007. 'Desastre cooperativista.' *El Universal*, 24 March.

Vanek, Jaroslav. 1971. *The Participatory Economy; An Evolutionary Hypothesis and a Strategy for Development*. Ithaca, NY: Cornell University Press.

Xiaoping, Deng. 1984. 'Building Socialism with a specifically Chinese character.' *The People's Daily*.

# 6
# From Managed Employees to Self-Managed Workers: The Transformations of Labour at Argentina's Worker-Recuperated Enterprises

*Marcelo Vieta*

## Introduction

Argentina's *empresas recuperadas por sus trabajadores* (worker-recuperated enterprises, or ERTs) began to emerge in the early 1990s. They became consolidated in the late 1990s to early 2000s as more and more small- and medium-sized enterprises (SMEs) began to fail or declare bankruptcy as a result of the country's sharp neo-liberal turn. Traditional union tactics were unable to address workers' needs, and an impotent state was on the defensive as social, economic and political crises rendered it incapable of responding to soaring immiseration and business failure. In this climate, some workers took matters into their own hands by occupying and reopening failing or failed firms, usually as workers' cooperatives. By late 2009, almost 9400 workers were self-managing their working lives in over 200 ERTs across Argentina's urban economy, in sectors as diverse as printing and publishing, metallurgy, foodstuffs, waste management, construction, textiles, shipbuilding, tourism and health provision (Ruggeri, 2010: 7).

While representing only a fraction of Argentina's 16.485 million formal and informal workers in its urban-based economy (Ministerio de Trabajo, 2010), labour sociologist Hector Palomino (2003) points out that ERTs have nevertheless inspired 'new expectations for [social] change' (71). Indeed, as outlined in this chapter, ERTs show workers' abilities to save their own jobs and to avoid the fate of precarious welfare plans or structural unemployment. They also highlight workers' capacities to innovate alternatives, and to cooperatively reorganize and self-manage their own working lives, even in the aftermath of financial, economic or socio-political crises inherent to the neo-liberal capitalist system.

The aim of this chapter is to explore ERTs as one promising form of alternative work organization in the light of the continued crises of capital and from the perspective of these firms' worker-protagonists. From the point-of-view of capital, these workers are 'rebellious subjects' (Dyer-Witheford, 1999: 64) who, in the process of reconstituting a formerly capitalist firm into a self-managed one, are at the same time resisting and challenging chronic unemployment and job insecurity, while also innovating ways to democratically reorganize their modes-of-production. More dramatically, and in contrast to purely for-profit business initiatives, these self-managed initiatives begin to consider and to include an affected community's members. In this chapter, the interplay is specifically examined between

(1) the macro- and micro-economic crises that spawned these self-managed firms in recent years;
(2) the challenges that arise for these workers in converting failing businesses into cooperatives;
(3) their lived experiences of micro- and macro-economic crises;
(4) some of the ways these rebellious subjects transform from managed employees to self-managed workers and, in turn, radiate these intersubjective transformations into the new labour processes they reconstitute.

Ultimately, this chapter studies how these workers invent, learn about and implement the innovations they forge out of the tensions, and the ongoing challenges they face in starting – and subsequently running – their cooperatives... and in the process reinvent themselves.

## The emergence of ERTs

By the mid-1990s, thousands of Argentine SMEs were losing market share while amassing unwieldy debt loads due to an admixture of shrinking local markets, trade deficits, and the incompetence or outright fraudulent practices of SME business owners and managers (Ministerio de Trabajo, 2008; Ruggeri, 2009). In the name of curbing hyperinflation and reducing a surging national debt that, paradoxically, continued to rise throughout the 1990s, Argentina's International Monetary Fund-sanctioned liberalizations included the 'dollarization' of the peso, the privatization of over 150 once-nationalized or public sector firms, the erosion of decades-old labour protections and the foreign capitalization of large portions of Argentina's industrial and agricultural base (Gambina and Campione, 2002; Petras and Veltmeyer, 2002).

By 1994 it was clear that these neo-liberal policies were negatively affecting the competitive advantage of Argentine products in foreign and national markets (Patroni, 2004; Damill, 2005). The large wave of privatization schemes, company downsizings, outsourcing and the deregulation of labour markets were underpinned by a mass outflow of capital to foreign economic interests, compromising the competitiveness of thousands of businesses throughout the country (Boron and Thwaites Ray, 2004; Patroni, 2004). Meanwhile, by the first quarter of 2002, well over 20 per cent of Argentina's active, urban-based workers had entered the ranks of the structurally unemployed (Levy Yeyati and Valenzuela, 2007). Those workers that were still employed often suffered maltreatment by bosses who could not keep their firms afloat. This often included not paying employees' back wages, overtime pay, holiday pay, the employer's portion of social security contributions or severance upon dismissal. And some business owners would enter bankruptcy proceedings only to then pay off court trustees, asset strip their own firms, and open up shop somewhere else with cheaper labour. By the apogee of the neo-liberal collapse in late 2001 and early 2002 – a period highlighted by the popular revolt of 19–20 December 2001 and the announcement of Argentina's default on its national debt a few days later – the national month-to-month business bankruptcy rate had reached its highest point in Argentina's modern history, soaring from an average of 772 per month in 1991 to over 2600 per month by December 2001 (Magnani, 2003: 37).

In the midst of this macro- and micro-economic crisis, some workers took matters into their own hands by occupying their failing or failed firms and then usually converting them into workers' cooperatives. Rather than being impelled by a revolutionary cause, traditional union demands or the leadership of mainstream political parties, these responses were, at first, highly risky and localized tactics carried out by desperate workers willing to face violent repression by the state and returning owners in order to save their jobs, continue to feed their families and safeguard their self-dignity. Initially, then, ERT protagonists took on the challenges of self-management out of indignation at their mistreatment by bosses and their deep worries of becoming structurally unemployed within a morally and financially bankrupt political and economic system that looked the other way while countless business owners engaged in nefarious schemes to save their dying firms at the expense of employees' wellbeing (Palomino, 2003; Rebón, 2004, 2007; Ruggeri, 2009).

These workers were not alone. With a dearth of options left for most working people during this period, class divisions crystallized into the strident radicalization of marginalized groups. Starting around 1996, a contagion of bottom-up popular resistance and horizontalism spread across Argentina's marginal sectors, witnessed in the widespread direct action tactics of property occupations and squats, the *piquetero's* now famous road blockages, spontaneous community mobilization, the formation of neighbourhood assemblies and directly democratic organizational structures (Dinerstein, 2002; Ghibaudi, 2006; Sitrin, 2006; Svampa and Pereyra, 2004). What spilled over from these grassroots mobilizations onto all forms of popular struggle throughout the urban *barrios* and industrialized towns of the country at the time was a renewed sense of collective purpose against the callous exploitation of workers and the marginalized; a growing ethos of self-organization and direct participatory democracy 'from below' (Colectivo Situaciones, 2002, sec. 10); and a massive 'reactivation' of 'communitarian social experience' (Svampa and Pereyra, 2004: 233). This contagion intermingled with a long history of working class militancy and workers' collective imaginary of Argentina's Peronist-led 'golden years' during the vice-presidency and first two presidencies of Juán Perón (1944–1955) and the 20 or so years of working-class resistance that followed (1955–1976). This included a strong and politically active labour movement, a prosperous working class and a mostly nationalized and self-sustaining economy. By the early years of the new millennium there was much cross-pollination between these grassroots social justice groups – highly visible in the diverse composition of those engaging in the daily protests that took place across the country's urban centres (Almeyra, 2004; Svampa and Pereyra, 2004). These are the most direct roots of Argentina's wave of workspace occupations and recuperations.

## The emergence of democratized labour processes and workers' conscientization

The most distinguishing characteristic of ERTs is that they were almost all formerly privately-owned firms in micro-economic trouble that were then recuperated and revived by some of their former employees and converted into workers' cooperatives. Surprisingly, while ERTs are present in a wide cross-section of Argentina's economy, and although most of their workers have not had previous experience of cooperativism or political activism, most ERT workers' collectives

(1) appropriated the former firm's property, machines and production processes, and re-conceptualized their work organization along cooperative principles;
(2) directly adopted democratic decision-making structures;
(3) developed egalitarian forms of remuneration and surplus distribution; and
(4) perhaps most innovative of all – opened up formerly capitalist workplaces to the community or engaged in community economic, social or cultural development projects.

These characteristics gradually emerged over the years as workers' pragmatic responses to the multifold challenges involved in reopening and self-managing formerly depleted capitalist firms. They are intimately linked to the concomitant transformation of these workers' subjectivities from employees to self-managed workers and their new outlooks on working life. In other words, these workplace conversions are rooted in the very subjective transformations that some of these workers go through as they collectively overcome micro-economic crises and work together to reopen and restart production under a new form of management: *autogestión*, or self-management. The intricacies of cooperatively managing their firms were developed praxically as ERT protagonists learnt from each other and discovered self-management together. Implicit throughout this chapter is the notion that, in essence, these four characteristics were the result of ERT workers gradually recuperating their own labour-power – an inherently human capacity that, nevertheless, becomes alienated from workers within the labour-capital relation when, in return for a wage, workers give up control of their skills, inventive capacities and the products they make to capitalist bosses in the standard employment contract (Braverman, 1974; Marx, 1987; Vosko, 2006).

I based my analysis of ERT workers' transformed subjectivities – their emergent class consciousness – on the tradition that has been called '"class struggle" Marxism' (Dyer-Witheford, 1999: 63). This subject-centred Marxism is present in phenomenological, autonomist and 'Open' Marxist currents, as well as in moments of the Frankfurt School of critical theory. Rather than focusing on the exploitative nature and iron-clad 'laws' of capitalism, 'class struggle' Marxism differentiates itself from objectivist 'one-sided' Marxism in that it views these laws as mutable – constantly influenced and challenged by the ongoing resistances and refusals of 'rebellious subjects seek[ing] a way beyond work, wage, and profit' (64). For these theorists, it is capital that needs labour for its valorization and existence. Labour, on the other hand, is not similarly reliant on capital. That is, it is labour, not capital, which can be seen as being *a priori* in the capital-labour relation. In the light of this, 'class struggle' Marxists highlight not only the dynamics and lived experiences of exploitation, alienation and class conflict within capitalism (Merleau-Ponty, 1962; Marcuse, 1964, 1966; Marx, 1967) but also the vitality of working class culture and workers' self-activity (Ranciere, 1989; Thompson, 1991; Williams, 2002); labourers' ongoing capacities to do something about their situation of exploitation within the capital-labour relation (Dyer-Witheford, 1999; Clever, 2000); workers' 'cultures of solidarity' forged to counter and move beyond these crises and conflicts (Fantasia, 1988); and the recognition of workers as active agents of history and how they, in turn, change themselves as they move history (Thompson, 1991; Lebowitz, 2003).

The experiences of Argentina's ERT workers are, I believe, illustrative of how such a collective working class consciousness arises: via spontaneous struggle, without vanguard leadership, in an unfinished and multilayered state of becoming, within the tensions inherent to complex social relations of production, conjuncturally formed and praxically driven by the crises and needs confronting a collective of workers. For instance, the formation of a working class consciousness among ERT workers is not – hearkening back to Maurice Merleau-Ponty's words in the *Phenomenology of Perception* (1962) – predetermined by an 'idea' of what 'the working class' should be. Rather, the collective practices of resistance and self-management experimented with by ERT protagonists emerge intersubjectively from the entanglements and ruptures of ERT workers' subjectivities that 'co-exist in the same situation and feel alike, not in virtue of some comparison, as if each one [of them] lived primarily within [themselves], but on the basis of [their shared] tasks and gestures' (444). That is, as individuals whose lives are 'synchronized' together and that 'share a common lot' (444) within the socio-economic crisis that Argentina recently found itself in at the turn of the millennium. And what are the commonly shared lived experiences, this 'common lot', that piqued in Argentina during the implosion of the neo-liberal model in recent years and that brought together some of its workers through their direct actions of occupying and self-managing firms? Shared feelings of frustration as thousands of firms were closing and declaring bankruptcy or were idle; commonly felt fear at being relegated to the growing ranks of the unemployed and the poor; an intensification of exploitation in the wake of dwindling salaries and benefits; feelings of helplessness and the loss of dignity as job security eroded. There are countless stories of domestic crises and the breakdown of families as a result of increased life precarization, and a myriad of other calamitous experiences Argentine workers were suffering everyday.

## From micro-economic challenges to cooperative self-determination

The process of workplace recuperation usually culminates in the firm becoming a self-managed, worker-run business under the legal rubric of a workers' cooperative and, as has been the case in 63 per cent of all ERTs, the temporary or permanent expropriation of the firm by provincial legislatures on behalf of the cooperative (Ruggeri, 2010: 24).[1] As of late 2009, 95.3 per cent of ERTs were self-organized under the legal framework of a workers' cooperative. What is astounding about this number is that, in most cases, while some ERT workers have had previous experience of union organization or community politics, most workers just starting an ERT have had no experience of any form of cooperativism (Olmedo and Murray, 2002; Fajn, 2003; Martí et al., 2004; Rebón, 2007). This fact adds to the many challenges these workers face in self-managing their firms: they not only have to self-organize depleted workspaces, they also have to learn the intricacies of forming and running a cooperative.

If learning how to become cooperators compounds the challenges ERTs face early on, then why is it that their workers overwhelmingly turn to cooperativism without having had any previous experience with the organizational form? One answer can be found in the public debates that were, in the early years of the ERT phenomenon, preoccupying workers, social economy activists, sympathetic academics and the phenomenon's first political leaders. One of the major issues on the table at the time was the legal framework ERTs were to take: nationalization under workers' control or workers' cooperativism (Fajn, 2003: 105–106; Ruggeri et al., 2005: 67). While nationalization under workers' control was historically plausible (see Petras and Veltmeyer, 2002), early ERT protagonists eventually scrapped this option when it became clear that the Argentine state was refusing to go along with the proposal (Fajn, 2003: 60). It was decided in these debates that the only practical and legally sound alternative for ERTs was – out of 'convenience'– to turn to the already viable and long-established cooperative model.[2] Especially in the light of a state that, because of its strong commitments to capitalist enterprise, could not set the precedent of nationalizing once-proprietary firms.

At first, these workers reopened their firms as cooperatives for pragmatic reasons: in order to re-establish the business as a formal productive entity as quickly as possible, legally recognized by the state, the financial system, providers, and its customer-base. At the same time, becoming a workers' cooperative rather than another form of entity (such as a partnership) protects the worker-members from the seizure of their personal property should the cooperative fail – offering a form of limited liability. Additionally, the cooperative model ensures that the ERT, due to Argentine cooperative law, does not have to pay taxes on revenue (2003: 106). Summarizing the view of a majority of the ERT workers I interviewed, one worker told me: 'We became *cooperativistas* out of obligation, not because we wanted to be *cooperativistas*'.[3] Despite these pragmatic beginnings, however, many ERT workers I interviewed also told me that they eventually came to realize that the workers' cooperative was indeed the most robust organizational model for restructuring their decision-making, production and remuneration processes. The workers' cooperative model essentially served to give procedural shape to their self-management and helped to organizationally express their desires for *compañerismo* (camaraderie or solidarity).

Of course, because most ERTs must still compete within capitalist markets once they restart production, they are constantly affected by the tensions that inevitably arise between the quotidian needs of workers and the production and market challenges that impose themselves palpably upon an already depleted firm. The most commonly shared challenges for ERT workers soon after converting the firm – often becoming chronic challenges as the months and years of self-managed production transpire – tend to be:

(1) underproduction, in large part due to a) depreciated or broken machinery and b) capitalization difficulties;
(2) burdensome and ongoing court cases for negotiating carried-over unpaid utility bills or even rent from the previous business;
(3) difficulties in reaching new markets and lost customers;

(4) the risk of hiring new workers and securing the future of the workers' cooperative if newer workers do not share the same values as its founders; and

(5) the continued precarious life conditions of workers due to fluctuating revenues and salaries, lost pension contributions from the days when the former firm was failing, and the lack of access to the comprehensive system of social security benefits, workers' compensation, and extended health insurance usually guaranteed to employees of privately owned or state-controlled firms (Ruggeri et al., 2005; Vieta, 2010).

Considering the conflictive beginnings of ERTs, the technological limitations of many ERTs due to inheriting deteriorated or depreciated production infrastructure, the reduced size of an ERT's workforce when compared to the firm under owner-management,[4] the lack of access to credit from banks, and the lack of governmental assistance for the movement in general, it is not surprising that most ERTs produce at between 30 and 60 per cent of their potential capacity when compared to their production runs during the 'best' days of private ownership (Ruggeri et al., 2005: 65–76).

## From transforming subjectivities to alternative labour processes

To illustrate some of the connections between ERT protagonists' transformations to self-managed workers and the horizontalized labour processes these firms adopt, I now draw on a selection of findings from key informant interviews and *in situ* observations of four diverse ERT case studies: (1) Artés Gráficas Chilavert, a small and emblematic print shop in the working class Buenos Aires *barrio* of Nueva Pompeya, currently consisting of 14 members; (2) the construction and parks maintenance cooperative Unión Solidaria de Trabajadores (UST) in the Villa Domínico *barrio* of the southern Buenos Aires municipality of Avellaneda, consisting of more than 90 members; (3) *Comercio y Justicia*, the worker-recuperated cooperative newspaper consisting of 71 members in the industrial city of Córdoba; and (4) the formerly private medical clinic, Clínica Junín, recuperated by its nurses and maintenance staff and now consisting of over 30 members, also in the city of Córdoba.[5]

In order to begin to assess how these ERT workers acquire and share the skills, values and attitudes needed to self-manage their firms and, in the process, personally and collectively transform themselves and their firms, I embedded a series of questions focused on workers' learning processes into the semi-structured interview protocol I deployed. These learning-based questions focused on ERT workers' reflections on four main areas: their personal changes in cooperative knowledge, skills, practices and attitudes and values since participating in their ERT projects.[6] What I found was that ERT protagonists' politicization, emergent conscientization, the acquisition of new cooperative values and attitudes, and their transformed subjectivities emerge from their collective actions, which respond to the conjunctures of the microeconomic crises they find themselves in. Their processes of learning how to be cooperators and their adoption of community-focused values and projects are learned via informal and intersubjective processes. Moreover, for these workers, the centring of their restructured labour processes along cooperative principles and their new found hope grows directly from their collective responses to their difficulties rather than from an enlightened vanguard; from within their collective moments of struggle, not from above or outside of them. As one of the founders of Chilavert eloquently articulates:

> Early on in the fight to reclaim our work we started fighting for our salaries, for getting out of our severe debt-loads that the boss had left us...But now I know, looking back on our struggle three years on. Now I can see where the change in me started, because it begins during your struggles. First, you fight for not being left out on the street with nothing. And then, suddenly, you see that you've formed a cooperative and you start getting involved in the struggle of other recuperated enterprises. You don't realize at the time but within your own self there's a change that's taking place...You realize it afterwards, when time has transpired...

## Cooperativized work organization and associated forms of labour

### Collaborative and informal learning

With all the ERT protagonists I interviewed, their acquisition of cooperative knowledge, skills, practices and values and attitudes – witnessed primarily in the transformation of their dispositions of individualist and competitive employees to ones of cooperativist *socios* (associates) – occurs informally as they unfold their self-management projects over time and struggle together to address the crises and challenges that face their cooperativized firms.[7] Moreover, these changes tend, on the whole, to happen immanently, at times by trial and error, and always in the evolution of the processes of self-management. As the former president of Clínica Junín told me, 'We learned the ins and outs of cooperativism *sobre la marcha, como todos acá* (on the path of doing, like all of us here).' A new *socio* from UST echoed this: 'Most of us here learned [cooperativism] from working here...'

Firstly, this learning occurs most noticeably intracooperatively via both the social bonds that form organically on shop floors from having to collectively self-manage a firm and from the attitudinal and behavioural examples of the ERT's leader(s), who most often have had previous experience of political or union organization. Secondly, this informal learning occurs intercooperatively, via the horizontal networks that form between ERTs, from the influence of ERT political and umbrella organizations,[8] and between ERTs and other social movement groups that forge affinity relations with specific ERTs. Intercooperative exchanges especially occur during an ERT's first days, weeks and months of high conflict, when other ERTs and social movement organizations come to support workers occupying a plant. During these moments of high political turmoil, supporting affinity groups begin to transfer their knowledge of the political and judicial system, and the values and attitudes of *compañerismo* (camaraderie or solidarity) and cooperativism to the new ERT workers. The former president of Júnin underscores this intercooperative, network-based informal learning process:

> Meanwhile, what continued to strengthen the processes [of workplace takeovers] was the unity and solidarity of other sectors helping out: students, sympathetic unions, neighbourhood groups, human rights organizations... That's what permitted all of these processes to sustain themselves over time... We've had close relations with other ERTs and we have participated in national gatherings of ERTs, as well. There is a common saying among ERTs: 'If they touch one of us they touch us all.' Ever since, if there were other ERTs that were being threatened with eviction, many of us would also go to support them... There's been a permanent exchange between many of us [for some time].

Subsequently, from out of this intracooperative and intercooperative informal learning, what, in practice, more *compeñerismo* tends to mean for ERT workers is that they are now much more likely to help out their workmates in situations when in the past they would have stuck to their own tasks and worried primarily about their own individual interests. As a founding member of Chilavert emphatically told me:

> Before, under owner-management, there was always someone marking out the rhythm of your work. You would work because you got paid. Things are now different. Now, we have other obligations based on our own responsibility to one another and our jobs... Everything we do [and produce] now passes through our own hands... Before we were 'workmates' but today we aren't workmates anymore. We're now more like 'associates', where the problem of one associate affects us all. And there are times when we have to look at the problems of each *compañero* and try to resolve them so they won't affect the entire society that we have formed here. Before, if something happened to someone it was the owner's responsibility... we were all just mere acquaintances, nothing more... But now, we're a much tighter unit, and what binds us together is the fact that we're all responsible for this cooperative as a society and we all have to contribute to moving it forward.

It must be pointed out, however, that these transformations into more solidarity-minded workmates, who recognize their increased 'obligations' and 'responsibility' to each other, are not a given for all ERT workers, nor are they present to the same degree in all ERTs. It was obvious from my interviews that tensions – and sometimes deep tensions – still exist between the commitment to cooperativism and *compañerismo* of some members and the continued individualism, competiveness or indifference of other members. Indeed, sometimes these tensions exist within the same worker. At times, some workers have said to me things such as: 'I didn't sign up for self-managing my workplace,' or 'All I ever wanted was to do an honest day's work and get my regular paycheque.' Some workers, it was obvious, are more aware of these tensions within themselves than others as they reflected critically on their own contradictions between the desire to self-manage and their longing, at times, for simpler days when they would only need to 'keep their heads down', work their shift and go home. When, for example, I asked workers what *autogestión* meant to them none of them would say to me 'more freedom' (which is what I had hypothesized they would say to me). Rather, what most workers would immediately say to me, at times in a begrudging voice, were things like '*autogestión* means more responsibility' and 'a larger amount of commitment to my work', complementing the comments of the Chilavert founder above. But when I asked them if they would ever consider returning to their previous work situation, even if they received more money, almost all of my key informants said that they would not. What was clear to me, in talking to workers and being present at dozens of ERTs, is that notions and practices of solidarity and *compañerismo* that infuse *autogestión*, although not uniformly conceived of and practised even within the same ERT by any means, palpably exist to some degree in all the ERTs I visited. This is, to say the least, a vast difference from the workplace atmosphere present at these firms when they worked for a boss, workers told me.

While more top-down and sometimes more formal types of learning processes occur when non-governmental organization-based or university-led affinity initiatives approach and work with ERTs directly, or when state-based institutions and ministries assist ERTs, on the whole ERT *socios* tend to learn the values and practices of cooperativism informally from each other or on a trial-and-error basis as they work out the daily practicalities of self-management together. Moreover, newer ERT workers are informally trained both in the ins-and-outs of cooperativism and in job-specific skills 'on-the-job' via apprenticing. This emulates the principal way that job training has traditionally happened in certain blue collar economic sectors in Argentina (Munck et al., 1987), but now, in ERTs, cooperative values and ideals are layered onto apprenticing scenarios on shop floors.

These informal and mentor-apprentice learning practices – as I have already pointed out – did not emerge from Argentina's traditional cooperative movement, with its more formalized training programmes rooted in the fifth Rochdale principle of cooperatives, but mainly from unionized workplaces identifying with Argentina's labour movement. Indeed, most ERT members I spoke with still perceive themselves as *laburantes* (workers) rather than *cooperativistas*. I asked a founding member of UST, and the plant's expert bulldozer operator, whether he felt more like a worker or a cooperator:

> No, I feel that I am a *laburante*, and I will continue to be one! When we go to community meetings, we go with our overalls. And wearing our overalls all the time while at work is important to remind us of where we came from. This is one of the things we keep on reminding our younger members of the coop, to always have their overalls on when they are at work and in the community during working hours.

Indeed, only 3 of the 31 ERT workers I interviewed had previous experience with cooperativism, while considerably more founding members of

ERTs interviewed had previous union-organization experience. Tellingly, ERT workers who have gone through these previous cooperative- or union-organization experiences are considered leaders within the firm, holding formal administrative positions or informal leadership roles in order to teach their *compañeros* how to organize workers' assemblies and how to carry out democratic decision making in practice.[9] A subset of workers I interviewed, who had either cooperative- or union-organization experience – that is, the three predominant leaders of Chilavert (one of whom is now the current president of the plant), the current president of UST and two former presidents of *Comercio y Justicia* – was instrumental in motivating their co-workers to take over the failing former plant and restart production as cooperatives.

*Changing the pace of work, and merging work and play*

Another way that *compañerismo* and *autogestión* takes shape at ERTs – and, in the process, relaxing and arguably even humanizing an ERT's labour process – is the incorporation of more flexible work processes, and the integration of unstructured moments of play and rest into the working day. This was present to some degree in all the ERTs I visited.

For example, I observed countless instances of job- or task-sharing; varying work hours on the basis of a specific deliverable, contract or job; and taking many breaks throughout the day. ERT workers have told me on numerous occasions that these less-intense production processes work well with their fluctuating work demands. They also facilitated taking care of workers' other ongoing life needs (e.g. attending to personal matters or medical visits) during working hours on slow days. Generally, workers told me, flexible work hours help to ease the tensions and stresses that come with the daily routines of work, while taking into account the life needs of the cooperative's *socios*.

I have also observed the importance of the incorporation of play and rest in the transformation of the rhythm of the working day at ERTs, which has the effect of rethinking and prefiguring another pace to working life. At Chilavert and UST, for example, worker-members make a point of eating and playing together regularly (i.e. daily communal lunches or weekly football games or barbeques). Another example of this merger of work and play, present at every ERT I visited in Argentina, is the privileged presence of the *mate* station on every shop floor. The shared gourd with its metal *bombilla* (straw), the bags of *mate* tea and the teapot or thermos were located at prominent and easily accessed places throughout the shops I visited, and there are often several *mate* stations throughout the plant. I have often seen workers making *mate*, meeting at the station and drinking throughout the working day. I even had the recurring pleasure of sharing the *mate* break on the shop floor with workers – together with the complementary *factura* (baked sweets) that are customarily eaten with *mate* in Argentina. I was told by several workers, especially at Chilavert and UST, that this particular act, for them, was not only a way to break up the monotony of the working day, but also a symbolic gesture that reclaimed for them their working class Argentine culture. It was, for them, a purposeful act that served to remind them of what they could not readily do when working for former bosses.

## Democratic decision-making structures within an ERT's labour processes

Because ERTs did not emerge from Argentina's traditional cooperative movement, and workers were not impelled – initially – to form the ERT because of pre-existing cooperative values, the specific form that cooperation takes tends to be worked out within each ERT pragmatically as it matures and lives out the intricacies of self-management within its particular economic sector. One area where informal learning and communication flows merge into more formal, consensus-based decision making and communication structures in an ERT relates to the second and third principles of cooperativism respectively: 'democratic member control' (MacPherson, 1995, par. 34) and 'member economic participation' (par. 46). On the whole, most ERTs tend to be administered by workers' councils made up of at least a president, a treasurer, a secretary and sometimes members-at-large elected from the *socios* and with a mandate of one or two years. Many ERTs also hold regular workers' assemblies that meet either on a regular periodic basis (weekly, bi-weekly or monthly) or when major issues arise, or both. Of my four case studies, only *Comercio y Justicia* held one compulsory meeting, its annual general meeting. Smaller ERTs, such as Chilavert, tended to administer themselves in a more relaxed way, relegating smaller day-to-day decisions to those most skilled in a particular task. Day-to-day concerns, especially in smaller ERTs, are more often than not worked out on an ad hoc basis on shop floors and in the adoption of production processes that are (re)organized around flexible work teams on a per-project basis. Issues that affect the cooperative as a whole, such as whether or not to enter new markets, deciding on buying new equipment, hiring decisions, or whether or not to reprimand a worker, primarily happen via the formal meeting of the workers' assembly on a per-need basis as issues arise. This is especially the case, for example, at Chilavert and

Junín, but also, interestingly, in the larger UST and *Comercio y Justicia*, which both tend to operate as a collection of smaller workers' collectives within each ERT organized around particular production tasks within predetermined divisions of labour.

Concerning the cooperative principle of 'member economic participation', in most ERTs revenue capitalization and salary amounts, salary adjustments due to the ebbs and flows of business cycles, and the social dividend each member is to receive are regularly debated, voted on, adjusted, and agreed upon by the workers' assembly. There is, however, no defining trend across ERTs concerning what percentage of revenue should return to the cooperative as capital, how much should be allocated to salaries and benefits, and whether a percentage of revenues should go to local community needs. More financially challenging months, for example, are usually bridged with consensus-based cuts to, most often, social dividends, salaries and community contributions for those firms that engage in community work.

These continued debates accentuate the importance (without them articulating it in this way) that most ERT protagonists give generally to the cooperative principle of 'democratic member control'. Indeed, more often than not, in the ERTs I visited I consistently witnessed a strong culture of active member participation 'in setting... policies and making decisions' (par. 34), which also means the implicit and, at times, explicit reprimanding of members that 'free load', steal or otherwise shirk their cooperative responsibilities. These flexible and democratically mitigated organizational policies highlight the strength of the cooperative structure mentioned in the literature, underscoring what Ian MacPherson has characterized as one of the 'remarkable special characteristics' of the International Cooperative Alliance's (ICA) cooperative principles: their 'inherent flexibility' to adapt to the economic and political particularities of a cooperative and to the collective needs of its members (1995, par. 37).

### Workers' control over the distribution of surpluses

Another way that researchers have assessed the degree to which *compañerismo* unfolds within an ERT has been to look at their remuneration strategies (Fajn, 2003; Ruggeri et al., 2005; Rebón, 2007). One influential survey found that 56 per cent of ERTs practise complete pay equity (Ruggeri et al., 2005: 67). Moreover, it seems that *the age* of an ERT correlates with whether or not, and the degree to which, pay equity is practised; older ERTs, recuperated around the turn of the millennium for example, are more likely to practise pay equity when compared to more recently recuperated firms (80). In addition, *the size* of the firm tends to also be linked to pay equity: 64 per cent of firms with 20 workers or less practise pay equity, compared to 47 per cent of firms having between 20 and 50 workers and 54 per cent of firms with more than 50 workers (81). Finally, the likelihood of pay parity is also specifically linked to an ERT's *level of conflictivity* (the level of suffering and intensity of worker-protagonists' struggles during the processes of taking over and converting the firm into a workers' cooperative). For instance, 71 per cent of ERTs that were involved in lengthy acts of occupation or other intense conflicts with former bosses or the state subsequently practise pay equity, compared to only 37 per cent of ERTs that were not occupied or had not experienced intense conflicts (80).

These trends in pay equity were supported in my four case studies, especially concerning the level of conflict that an ERT went through during its founding. Chilavert and Clínica Junín, for example, both with highly conflictual beginnings and the two smallest ERTs of my four cases, practise complete pay equity among full members. UST, the newest ERT in the study (founded in 2004) and the largest of my four cases at more than 90 members, practises almost complete pay equity – differentiating some salaries with respect to seniority, tasks or skill sets. On the other hand, the newspaper *Comercio y Justicia*, also with a relatively large membership base, has the least conflictual founding story and also has the most differentiated salary scheme of the four cases I studied based on experience, seniority and position. In fact, *Comercio y Justicia* in many ways continues the same hierarchical structure that the previous private iteration of the newspaper had.

There are several other phenomenological explanations for these differing remuneration practices linked to the age, size and level of conflictivity of an ERT. Most notably, my qualitative data, as with Ruggeri et al.'s (2005) quantitative data, suggest that the collective of workers belonging to smaller ERTs spend more time interacting with each other on a daily basis when compared to larger ERTs, and thus have more intimate knowledge of each other's jobs, personal lives and concerns. For example, Chilavert and Junín, in particular, tend to experience less factionalism, individualism and shop floor competition, compared to larger ERTs such as UST and *Comercio y Justicia* which, not surprisingly, also have more dispersed work teams. Another reason some ERTs tend towards pay equity, more so than others, is because workers from more egalitarian ERTs (as my case studies also show), have usually known each other for longer periods of time or have a longer history of experiencing struggles together.

These attitudinal and practical changes are not as strong at the newspaper *Comercio y Justicia*, underscoring the flip side of Ruggeri et al.'s findings: as already mentioned, *Comercio y Justicia*'s beginnings were not as conflictual as the other ERTs in my study. In particular, this ERT happened to be the first to have negotiated a lease-back-to-own settlement with bankruptcy courts. Its workers neither had to occupy the firm for an extended period of time nor did they have to actively confront the former owners who had abandoned the plant. Its founders, probably in part because many of them are also professional journalists working – coincidentally – in the field of judicial and business news, decided to take the path of negotiating with bankruptcy courts rather than the more usual 'occupy and resist' path taken by ERTs. Indeed, as my interviews at the newspaper reveal, most of its journalist members possess the strong critical writing and thinking skills, as well as the social capital, necessary to negotiate the legal quagmire of bankruptcy. Moreover, its leaders have had experience of workplace organization, mostly via previous work in their local journalists' union.

In addition to Ruggeri et al.'s positive correlations between the level of conflictivity and the egalitarian nature of an ERT, one further observation that deserves mention here is that *Comercio y Justicia* is involved in the most competitive market of the four ERTs I worked with; one which is dominated by Argentina's largest media and newspaper group, Grupo Clarín. As such, and highlighting the thesis put forward by Fajn and Rebón (2005), this highly competitive market has encouraged this ERT to continue to organize itself within a hierarchical production process, emulating the divisions of labour of privately owned newspapers. For example, each of the newspaper's sectors is headed by an appointed *encargado*, or chief, as in 'chief correspondent', 'editor-in-chief', 'chief of publication', and so on. Not surprisingly, it was evident in my visits to this ERT that it tends to mostly focus on the task of producing a newspaper rather than further consolidating and horizontalizing their cooperative model. This is exemplified in the fact that attendance at workers' assemblies is not mandatory at this ERT as it is in the other three cases. Moreover, the members I interviewed here also tended to have the fewest personal changes in community-focused values and attitudes, reflected in their workers' lack of involvement in community events or political work.

### The opening up of workplaces to the community and community economic development

Like other social economy businesses, some ERTs tend to have strong social missions and objectives that look beyond the inside walls of the cooperative (Quarter et al., 2009). For ERTs, new forms of *social production* and, as cooperatives, the social wealth they generate and redistribute among members tend – with some of the most promising ERTs – to extend out to include provision for the social and economic needs of surrounding communities. Some ERTs, for instance, are always open to the neighbourhood – doubling as cultural and community centres, free community health clinics, areas for popular education programmes for marginalized children and adults, alternative media spaces or community dining rooms – run by workers, neighbours or volunteers. Two of the four ERTs I worked with – Chilavert and UST – like other emblematic ERTs (e.g. the ceramics ERT Zanón/FaSinPat, the IMPA metal shop and the Hotel BAUEN), regularly open up their workspaces to other uses besides their business goals. Hosting such cultural and community spaces and involving themselves with the needs of local communities is not just a way of giving back to the neighbourhood out of corporate 'goodwill'. Instead, ERTs that host community projects tend to see their workplaces as continuations of, and integral players in, the neighbourhoods in which they are located.

For instance, Chilavert hosts the ERT Documentation Centre, run by student volunteers associated with the University of Buenos Aires' Faculty of Philosophy and Letters' Extension Program and used frequently by national and international researchers. A vibrant community centre called *Chilavert Recupera* (Chilavert Recuperates) also operates on its mezzanine level – hosting plays, art classes, music concerts and community events often linked to Argentina's social justice movements. Furthermore, Chilavert houses an adult high school equivalency programme focused on a popular education curriculum that is heavily used by local marginalized communities. IMPA, a large metallurgic ERT in the Caballito *barrio* of Buenos Aires, is also known as *La Fábrica Cultural* (The Cultural Factory) because it dedicates a large portion of its space to an art school, silk-screen shop, free health clinic, community theatre and an adult education high school programme. And Artes Gráficas Patricios, in the southern Buenos Aires neighbourhood of Barracas, also hosts a popular school, a community radio station and a dental and medical clinic, all run voluntarily by neighbours, social movement groups and health practitioners.

Looking at the entire sample of ERT workers I interviewed, personal transformations in the desire for solidarity practices extending into the neighbourhoods and communities that exist beyond the walls of the ERT, while less noticeable than the changes in the values, attitudes and practices of cooperativism within the walls of an ERT, were, nevertheless – for most of them – at the forefront of their minds. Again, this is a marked difference from their individualistic practices when employed by a boss. Participation in community projects was most evident in the four cases at Chilavert and UST, and even among some members of Clínica Junín and *Comercio y Justicia* – which are, for various reasons, less involved in community work outside of the ERT (Junín's workers have little time for non-health related community work, while *Comercio y Justicia*'s workers have not been similarly seized with the need for such work). There was a tangible sense of the importance of their projects for a different, less individualistic and more communitarian kind of social and economic project for Argentina with all workers I interviewed at all four firms. A member nurse at Junín explained why the clinic is not as involved in more community activism:

> No, I was never involved in a community project of any sort before helping to start this coop…And now I am only, unfortunately, involved in this coop, not in other movements. I just don't have the time. I'd like to do more work in a disadvantaged neighbourhood, for example, or some such thing. But time is limited! For us, it's about doing as much as we can for the community from here, our coop.

My data also suggest that, after having worked at the ERT, some workers do experience a strong desire to personally take up community practices beyond the ERT, such as speaking to neighbours about community issues and attending community meetings. As a young and novice 21-year-old member of UST told me:

> I never worried about community problems or problems in my neighbourhood before coming to work here. I just couldn't see them before, in reality. Now, from here, you start to see these problems and you start to work [to alleviate them].

Apart from five of the workers I interviewed, who had community-activist or union-activist backgrounds, it is important to underscore here that most of my key informants did not have previous experiences with community organization or activism and it was the specific involvement with the ERT project that fundamentally changed them into more community-minded individuals.

While some ERTs open up their doors to the community, the changes in community values and attitudes experienced by some ERT workers

have encouraged some ERTs to integrate into their very business practices social missions that see them *sharing* portions of their revenue
with the community, which essentially extends their productive efforts
out into the surrounding neighbourhoods spatially, co-producing social
wealth. Some of the most celebrated ERTs (e.g. UST and Zanón/FaSinPat)
have expanded their business focus to include community economic
development projects as their *raison d'être*. UST and Zanón/FaSinPat, in
particular, are renowned for their practice of sharing revenue between
the capitalization needs of the firm, workers' salaries and community
service.

UST is an especially promising case of how to rethink the social,
cultural and economic role of a social business within the immediate
geographic spaces and the myriad of communities that it finds itself
in. This is especially promising in Argentina, given the depleted and
neglected reality of many working class neighbourhoods that, unfortu-
nately, still remain far from the reach of government development programmes. Like Zanón/FaSinPat, UST consistently redirects a significant
portion of its revenues to community development, such as an afford-
able housing project for its workers and the surrounding community.
This initiative has built 100 attractive town homes to replace precarious
housing for its own members and the neighbourhood. In addition, UST
built, and continues to support, a youth sports complex in the *barrio*
and an alternative media workshop and radio programme, while also
heading a unique plastics recycling initiative for the large low-income
housing project located near its plant. The current president of UST told
me, in several extended conversations I had with him, that providing
for the life needs of workers and the surrounding neighbourhood in
areas such as decent housing, sports, education and eradicating illiteracy
among workers and neighbours are key motivators for the cooperative.
Indeed, he added, the cooperative is not only in the park maintenance
and construction business but is now also in the business of assisting
with the provision of the life needs of its workers and neighbouring
communities.

## Conclusions

Despite having emerged from privately owned firms in trouble, ERTs
generally fit the broader definition of a workers' cooperative found
in the literature. ERTs, for example, are, like most workers' cooperatives, voluntary associations of workers cooperating in the running of
a productive entity wherein each worker has an 'equal say' (Mathews,

1999: 198) via workers' boards, assemblies or councils elected from its membership base (Quarter, 1992: 27). ERTs are also productive entities whereby 'labour hires capital' (Smith et al., 1988: 25), where 'work' is the common contribution of each member (INAES, 2007), where 'control is linked to work' (Oakeshott, 1990: 27) and where revenues are the common property of the cooperative's members (Quarter et al., 2009). And, as with the workers' cooperative movement historically and worldwide, how to distribute surpluses to members and reinvest revenues back into the firm remains an open question, continuously debated within each individual ERT (Escobedo and Deux Marzi, 2007; Vieta and Ruggeri, 2009).

But in other ways, Argentina's ERTs can be seen as delineating new experiments in workers' cooperativism and self-management when compared to workers' cooperatives in other conjunctures. As I discuss throughout this chapter, ERTs emerge not because their workers had predetermined values of cooperativism nor because they sought radical social change. Rather, ERTs tend to emerge out of necessity and immanently out of their workers' experiences of micro-economic crises on shop floors, and the injustices they suffered because of the actions of former bosses. In addition, ERT protagonists' transformations from managed employees to self-managed cooperators, and the horizontalized work processes they subsequently adopt in their firms, tend to be learned, developed and consolidated informally, by trial-and-error, and over time as the collective of workers learn the intricacies of self-management both intracooperatively with other ERTs, ERT umbrella organizations, and sympathetic social movements, and intercooperatively from each other within the same ERT.

The degree to which ERT protagonists experience situations of conflict with former bosses or the state when taking over the former troubled firm that hired them, the collective actions these workers resort to in order to consolidate their cooperative and stay afloat, and the forging of a common cooperative project together interplay intimately and immanently with, as Paolo Freire (1970) names it, these workers' *concientização* (conscientization) as the workers are now in control of their own working lives. On the whole, then, and as the empirical findings I report on in this chapter suggest – paralleling Merleau-Ponty's theorization of emergent and collective working class conscientization – a tight and intersubjective social structure rooted in necessity, common bonds of solidarity, and shared experiences of conflict and crises permeate the ways ERT workers transform into self-managed workers and how these transformations radiate onto their cooperatively reorganized labour processes and influence their new and promising community projects. Furthermore, it is true that not all ERTs practise completely egalitarian salary schemes, that the degree to which organizational models are flattened at ERTs differs, and how ERTs engage in community projects may vary. Nevertheless it is clear that there is strong tendency for ERTs to practise far more egalitarian forms of remuneration and horizontal organization models. ERTs are also infinitely more likely to adopt community development projects than when these firms were under the control of bosses and owners. Thus, ERT protagonists' collective actions that first strive to overcome micro-economic crises at the point-of-production, the ways in which these workers subsequently work together to overcome their challenges, and their emergent sense of the social value of their collective labour – not particular skill-sets, the pursuit of profit or hierarchical divisions of labour – tend to dictate how cooperation unfolds within and beyond the walls of these new, alternative work organizations.

## Acknowledgements

This chapter is dedicated to the memory of Professor David F. Noble (1945–2010), my teacher and friend.

## Notes

1. The law of expropriation (*ley de expropiación*) is vitally important to these workers because it legally suspends, either temporarily or permanently, further bankruptcy proceedings against the firm while giving the workers' cooperative more secure control of the plant. Expropriation is granted in Argentina as case-specific bills passed by regional legislatures on behalf of an ERT in order to give the workers' cooperative the right to use the firms' machines, inventories, assets, buildings and sometimes trademarks and patents in usufruct. More often than not, an ERTs' members must pay back the cost of the expropriation to the state, usually over a period of 20 years. In no small part, this use of state expropriation laws has been possible due to the lobbying efforts of ERT umbrella organizations such as the National Movement of Recuperated Enterprises (Movimiento Nacional de Empresas Recuperadas, or MNER) and the National Movement of Worker-Recuperated Factories (Movimiento Nacional de Fábricas Recuperadas por sus Trabajadores, or MNFRT). ERTs that have not been able to secure expropriation have had to cobble together various other types of working arrangements. These include: co-ownership schemes with former owners or with the management that remained; renting the firm from former owners or the state; leasing back the firm from bankruptcy courts or the state in order that the workers' cooperative may eventually own the plant and its assets (as is the case with one of my case studies, *Comercio y Justicia*);

taking on part of the debt left by former owners; or arrangements with union locals to assist in these varied schemes.

2. Argentina's bankruptcy law was first revised in May 2002, in part to stem the tide of bankruptcies at the time. It stipulates the following concerning employee ownership of a failed firm: '[T]he continuity of the enterprise [in the case of bankruptcy] will consider the formal requests of its employees in their dependency…or as labour creditors, who must act in the subsequent period of continuity under the form of a workers' cooperative' (Ministerio de Economía y Producción, 2007). In 2006 and in 2011 this law was again revised to further benefit the country's self-managed workplaces, facilitating the conversion of failing firms into worker cooperatives *before* entering bankruptcy proceedings.

3. For similar findings, see Rebón (2007: 184).

4. On average, most ERT workforces shrink by about 80 per cent when compared to their most robust numbers when under previous owner-management (Ruggeri et al., 2005: 43). Moreover, most of the workers that decide not to be a part of an ERT project tend to be younger or have more transferable administrative or specialized skills than those that decide to stay, meaning that there is a paucity of professional, technical and administrative staff left at most ERTs by the time the remaining worker collective decides to take over a failing firm.

5. Following the example of Atzeni and Ghigliani's (2007) method of selecting ERT case studies, in selecting my cases I too used the criteria of 'diversification' (658). The four ERTs selected for this study are exemplary because of their varied sizes; the different business sectors they are in; the different labour processes they employ; their diverse histories of owner abandonment, worker occupation, and paths to self-management; and the unique political, cultural, and regional contexts they find themselves in.

6. The development of these questions and the subsequent analysis I embarked on was informed by Livingstone and Roth's (2001) worker lifelong learning research; Quarter and Midha's (2001) investigations into informal learning processes within workers' cooperatives; and Foley's (1999), Schugurensky's (2000), and Hall and Clover's (2005) theories of social movement and social action learning. What all of these studies have in common is to show how politically-active and unionized workers on shop floors, participants in social movements, or cooperative members tend to mostly learn their political, democratic and cooperative skills *informally*, in the act of 'doing' or engaging in their micro-politics or cooperative practices.

7. For Daniel Schugurensky (2000) *informal learning* 'includes all learning that occurs outside the curriculum of formal and non-formal educational institutions and programs' (1), is social in nature, and often the learner is not aware that he is learning but rather engages in tacit learning.

8. The most important of these organizations includes, among others: the National Movement of Recuperated Enterprises (Movimiento Nacional de Empresas Recuperadas, or MNER), the National Movement of Worker-Recuperated Factories (Movimiento Nacional de Fábricas Recuperadas por sus Trabajadores, or MNFRT), the National Association of Self-Managed Workers (Asociación Nacional de Trabajadores Autogesionados, or ANTA), and the Argentine Federation of Self-Managed Worker Cooperatives (Federación Argentina de Cooperativas de Trabajadores Autogestionados, or FACTA).

9. Argentine trade unionism has a long tradition of shop-floor *asambleas* (assemblies) and a high turnout rate among the rank and file when electing shop stewards (in Argentina, *delegados*), who then vote on key national union issues in Argentina's two union centrals. While union support for ERTs has been sketchy at best (for more, see Vieta, 2010), many ERTs used to be former union shops when owner-run. Most ERT workers that belonged to unions before still belong to their unions. ERTs' current practices of holding regular workers' assemblies and electing the cooperative's administrative positions have deep roots in these syndicalist shop floor practices (Clarke and Antivero, 2009).

# References

Almeyra, G. (2004). *La Protesta Social En La Argentina, 1990–2004: Fábricas Recuperadas, Piquetes, Cacerolazos, Asambleas Populares*. Buenos Aires: Ediciones Continente.

Atzeni, M. and Ghigliani, P. (2007). Labour process and decision-making in factories under workers' self-management: Empirical evidence from Argentina. *Work, Employment and Society*, 21(4), 653–671.

Boron, A. and Thwaites-Rey, M. (2004). La expropiación en la Argentina: Genesis, desarrollo, y los impactos estructurales. In J. Petras and H. Veltmeyer (Eds.), *Las Privatizaciones Y La Desnacionalización De América Latin* (pp. 113–182). Buenos Aires: Promoteo Libros.

Braverman, H. (1974). *Labor and Monopoly Capital: The Degradation of Work in the Twentieth Century*. New York: Monthly Review Press.

Clarke, G. and Antivero, J. (2009). La intervención sindical en las empresas recuperadas en la Argentina: Hacia la reconstrucción selectiva de un modelo de justicia social. In A. Ruggeri (Ed.), *Las Empresas Recuperadas: Autogestión Obrera En Argentina Y América Latina* (pp. 125–138). Buenos Aires: Facultad de Filosofía y Letras, Universidad de Buenos Aires.

Clever, H. (2000). *Reading Capital Politically*. Oakland, CA: AK Press/AntiThesis.

Colectivo Situaciones. (2002). Asambleas, cacerolas, y piquetes (Sobre las nuevas formas de protagonismo social). Buenos Aires: Colectivo Situaciones, Boradores de Investigación, No. 3. Retrieved 19 October 2005 from http://www.nodo50.org/colectivosituaciones/borradores_03.html.

Damill, M. (2005). La economía y la pólitica económica: Del viejo al nuevo endeudamiento. In J. Sariano (Ed.), *Nueva Historia Argentina, Vol. 10: Dictadura Y Democracia (1976–2001)* (pp. 155–224). Buenos Aires: Editorial Sudamericana.

Dinerstein, A. (2002). The battle of Buenos Aires: Crisis, insurrection and the reinvention of politics in Argentina. *Historical Materialism*, 10(4), 5–38.

Dyer-Witheford, N. (1999). *Cyber-Marx: Cycles and Circuits of Struggle in High-Technology Capitalism*. Chicago: University of Illinois Press.

Escobedo, M. and Deux Marzi, M. V. (2007). *Autogestión Obrera En La Argentina: Historia Y Presente*. Rosario: UNR Editoria/Universidad Nacional de Rosario.

Fajn, G. (2003). *Fábricas Y Empresas Recuperadas: Protesta Social, Auotgestión, Y Rupturas En La Subjectividad*. Buenos Aires: Centro Cultural de la Cooperación, Instituto Movilizador de Fondos Cooperativos.

Fajn, G. and Rebón, J. (2005). El taller ¿sin cronometro? Apuntes acerca de las empresas recuperadas. *Herramienta*, 28. Retrieved 23 January 2006 from http://www.herramienta.com.ar/print.php?sid=300.

Fantasia, R. (1988). *Cultures of Solidarity: Consciousness, Action, and Contemporary American Workers*. Berkeley, CA: University of California Press.

Foley, G. (1999). *Learning in Social Action: A Contribution to Understanding Informal Education*. London: Zed Books.

Freire, P. (1970). *Pedagogy of the Oppressed*. New York: Continuum.

Gambina, J. and Campione, D. (2002). *Los Años De Menem: Cirugía Mayor*. Buenos Aires: Centro Cultural de la Cooperación.

Ghibaudi, J. (2006). Una aproximación comparativa a las empresas recuperadas argentinas y la autogeridas en Brasil [Electronic Version]. *LabourAgain: International Institute of Social History*. Retrieved January 6, 2009, from http://www.iisg.nl/labouragain/argentineantakeovers.php

Hall, B. and Clover, D. (2005). Social movement learning. In L. M. English (Ed.), *International Encyclopedia of Adult Education* (pp. 584–589). Hampshire: Palgrave Macmillan.

INAES (2007). *Que es una cooperativa: Difinición, valores, principios, tipos*. Instituto Nacional de Asociativismo y Economía Social, Ministerio Nacional de Desarollo Social. Retrieved 14 May 2007 from http://www.inaes.gov.ar/es/Entidades/cooperativas.

Lebowitz, M. (2003). *Beyond Capital: Marx's Political Economy of the Working Class*. Basingstoke, Hampshire, UK: Palgrave Macmillan.

Levy Yeyati, E. and Valenzuela, D. (2007). *La Resurrección: Historia De La Poscrisis Argentina*. Buenos Aires: Editorial Sudamericana.

Livingstone, D. and Roth, R. (2001). Workers' knowledge: An untapped resource in the labour movement. *New Approaches to Lifelong Learning Working Papers, 31*. Retrieved 25 September 2010 from http://www.nall.ca/res/31workers.htm.

MacPherson, I. (1995). Co-operative principles, ICA review 1995. International Co-operative Information Centre. Retrieved 14 June 2007 from http://www.uwcc.wisc.edu/icic/def-hist/gen-info/

Magnani, E. (2003). *El Cambio Silencioso: Empresas Y Fábricas Recuperadas Por Los Trabajadores En La Argentina*. Buenos Aires: Promoteo Libros.

Marcuse, H. (1964). *One-Dimensional Man: Studies in the Ideology of Advanced Industrial Society*. Boston, MA: Beacon Press.

Marcuse, H. (1966). *Eros and Civilization: A Philosophical Inquiry into Freud*. Boston, MA: Beacon Press.

Martí, J. P., Bertullo, J., Soria, C., Barrios, D., Silveira, M., Camilletti, A. et al. (2004). Empresas recuperadas mediante cooperativas de trabajo: Viabilidad de una alternativa. *UniRcoop, 2*, 80–105. Retrieved 25 June 2007 from http://www.unircoop.org/unircoop/?q=node/35.

Marx, K. (1987). *Economic and Philosophic Manuscripts of 1844*. Buffalo, NY: Prometheus Books.

Mathews, R. (1999). *Jobs of Our Own: Building a Stake-Holder Society: Alternatives to the Market and the State*. Sydney: Pluto Press.

Merleau-Ponty, M. (1962). *Phenomenology of Perception*. New York: Humanities Press.

Ministerio de Economía y Producción. (2007). *Concursos y Quiebras, Ley 25.589, Modificación de las Leyes 24.522 y 25.563*. Buenos Aires: Ministerio de Economía y Producción, Gobierno de la República Argentina. Retrieved 7 July 2007 from http://infoleg.mecon.gov.ar/infolegInternet/anexos/70000-74999/74331/norma.htm.

Ministerio de Trabajo. (2008). *Dinámico del empleo y rotación de empresas.* Buenos Aires: Ministerio de Tabajo, Empleo, y Seguridad Social, Gobierno de la República Argentina. Retrieved 27 March 2010 from http://www.trabajo.gov. ar/left/estadisticas/descargas/oede/INF_dinamica200804.pdf.

Ministerio de Trabajo. (2010). *Situación ocupacional de la población urbana total.* Buenos Aires: Ministerio de Tabajo, Empleo, y Seguridad Social, Gobierno de la República Argentina. Retrieved 9 March 2011 from http://www.trabajo.gob.ar/ left/estadisticas/bel/belDisplayCuadro.asp?idCuadro=2&idSubseccion=1.

Munck, R. M., Falcon, R. and Galitelli, B. (1987). *Argentina from Anarchism to Peronism: Workers, Unions, and Politics, 1855–1985.* London: Zed Books.

Oakeshott, R. (1990). *The Case for Workers' Co-Ops* (2nd ed.). Basingstoke: Macmillan.

Olmedo, C. and Murray, M. J. (2002). The formalization of informal/precarious labor in contemporary Argentina. *International Sociology,* 17(3), 421–443.

Palomino, H. (2003). The workers' movement in occupied enterprises: A survey. *Canadian Journal of Latin American and Caribbean Studies,* 28(55), 71–96.

Patroni, V. (2004). Disciplining labour, producing poverty: Neoliberal structural reforms and political conflict in Argentina. *Research in Political Economy,* 21, 91–119.

Petras, J. F. and Veltmeyer, H. (2002). Autogestión de trabajadores en una perspectiva histórica. In J. F. Petras, E. Carpintero and M. Hernández (Eds.), *Produciendo Realidad: Las Empresas Comunitarias* (pp. 53–81). Buenos Aires: Topía.

Quarter, J. (1992). *Canada's Social Economy.* Toronto: James Lorimer.

Quarter, J. and Midha, H. (2001). Informal learning Processes in a worker cooperative. *New Approaches to Lifelong Learning Working Papers,* 37. Retrieved 25 September 2010 from http://www.uwcc.wisc.edu/info/worker/nall37.pdf.

Quarter, J., Mook, L. and Armstrong, A. (2009). *Understanding the Social Economy: A Canadian Perspective.* Toronto, Buffalo: University of Toronto Press.

Ranciere, J. (1989). *The Nights of Labor: The Workers' Dream in Nineteenth-Century France.* Philadelphia, PA: Temple University Press.

Rebón, J. (2004). *Desobedeciendo Al Desempleo: La Experiencia De Las Empresas Recuperadas.* Buenos Aires: Ediciones PICASO/La Rosa Blindada.

Rebón, J. (2007). *La Empresa De La Autonomía: Trabajadores Recuperando La Producción.* Buenos Aires: Ediciones PICASO.

Ruggeri, A. (Ed.) (2009). *Las Empresas Recuperadas: Autogestión Obrera En Argentina Y América Latina.* Buenos Aires: Facultad de Filosofía y Letras, Universidad de Buenos Aires.

Ruggeri, A. (Ed.) (2010). *Informe Del Tercer Relevamiento De Empresas Recuperadas Por Sus Trabajadores: Las Empresas Recuperadas En La Argentina, 2010.* Buenos Aires: Programa Facultad Abierta, Facultad de Filosofía y Letras, Universidad de Buenos Aires.

Ruggeri, A., Martínez, C. and Trinchero, H. (2005). *Las empresas recuperadas en la Argentina: Informe del segundo relevamiento del programa.* Buenos Aires: Facultad Abierta, Facultad de Filosofía y Letras, Universidad de Buenos Aires, Programa de Transferencia Científico-Técnica con Empresas Recuperadas por sus Trabajadores (UBACyT de Urgencia Social F–701).

Schugurensky, D. (2000). The forms of informal learning: Towards a conceptualization of the field. *New Approaches to Lifelong Learning Working Papers,* 19.

Retrieved 14 December 2009 from https://tspace.library.utoronto.ca/bitstream/ 1807/2733/2/19formsofinformal.pdf.

Sitrin, M. (Ed.) (2006). *Horizontalism: Voices of Popular Power in Argentina*. Oakland, CA: AK Press.

Smith, P., Chivers, D. and Goodfellow, G. (1988). *Co-Operatives That Work: New Constitutions, Conversions, and Tax*. Nottingham: Spokesman.

Svampa, M. and Pereyra, S. (2004). *Entre La Ruta Y El Barrio: Le Experiencia De Las Organizaciones Piqueteras*. Buenos Aires: Editorial Biblos.

Thompson, E. P. (1991). *The Making of the English Working Class*. London: Penguin Books.

Vieta, M. (2010). The social innovations of *autogestión* in Argentina's worker-recuperated enterprises: Cooperatively organizing productive life in hard times. *Labor Studies Journal*, 35(3), 295–321.

Vieta, M. and Ruggeri, A. (2009). The worker-recovered enterprises as worker cooperatives: The conjunctures, challenges, and innovations of self-management in Argentina and Latin America. In J. J. McMurtry and D. Reed (Eds.), *Co-Operatives in a Global Economy: The Challenges of Co-Operation Across Borders* (pp. 178–225). Newcastle-Upon-Tyne: Cambridge Scholars Press.

Vosko, L. F. (2006). *Precarious Employment: Understanding Labour Market Insecurity in Canada*. Montreal: McGill-Queen's University Press.

Williams, R. (2002). Culture is ordinary. In B. Highmore (Ed.), *The Everyday Reader* (pp. 91–100). London: Routledge.

# 7
# Institutional Analysis and Collective Mobilization in a Comparative Assessment of Two Cooperatives in India

*Anita Hammer*

## Introduction

Cooperatives as a form of economic organization represent one of the main alternatives to shareholder-based capitalism. There are over 1 billion members of cooperatives worldwide, and they employ more than 100 million women and men – 20 per cent more than multinational enterprises (International Cooperative Alliance, ICA, 2011). The ICA (2011) defines a cooperative as 'an autonomous association of persons united voluntarily to meet their common economic, social, and cultural needs and aspirations through a jointly-owned and democratically-controlled enterprise'. The United Nations estimated in 1994 that the livelihood of nearly 3 billion people was supported by cooperative enterprise, underlining their significant economic and social roles in their communities. It is a testimony to their economic and social significance that the International Labour Organization has declared 2012 to be the International Year of Cooperatives.

Arguably there is a strong case for studying cooperatives as alternative forms of work organization. However, their significance is contested, as the debate between the proponents and sceptics of cooperatives has remained at a high level of abstraction – mobilizing a number of key factors to a varying degree. The main questions revolved around their alternative potential as an emancipatory organizational form; their sustainability in a hostile market-oriented environment where they need to generate counter-institutional support and a context of radical struggles that is difficult to sustain indefinitely; also, the degeneration of their principles and values when distorted by the market competition of the capitalist system.

In contrast, this chapter argues that an institutional analysis, in conjunction with the role of collective mobilization, may yield a more fruitful way forward in the assessment of cooperatives. It is important to take into account the variation in institutional contexts and the nature of mobilization, because they shape constraints and opportunities available to cooperatives in different ways. This approach conceptualizes institutions (and cooperatives) as a settlement of political processes, thereby emphasizing contestation and multiple and competing logics inherent in them. Rather than setting cooperatives against an abstract capitalist system, an analysis of cooperatives at the intermediate level helps to explain the emergence of different forms of cooperatives; how they are shaped by their specific institutional and mobilization contexts; and how they take advantage of the constraints and opportunities available to them. Significantly, it also incorporates the possibility of change within cooperatives as well as in the wider context, shaped as they are by a dynamic interaction of institutions and social movements.

This chapter undertakes a comparative institutional analysis of two cooperatives in two different states of India (Kerala and Gujarat). The case studies are examples of two successful, but fundamentally different, cooperatives that continue to survive in changing conditions and the increasing marketization of the economy. The cooperative in Kerala is a workers' cooperative that has a radical and emancipatory potential supported by the institutionalization of radical class mobilization in a favourable context. On the other hand, the cooperative in Gujarat is a producers' marketing cooperative that mobilizes institutional-political context in a way that reinforces existing power relations in socio-economic and political spheres. The aim is to show that it is the dialectics of institutional development and class mobilization that influence and determine the differing nature and trajectory of cooperatives in the two states. The chapter is structured as follows: the next section details the analytical framework. Then, an outline of cooperatives in India and the two case studies are presented in detail, before they are assessed and analysed in the subsequent section. The concluding section brings together the main analytical points raised through these case studies.

## Institutions and collective mobilization in the analysis of cooperatives

Cooperatives span a wide range of contexts and this comparative study of cooperatives in Kerala and Gujarat in India shows that, even within one societal context, institutions provide very different opportunities and are the products of different social constellations and social movements/collective mobilization. Within the wider debate on the nature as well as potential of cooperatives, this chapter engages with one aspect: why do particular types of cooperatives emerge? Drawing upon earlier works by Egan (1990) and Baldacchino (1990), this chapter utilizes the more recent analytical framework of Schneiberg and Lounsbury (2008) of an integrative institutional-social movement analysis of cooperatives that helps account for the variety of cooperative forms and their significance. The authors argue that cooperatives, as institutions, are influenced by politics and collective action; mobilization and conflict shape their institutional development. The analytical framework conceptualizes the institutional context – as well as cooperatives – as settlements of political processes, emphasizing contestation and multiple and competing logics inherent in them. Such dynamic conceptualization helps to explain the role of the institutional-political context in shaping the different forms of cooperatives.

According to Ellerman (1988), a workers' cooperative is the fullest expression of workplace democracy. However, when faced with market competition in the capitalist system, they often face degeneration, reproducing the shortcomings of the prevailing system. Egan (1990) counters such scepticism towards workers' cooperatives as incapable of transforming the capitalist mode of production by emphasizing their radical and democratic potential. He argues that provided with certain conditions, for example, a context of radical working-class self-organization as well as an appropriate strategy to counter the sources of degeneration, they could survive against market odds. Baldacchino (1990) underlines the importance and role of institutional, political and cultural supportive mechanisms in the success of workers' cooperatives. Mobilizing the Gramscian concept of 'hegemony', he identifies how cooperatives often fall prey to the hegemonic structure and end up reinforcing existing power relations, most noticeably in the developing countries. It is the specific institutional and cultural environment that plays a role in the cooperatives' success or failure. Moreover, the long-term success of cooperatives depends on how successful counter-hegemonic forces are in transforming the institutions and dominant values that become supportive of cooperatives as normal and legitimate organizations.

The case study from Kerala in this chapter certainly underscores Egan's emphasis on the role of working class reorganization, as well as Baldacchino's emphasis on the relevance of institutional and cultural environment being crucial to this cooperative's success. However, cooperatives may also be producer-owned or consumer-owned.

A producers' cooperative is typically operated by farmers, producers of goods, or small businesses. Farmers and producers organize cooperatives in order to process and market their goods as well as to acquire credit, equipment and production supplies. They are common in agricultural products (cotton, sugar, dairy), retail trade, housing, financial institutions and health care, and less common in the manufacturing sector. It is significant that consumer or agricultural producers' cooperatives have been more successful than workers' cooperatives. This is true of the second case study in this chapter: a cotton cooperative in Gujarat.

A comparative assessment of the two cooperatives poses the problem of how to explain the success of both cooperatives while they remain fundamentally different in nature. It is the contention of this chapter that institutional analysis, integrated with social movements, as argued for by Schneiberg and Lounsbury (2008), provides a useful framework to explain the difference, and in the process reframe the debate on cooperatives. The approach conceptualizes institutions as settlements of political struggles. The process of institutionalization here is a result of a combination of contestation and mobilization outside as well as within the institutions. Such dynamic conceptualization analyses the underlying institutions, interests and processes that account for the emergence and significance of the variety of cooperative forms. It considers how the institutional context shapes political/institutional opportunity structures, institutional mediation and institutional contingency to explain organizational outcomes for cooperatives. Therefore, what role do the institutions at multiple levels play in shaping the differing nature of the cooperatives in Kerala and Gujarat? How does the institutional mediation of wider market competition translate for the nature of cooperatives, particularly in neo-liberal Gujarat?

In analysing cooperatives, the approach examines, first, the rise and effect of movements on institutions. This emphasizes movements as forces *against* institutions that contest and disrupt existing arrangements, as well as forces *within* institutions (i.e. political processes that emerge from and exploit contradictions or multiple logics within the institutional structures and processes to mobilize and change). For example, in their study of cooperatives in the USA, Schneiberg et al. (2008) study the movement effect on the organization of cooperatives and identify how mobilization, counter mobilization and political opportunity shape economic organization. The same is evident in the emergence, as well as the functioning, of the Kerala workers' cooperative. In Gujarat, on the other hand, the dominant groups have a firm grip of the social, political and electoral arena that is reproduced in the cooperatives in the absence of a collective mobilization of the lower classes. Second, the approach examines how contexts shape contestation and collective action (i.e. how institutions constrain and enable mobilization, create openings for challengers and shape their capacity to produce change or to keep existing structures intact, highlighting how movements and change are endogenously shaped by institutions). As the case studies will show, institutions in Kerala have enabled restructuring in the sphere of production while the same institutions constrain it in Gujarat, where almost neo-feudal relations persist in the sphere of production. At the same time, the institutional regime in Gujarat has created opportunities for the cotton producers/traders in the sphere of market competition, which they take advantage of through their cooperatives. Third, the approach engages with the question of how to explain institutional emergence and change. Change can be disruptive when movement from the outside disrupts existing established institutions. However, it can also work in an incremental and embedded fashion when contradictions and multiple logics that exist within institutions and movements are mobilized. Therefore, change as conceptualized by institutionalist scholars (Streeck and Thelen, 2005) can result in path creation, recombination or layering, and new or alternate organizational forms. This allows for a possibility of emergence of and change within cooperatives, or a change in the wider institutional context by them. Though outside the remit of this chapter, this aspect is relevant to a longitudinal assessment of cooperatives.

## A story of two cooperatives: A beedi cooperative, Kerala and a cotton cooperative, Gujarat

This section briefly outlines the development and role of cooperatives in India. Then, the case studies of two cooperatives that operate in two different states in India – Kerala and Gujarat – are presented. Kerala, for its unique development model with high human development indicators; Gujarat, for its business-friendly and entrepreneurial model that has translated into high economic growth. The two case studies are similar in that both cooperatives are rural in nature and have been operating successfully for a long time in their respective regions. They are different in that the Kerala case study is a workers' cooperative whereas the Gujarat cooperative is a farmers' marketing cooperative (see Table 7.1). The aim is to provide a more nuanced assessment through an analysis of the underlying institutions and interest constellations to explain the differing nature and trajectory of cooperatives.

*Table 7.1*   Comparison between two cooperatives in India

| Dimensions of a cooperative | Kerala: rural, workers' cooperative | Gujarat: agricultural, marketing cooperative |
| --- | --- | --- |
| Nature of organization | Workplace democracy, autonomous | Capitalist, certain groups/interests |
| Nature of membership | Workers as co-owners and managers, voluntary | All producers are members but dominated by a particular caste (Patidars) |
| Nature of worker democracy | Direct democracy at shop floor level and delegated control to worker representatives and managers at the central level | Autonomy of cooperatives at each level but class and caste dominance at board of directors and leadership level |
| Governance/decision-making structures | Voluntary delegation of control within a hierarchical management structure | Vertically integrated from local, district to state level |
| Wage structure/profit distribution | Egalitarian | Distribution of income a matter of inter-faction contention |
| Accumulation of capital and long-term viability | Workers' interest in preserving long-term viability and therefore investment in the cooperative | Members' interest in preserving the viability, for obtaining the best price and for political clout |
| Diversification | Diversified into other products | None |
| Nature of institutional/state intervention | Initial start-up capital as well as continued support provided but minimum interference | Closely intertwined relations with the state and political processes based on caste, class and business interests |

## Cooperatives in India

India has over 239 million cooperative members, and the coopera-tives play a significant role in economic and development arenas. The Indian government has invested massively in cooperatives for rural development, as have many international agencies, including the World Bank. Cooperatives assumed a great significance after independence in 1947 – in poverty removal and to engender faster socio-economic growth. There was substantial growth of this sector in diverse areas of the economy between the 1950s and 1990s. With the advent of the planning process, cooperatives became an integral part of the five-year plans. As a result, they emerged as a distinct segment in the national economy. Different states drew up schemes for the cooperative movement in order to assist the organization of large-size societies and to provide additional support through state partnerships. In 1958 the National Development Council recommended a national policy on cooperatives and in the 1960s, further efforts were made to re-organize and consolidate cooperative societies. The process of encouragement and consolidation continues under the tenth plan.

In some of their activities such as cotton dairying, urban banking and housing, sugar and handlooms, cooperatives have achieved considerable success (e.g. the Self Employed Women's Association [SEWA] or Amul, a dairy cooperative); however, there are large areas where results have been more mixed. The weakness and failure of cooperatives in the country has been attributed to a combination of factors. These include: dormant membership and lack of active participation of members in the management of cooperatives; mounting arrears in cooperative credit institutions; lack of mobilization of internal resources and over-dependence on government assistance; lack of professional management and bureaucratic control and interference in the management; political interference and over-politicization of cooperatives; and a predominance of vested interests which continues to disadvantage those groups the cooperatives are supposed to benefit.

A review of literature on cooperatives in India emphasizes certain aspects significant for analysing cooperatives. Firstly, the nature of a cooperatives' governance structure, and how control and delegation operate in what may be hierarchical or vertically integrated management structures of a cooperative. Secondly, the nature and extent to which a cooperative manages accumulation of capital, and to preserve its long-term viability as an enterprise. Thirdly, the role the state may play in influencing the nature and trajectory of a cooperative (Rajaram, 1999; Ebrahim, 2000; Bhowmik and Sarker, 2002; Gulati et al., 2002).

Attwood and Baviskar (1987) argue for a comparative analysis of cooperatives, and particularly on how the informal network of interests and alliances within them affects their formal operation. In a study of sugar cooperatives, they show that both the internal structure of class interests and the external environment of social relations (caste, clan, regional politics and power) help to determine the success or failure of cooperatives. They raise important questions which decide whether cooperatives are likely to succeed in a given context. In particular, whether the more powerful members have any real economic interest in encouraging participation by the less powerful members. If the powerful members have an economic stake in the participation of the smaller cooperatives, the cooperative is more likely to be run equitably and efficiently. Cooperatives which work very well in one region may not fit at all in others. This chapter draws upon their valuable insight while placing the analysis in a more detailed institutional-social movement framework.

## Kerala: A beedi cooperative

The south-western Indian state of Kerala provides the context for the first case study, the Kerala Dinesh Beedi Workers Central Co-op Society (KDB), one of the largest industrial cooperative societies in India (the case study draws on two bodies of primary research, in particular Gulati et al., 2002). Despite being dominated by an agrarian economy, and a fairly low per capita gross domestic product (GDP) of US $470/year, Kerala has performed consistently high on human development indicators, having achieved total literacy, highest life expectancy, lowest birth rate and lowest infant mortality in the country. It has seen long periods of elected communist governments that have supported a model of development characterized by investment in health and education along with redistributive reforms. The main product of the KDB workers' cooperative, beedis are cheap hand-rolled cigarettes that are smoked by the working classes in India, produced in a sequence of simple tasks without any tools. KDB was established in 1969 and has been operating successfully for 38 years. It is based at Kannur with operational units in the three northern districts of Kerala – Kannur, Kasargod and Kozhikode.

KDB emerged in 1969 in response to the relocation of the company and the associated job losses by experienced workers. In fact, employers had attempted to organize production through contracting and piece-work compensation. This resulted in worker mobilization against the threat of lower wages, as well as difficulties in organizing and implementing the minimum wage law. Kerala's communist government and its support of unions and labour unrest also played a role in the employers' decision to move to the adjoining state of Karnataka, where workers were perceived to be less organized and more malleable. Faced with mass unemployment, the workers formed a cooperative, supported initially by capital from the state and with the help of veteran trade union leaders. The cooperative had a five-member board of beedi workers, with two additional non-voting members from the government: the president, who was an effective official with experience of having worked with workers' cooperatives, and the secretary. In addition, KDB focused on the production of a high quality product and mobilized support among other workers to buy their beedis as a sign of support. The cooperative has had 35,000 members at times who live in close proximity and join voluntarily. Membership has declined in recent years but is offset by diversification into other products.

In terms of worker democracy, KDB operates with a twin system, in the area of production on the one hand, and of support functions on the other. Furthermore, worker democracy operates across three hierarchical levels: the shop floor; the primary cooperative; and the central cooperative organization. At the first level, shop floor direct democracy covers production and discipline, as well as delegated decision making to worker representatives at the level of the primary cooperative. They are constituted by 7–12 shop floors and organize around 75–125 workers; the primary cooperative level also has a factory committee for daily supervision and management of the floor. There are 18 such primary cooperatives at KDB. The direct participation at the shop floor level plays an important role in the supervision of workers. Although the supervisor cannot hire, fire, transfer or fine a worker, the worker can complain against the supervisor to the factory committee. At the same time, supervisors are selected from the most senior workers, enforce discipline, and monitor and train those lagging behind in production; in this case the workers have no say in hiring, firing or wages of supervisors. Peer pressure at work and through the social settings of shared living areas and/or the same village help reinforce the supervisor's authority in dealing with low quality and productivity. The workers are pressured into rectifying their deficiencies in order to avoid negative mention at the annual general body meeting. In addition, campaigns to emphasize the role of quality and productivity in the survival and success of the cooperative reinforce the peer pressure and the supervisor's decisions. The workers are also organized in trade unions which negotiate wages and benefits at the central cooperative level. Thus, workers participate directly in the decision making that affects their immediate working conditions.

The other, almost corporate-style structure covers support functions such as pricing, marketing, quality control and the overall operation of the cooperative. This area of participation operates at the level of the primary cooperative as well as that of the central cooperative. The primary cooperative has a board of directors which is directly elected by the workers. This board manages the primary cooperative as an independent profit and loss centre; supervises the production process; makes modest expenditures to improve working conditions; and settles disputes between workers and supervisors that are not resolved at the shop floor level. This board of directors is replicated at the level of the central cooperative, and elected for a three-year term by the boards of directors at the primary cooperative level. Thus, worker democracy operates alongside and within a hierarchical governance structure; it is relevant as direct participation at the shop floor with respect to the labour process, and as delegated participation at the central cooperative level with respect to market-related decisions. The central board's decisions are subject to discussion and alteration at the annual general meeting of the representatives of the primary cooperatives.

KDB's wage structure exhibits distinct egalitarian features that are often found in cooperatives. This concerns the structure of wages as well as the distribution of bonuses. With regard to the former, the overall wage is constituted by two parts: a piecework component based on the number of beedis rolled, and a fixed sum of dearness allowance that amounts to 50 per cent of workers' daily wages. Every worker receives the dearness allowance if s/he has rolled a minimum number of beedis. Regarding the latter, despite differences in productivity levels among the current 18 primary cooperatives, annual bonuses are nevertheless distributed uniformly, with the remainder spent on improvements to the working conditions on shop floors, based on the needs of the primary cooperatives.

Both dimensions of the wage structure have led to resentment and debate at all levels of the cooperative. More productive primary cooperatives express unhappiness with the uniform distribution of bonuses, while the younger and quicker workers resent the reduction in the minimum number of beedis to be rolled that allows older and slower workers to qualify for the dearness allowance. Though not completely resolved, a compromise was reached: relatively unproductive cooperatives are reprimanded and closely monitored, while the minimum number of beedis required to receive the dearness allowance was raised – at the same time, though, older workers are allowed to carry over their quota to the next day. Managers at KDB have lower compensation than in other firms; however, this is made up for by their belief in the cooperative and the status benefits that accrue to them in the short as well as long term. Although the tensions between material incentives and egalitarianism exist, the workplace compromises are characterized by a fundamental solidarity.

As a workers' cooperative, KDB has also been able to accumulate capital and to invest in physical assets. As participation is fairly encompassing, workers are, instead of maximizing wages, satisfied with a compensation system that pays at least minimum wages along with regularly increasing benefits such as pensions, holidays, medical benefits and access to loans. The latter constitute almost 50 per cent of their wages and have contributed to a steady improvement in workers' real earnings, while in private sector firms minimum wages are ignored and benefits are often non-existent. This is accompanied by cyclical membership drives in which new members are recruited only in good times with high accumulation levels. All this translates into a relatively higher compensation package for workers, higher job satisfaction, absence of labour disputes and healthier working conditions for workers at KDB than its private sector counterparts.

These factors contribute to an interest in the long-term survival of the firm, and hence a commitment to long-term investments in order to achieve this goal. In this respect, KDB has also managed to successfully diversify into other products (e.g. garments, software, umbrellas, food-processing) when demand for beedis declined and cheaper beedis from other states became available in the 1990s (www.keraladinesh.com).

## Gujarat: A cotton cooperative

The second case study, a cotton cooperative, is set in the state of Gujarat on the western coast of India (this section draws on primary research by Rajaram, 1999, and Shah et al., 2009). The state has a long tradition of cooperatives, especially in agricultural products such as cotton, sugar and milk; the first cotton cooperative, for example, was established in 1919. Gujarat is considered to be one of the most business-friendly states in India and has seen the centre-left Congress party and the right-leaning Bharatiya Janata Party alternating in government in recent decades, both pursuing neo-liberal policies. Flexible labour laws and the lowest labour days lost in the country provide the context for an average annual growth rate of 10.4 per cent in the last five years, the highest share of foreign direct investment (12.7%), and a contribution of 16 per cent of industrial production and 22 per cent of exports of the country. Per capita income has risen from $641 in 2004–2005 to $1094 in 2008–2009 (Socio-Economic Review, Gujarat state 2009–2010, www.gujaratindia.com), while the literacy rate stands at 80 per cent. The state has also clocked high and steady growth at 9.6 per cent per year in agricultural state domestic product since 1999–2000. The Gujarat government has aggressively pursued an agriculture development programme driven by liberalizing markets, inviting private capital, reinventing agricultural extension, improving roads and other infrastructure.

With a strong export demand, Gujarat has emerged as India's largest cotton-producing state and a major cotton supplier to China. The highly remunerative minimum support prices (MSPs) for cotton, announced by the central government (that has a sizeable procurement operation in the state), have provided a strong incentive to farmers to increase production. Gujarat's cotton boom has also been aided by the availability of reasonably priced quality cottonseed, regulated by the state government that imposed a ceiling of Rs 750 per packet to ensure that farmers could buy seeds at a reasonable price. Since then, cottonseed production in Gujarat has increased rapidly. The steep fall in the price of cottonseed from Rs 1600 to Rs 650 for a 450 g packet has helped spread the expansion of cotton cultivation in Gujarat. In addition, policies such as increased market access, technical support, credit, improved canal irrigation and management of groundwater and provision of infrastructure have helped the boom (Shah et al., 2009).

The cotton economy is characterized by close interaction between the farmers operating through the cooperatives, the traders, the mill/textile lobby and the central government that sets support prices for cotton. The farmers themselves – responsible for 75 per cent of total cotton production in the country – are predominantly members of the rural poor. Often, they cultivate cotton on plots of less than one-half hectare, or on part of their farms as a means of supplementing their livelihoods. The less salubrious aspect of the same industry is the nature of labour usage, especially the use of child labour and a large female workforce. Of the top seven cotton producers in the world, all, apart from the USA, have been reported to use children in the field. Children are recruited for a variety of tasks, from hybrid cottonseed production to pest control (EJF, 2007). Since the crop can be hand-picked by underpaid workers or free labour, there is often little incentive for the mechanization of the industry. There is a high presence of marginalized women – almost two thirds – as small and marginal farmers, landless agricultural sharecroppers and casual labourers working in agriculture-related, on-farm activities such as cotton pod shelling. They own less than one-tenth of the land and end up working as cheap labour.

The cotton cooperative under discussion is vertically integrated. This means that farmers in the villages are organized into marketing/ multipurpose/ginning and processing cooperatives at a primary level.

These primary cooperatives are members of a district-level union of cooperatives which in turn federate to form a state-level federation of cooperatives. The cooperative at each level is a legal separate entity with its own structure and area of operation, and enjoys autonomy. The cooperatives operate a 'pooling system', where farmer members pool their cotton in order for it to be processed and then sold at an appropriate time during the year to realize the best possible returns. The cooperative then deducts the expenses incurred before calculating the price for raw cotton. It also provides financial support to members facing particular needs. This form of cooperative primarily gives rise to disputes over the distribution of income in both a horizontal as well as a vertical dimension. At the primary level, this is about how income should be distributed to the members as opposed to set apart for reserve funds; in the vertical dimension, it is disputes about the redistribution of extra income from higher levels to primary cooperatives, for example from exports, that need to be solved.

These disputes are further shaped by underlying class-caste politics. It is significant, for example, that membership of the cooperative is dominated by the *Patidar* caste – landholding peasant communities who generally enjoy high social and economic status in the region. They own most of the land and occupy positions of leadership in the cooperatives as well as local political institutions. In this respect, cooperatives have become a terrain to promote and protect *Patidar* interests and serve as a platform for their business ventures. Similar dynamics can be observed in other regions of Gujarat, for example, in case studies of sugar cooperatives in Bardoli by Breman (1978, 1985, 1996) and Ebrahim (2000). Facets of *Patidar* dominance also affect the different levels of the cooperatives: on the one hand, locally dominant *Patidars* are able to secure election and representation at the boards of directors at district level, on the other hand, where competing primary level leaders are elected to district level boards, their differences are also carried to that level. Thus, conflicts within and between cooperatives are often factional conflicts between groups of rich *Patidars*. These processes were reinforced, but also modified to some extent, when representation at higher-level boards was made dependent on performance. Following changes in the cotton economy in the 1980s that led to surplus production and volatility, the balance of functional representation and the accompanying political networks was disturbed. In this context, performance became a factor in determining the number of representatives a cooperative could have on the board.

This emphasis on performance was pushed, in particular, by political leaders who may have known little about cotton but used the terrain and networks of cotton cooperatives in order to further their political aspirations. This development is a natural corollary of the two-way link that exists between cooperatives and politics at various levels. The cooperatives span village, district and state levels in their membership coverage and give rise to complex multi-level networks across industry and politics. On the one hand, for example, the political standing of the cooperative leader plays an important role in promoting and protecting the interests of the farmers and cooperatives. Cooperative leaders are often members of political parties as well as of state legislature, district and village bodies. These overlapping networks allow cooperatives to protect their narrow operational as well as wider caste interests, for example, with regard to financial and agricultural policies as well as the intricacies of state politics in a broader sense. This is important, given that the state decides on the level of the support price for cotton as well as on exports and imports, which in turn determines the amount of credit available to the cooperative. Not surprisingly, political leaders, on the other hand, try to get their supporters inducted into various positions in cooperatives at all levels in order to extend their influence. Aspiring politicians often use the cooperative route to fulfil their ambitions.

In addition to political influences, there are also business practices that threaten to disrupt the fragile compromises between cooperatives. This becomes evident, for example, in some cooperatives' practices of acquiring additional cotton from non-members, usually from traders. This has been criticized for increasing the influence of traders on the functioning and performance of cooperatives; for risking the reputation of the cooperative if the quality of cotton is dubious; and as well as for destabilizing the political balance between cooperatives. What is clear is that economic gains may at times override the principles of a cooperative. At the same time, it is significant that despite factions and rivalries, cooperatives continue to function. This can be explained through the stability of class and caste interests of the members (who are largely *Patidars*) at the village level, and the leaders of the cooperatives at higher levels who are rich *Patidars*. This comes into focus when local rivalries are forgotten in the face of threats to common interests. Moreover, recent decades have seen an overlap between members-leaders of cooperatives who are simultaneously farmers, business people (civil contractors) as well as politically active and influential cooperative leaders. This development gives a unique dimension to the nature of the cooperative that often veers towards being a capitalist enterprise, driven by short-term and profit motives. It represents the interest of a particular caste-class group of members, who are certainly interested in the long-term viability of the cooperative and accumulation of capital, and for that purpose are closely intertwined with the politics of the state at various levels.

## Institutional context and collective mobilization in analysing cooperatives

This section analyses the basis of the fundamental differences in the nature, operation and outcome of the two cooperatives along dimensions identified in the theoretical section. Firstly, the role of movements and mobilization from 'outside' and 'within' the institutions (labour regime, state institutions as well as the cooperative) are assessed. Secondly, how the institutional context has shaped the nature of movements that influence the two cooperatives is examined.

### Collective mobilization challenging (reinforcing) institutions

Movements from outside of established institutions help to assert new order, disrupt the existing system or secure concessions from the established order. Such an approach allows conceptualizing institutions as settlement of political processes, that arise through a sequence of contestation and mobilization, fuel new paths and change, and often result in the rise of alternate organizational forms (Schneiberg and Lounsbury, 2008). Kerala is an exemplar. The state had a class of upper caste landlords that had absolute social and economic power in a largely agrarian society. The labour regime was characterized by dependent patron-client relations that were embedded in the caste structures. In this context, a combination of social reform movements that challenged caste hierarchies in the early part of the 20th century, the agrarian movement of tenants and landless labourers that pushed through land reforms and labour legislation, as well as the wide and inclusive nature of unionization from the 1930s all contributed towards weakening class and caste hierarchies. Lower class mobilization challenged pre-capitalist institutions of landlordism and the caste-based organization of labour, in consequence also changing the relations of production. These developments were accompanied by an actively intervening state at all levels – local as well as provincial.

Conversely, in Gujarat, the middle class/middle caste dominance achieved under the different ruling estates by specific groups has not been challenged in the same fashion as in Kerala. Domination by richer elements in the rural elite that characterized cooperatives in the colonial period continues to be an abiding feature of these institutions even after independence. The same dominance has been extended into the political and electoral arena. One of the dominant groups, the *Patidars*, acquired land at the beginning of the 20th century when cotton cultivation became popular and took advantage of the cotton boom after World War I to raise their financial and social status. They formed cooperatives to establish economic dominance in the region. Thus, the caste-class alliance has reinforced social differentiation between dominant groups and excluded low-caste landless labour, women and migrants, and further strengthened the exploitative organization of production.

## Collective mobilization as an institutional process

Institutionalists recognize that movements occur inside institutions, that is, emerge and operate within established power structures, to drive change (Fligstein, 1996). The integrative approach supplements the conceptualization of institutional change as disruptive, with how change can be incremental and embedded producing change as recombination or layering (Streeck and Thelen, 2005; Schneiberg and Lounsbury, 2008). Here, confrontation is eschewed in favour of a mobilization of multiple logics for change. In Kerala, movements from *outside* established structures (social reforms and inclusive unionization from the turn of the century) resulted in the creation of a progressive welfare state that has undertaken significant redistributive reforms and invested in health and education (Kerala scores exceedingly high on all human development indicators). Sustained lower-class mobilization *within* the political structures and local state institutions has led to the political and economic incorporation of the lower classes into shaping an institutionalized democracy. High unionization and the organizational strength of the working class, combined with state intervention, have changed the political structure of class relations. Highly confrontational mobilization has weakened with the development of an institutional framework to regulate class conflict and to some extent negotiate a compromise between labour and capital (Heller, 1999). The cooperative under study is an organizational outcome of the institutionalization of the sustained class movement in Kerala. Characterized by workplace democracy, egalitarian wage structure and a highly unionized workforce, it succeeded because of initial support from the state and the party structures. Thereafter, it operated via negotiation on most aspects, in particular governance/decision-making structures; wages; capital accumulation and investment, as well as product diversification in response to market demands. There is minimum state interference in its current operation.

Mobilization can also seek to keep existing structures intact by the elite (Fligstein, 1996). In Gujarat, the traditional use of local low-caste landless labour has been replaced by migrant wage labour from surrounding regions. This is a result, as agriculture became increasingly commercialized, of the decline of the traditional feudal *halipratha* system of patronage and bondage that existed between the upper caste/upper class farmer and local labour. Unlike Kerala, where the traditional labour regime was replaced by organized, unionized and institutionally supported wage labour with minimum social cost, in Gujarat, the traditional exploitative system is replaced by migratory displacement, insecurity and exclusion of local labour while reducing the labour costs of capitalist farmers (Breman, 1996). Cooperatives have consolidated capitalist production, economic strength and political influence of the dominant group at the cost of subordinate class/low caste groups.

### Institutional context shaping mobilization

Adopting an integrative approach allows an analysis of how the institutional contexts shape mobilization, and the capacity for producing change, in a more sophisticated analysis of power and agency. For example, to consider how institutions can block access or provide opportunities for action. Features include legacies of prior movements and policies; receptiveness of institutional authorities to challenges; opportunities provided by the multi-level nature of institutions. The role of the state and political parties in the creation and operation of the labour regime helps the outcomes for mobilization (or not) and the nature of cooperatives in the two states to be understood.

### Labour regimes

The two states have labour regimes that are composed of predominantly rural labour where employers/producers often relied and/or continue to rely on middlemen, subcontractors and the use of children in the production process. However, that is where the similarity ends. While workers, unions and the government in Kerala actively countered such practices through the establishment of the cooperative, in Gujarat the labour regime (composed of landless labourers, women and children) forms the underbelly of the cooperative of a particular social and economic group that often reinforces such regimes.

In Kerala, the beedi workers at KDB are fairly homogenous, both as a social group as well as in the labour process. They come from the same area, often living in close proximity in the same village/community, and ties of the workplace extend into the living areas. While in the beginning, workers were predominantly men, in recent years the balance has changed to a 50 per cent female workforce. The factory regime is based on workplace democracy. The wage structure is egalitarian and the workforce is highly unionized, with almost 80 per cent being either members or sympathetic to the left parties. This can be traced back to social reform movements, class mobilization and extensive unionization in the early 20th century, discussed earlier.

In Gujarat, on the other hand, the labour regime in the cotton industry continues to be predominantly composed of women, children and low-caste landless labour. According to an Environmental Justice Foundation (EJF) report on child labour in the cotton industry (2007), the children are often bonded by loans given to their parents, while others are only guaranteed payment at the end of several months' work, effectively trapped in debt-bondage by farmers and middlemen. Subcontractors hire children, while allowing farmers to overlook age and working conditions. They are paid daily wages of Rs 40–52 ($1.00–1.30), whereas provisions supplied at the workplace (e.g. one-way transport, expenses incurred for medicines) are deducted from the wage. If children leave mid-season, they receive no payment. Most of the children working in the fields in India are girls, accounting for around 67 per cent of the children working in cottonseed production. Cottonseed producers claim girls have greater dexterity and patience, and are more obedient and diligent, with boys more likely to go to school, reflecting prevalent forms of gender discrimination. In addition to the difficult and arduous labour, children are vulnerable to health and safety risks and sexual harassment.

Moreover, the use of child labour has a debilitating economic impact on adults, particularly women who are also employed in large numbers in cotton production and whose bargaining power is consequently undermined. The agricultural sector tends to be less regulated than other industries, which means that adequate legal protection is often lacking, and child and women labourers usually have no institutional recourse. In some cases, children and women are often not formally registered as workers, but work with their family to ensure the high daily work quotas demanded by land owners are met (Reports by Self

Employed Women's Association [SEWA] who work with women agricultural workers in North and West Gujarat). A similar situation is
also prevalent among landless labour. Research by Breman (1978, 1985,
1996) and Ebrahim (2000) on the sugar industry in South Gujarat shows
that the conditions described above are not confined to the cotton
industry.

### State institutions, party politics and movements

Such differing labour regimes arise out of the social structures in the
two states and the different nature of organization and mobilization
(or lack thereof) of class-caste interests. In Kerala, a combination of
class-based movements, in conjunction and overlapping with union
movements, have come together to create the social basis for the
state and institutions. Mobilization and militancy led to the organizational solidification of the working class, and its political influence.
High levels of unionization, accompanied by state intervention in the
labour market as well as in the social arena, increased the power of
labour which has also found an expression in the form of increased
local participation at all levels of the state. Also, a developmental,
autonomous state in Kerala has actively intervened to create progressive
institutions. A coalition of left-leaning parties, democratically winning
elections for long terms, helped this process (Dreze and Sen, 1995;
Kannan, 1998; Heller, 1999). The KDB cooperative exemplifies this
in the support, both politically as well as economically in the form
of initial start-up capital that the state provided to aid the formation and survival of the cooperative while refraining from operational
interference.

Gujarat has a long history of successful cooperatives and social movements, some of them, such as SEWA, having a long and progressive
history. However, the broader social structures remain conservative
and entrepreneurial. State institutions as well as political parties reflect
the interests of the dominant socio-economic groups, which is further expressed by a succession of business-friendly governments. The
case study shows in detail the link between cooperatives, industry and
politics that exist at village, district and state levels. Cooperatives and
cooperative leaders are often members of political parties as well as of
state legislative, district and village bodies. This allows the cooperative
to protect its operational as well as wider caste interests. Political leaders, on the other hand, try to extend their influence in cooperatives.
The cooperative operates to cement existent socio-economic structures

and dominant interests rather than emergent forms of radical and emancipatory organization.

## Conclusions

This chapter undertook a comparative assessment of two cooperatives in two different states of India. The cooperative in Kerala had a radical and emancipatory potential, whereas the one in Gujarat reinforced existing power relations in socio-economic and political spheres. The problem was how to explain these differences as well as the context in which particular forms of cooperatives can emerge. Cooperatives span a wide range of contexts and the study of cooperatives in Kerala and Gujarat in this chapter has shown how, even within one societal context, institutions provide very different opportunities and are the product of different social constellations. This chapter argued for an embedded analysis of the interaction of institutions and mobilization that may help account for the variety of cooperative forms and their significance.

Through comparative assessment, this chapter demonstrated that it is the dialectics of institutional development and class mobilization that influence and determine the differing nature and trajectory of cooperatives. The interlinkages of class organization, political mobilization and institutional development and density in Kerala account for the formation and operation of the cooperative marked by workplace democracy, co-ownership of workers, egalitarian wage structure, long-term viability and state support. This supports the perspectives of Egan (1990) and Baldacchino (1990). In Gujarat, similar interlinkages have seen a dominant alliance of middle class and middle caste reinforce extant social differentiation and exclude low-caste landless labourers, women and migrants, thereby further consolidating an exploitative labour regime. Instead of challenging and restructuring socio-economic and political structures as in Kerala, the cooperative represents the interests of the dominant socio-economic groups that have extended into the political and electoral arena, where political parties reflect the close alliance between caste, class and business. The cooperative, as feared by Bernstein, tends towards exclusiveness and oligarchy rather than arising as an agent of equity.

Furthermore, the study opened the analysis beyond the national level/framework to the subnational level, which helps account better for variations. Kerala and Gujarat, though both part of India, have very different social and political trajectories, interest coalitions and state interventions. Also, both states have had very different relations with the central institutions, depending on the orientation of the national government, which has implications, for example regarding resource allocation and thereby policy interventions.

At a broader level, the case studies of cooperatives pose an interesting dilemma: is the 'social development' and political mobilization model (that has seen limited capital investment and rising unemployment in recent times in Kerala) sustainable? Does the 'market-friendly' model of Gujarat represent a triumph of neo-liberal economics and 'trickle down' theory? It would be worthwhile to note that while social conflict in Kerala has engendered flight of capital and unemployment in the short term, mobilization and state intervention has also transformed social structures and laid deep democratic institutions to regulate class conflict and to some extent negotiate class compromises. This, along with the social investment in health and education that has created a skilled workforce, would bring returns in the long term. On the other hand, in Gujarat the social relations of class-caste domination/subordination are pervasive in the sphere of production and reproduction and closely intertwined with institutions, political processes and business interests. Social conflict, though subterranean and suppressed at the moment, is a possibility, and the outcome in the absence of relevant political avenues and structures is unpredictable.

## References

Attwood, D.M. and Baviskar, B.S. (1987) 'Why Do Some Co-operatives Work but Not Others? A Comparative Analysis of Sugar Co-operatives', *Economic and Political Weekly* 22(26): 38–56.

Baldacchino, G. (1990) 'A War of Position: Ideas on Strategy for Worker Cooperative Development', *Economic and Industrial Democracy* 11(4): 463–482.

Bhowmik, S.K. and Sarker, K. (2002) 'Worker Cooperatives as Alternative Production Systems: A Study in Kolkata, India', *Work and Occupations* 29(4): 460–482.

Breman, J. (1978) 'Seasonal Migration and Cooperative Capitalism: Crushing of Cane and Labour by Sugar Factories of Bardoli', *Economic and Political Weekly* 13: 1317–1360.

Breman, J. (1985) *Of Peasants, Migrants and Paupers: Rural Labour Circulation and Capitalist Production in West India*, Delhi: Oxford University Press.

Breman, J. (1996) *Footloose Labour: Working in India's Informal Economy*, Cambridge: Cambridge University Press.

Dreze, J. and Sen, A. (1995) *India: Economic Development and Social Opportunity*, Delhi: Oxford University Press.

Ebrahim, A. (2000) 'Agricultural Cooperatives in Gujarat, India: Agents of Equity or Differentiation?', *Development in Practice* 10(2): 178–188.

Egan, D. (1990) 'Toward a Marxist Theory of Labor-Managed Firms: Breaking the Degeneration Thesis', *Review of Radical Political Economics* 22(4): 67–86.

EJF (2007) *The Children Behind Our Cotton*, London, UK: Environmental Justice Foundation.

Ellerman, D.P. (1988) 'The Kantian Person/Thing Principle in Political Economy', *Journal of Economic Issues* 22(4): 1109–1122.

Fligstein, N. (1996) 'Market as politics: A political-Cultural Approach to Market Institutions', *American Sociological Review* 61: 656–673.

Gulati, G.M., Thomas Isaac, T.M. and Klein, W.A. (2002) 'When a Workers' Cooperative Works: The Case of Kerala Dinesh Beedi', UCLA *Law Review*, 49: 5, Research Paper Series, No 02-13: 1417–1455.

Heller, P. (1999) *The Labor of Development: Workers and the Transformation of Capitalism in Kerala, India*, Ithaca and London: Cornell University Press.

International Cooperative Alliance (ICA) (2011) 'Statistical Information on the Co-operative Movement', http://www.ica.coop/coop/statistics.html (accessed October 2011).

Kannan, K.P. (1998) Political Economy of Labour and Development in Kerala: Some Reflections on the Dilemma of a Socially Transforming Labour Force in a Slow Growing Economy, Paper presented at a workshop in Centre for development studies, Trivandrum.

Rajaram, N. (1999) 'Politics and Cotton Cooperatives in Central Gujarat', *Economic and Political Weekly*, July 24: 2095–2103.

Schneiberg, M., King, M. and Smith, T. (2008) 'Social Movements and Organisational Form: Cooperative Alternatives to Corporations in the American Insurance, Diary and Grain Industries', *American Sociological Review* 73(4): 635–667.

Schneiberg, M. and Lounsbury, M. (2008) 'Social Movements and Institutional Analysis', in Greenwood, R., Oliver, C., Sahlin-Andersson, K. and Suddaby, R. (eds.) *The Handbook of Organisational Institutionalism*, London: Sage.

Shah, T., Gulati, A., Hemant, P., Shreedhar, Ganga. and Jain, R.C. (2009) 'Secret of Gujarat's Agrarian Miracle after 2000', *Economic & Political Weekly* XLIV(52): 45–55.

Streeck, W. and Thelen, K. (2005) *Beyond Continuity: Institutional Change in Advanced Political Economies*, Oxford: Oxford University Press.

# 8
# Self-Help Groups in Nairobi: Welfare Strategies or Alternative Work Organizations?

*Martino Ghielmi*

## Introduction

Nairobi[1] is one of the most unequal cities in the world. It has been described as 'a paradox' (Dafe, 2009: 5), 'a city under constant de(re)composition' (Katumanga, 2005: 518), and a place where 'the North and the South live a few yards from each other' (Floris, 2006: 19). Looking at Kenya's capital through *Google maps* or other satellite reconnaissance gives us a clear idea of the city's disparities. The western high ground – the old colonial settlements – consists of affluent residential estates of detached houses with green gardens, while the eastern side appears as a vast stretch of overcrowded shanty houses. The city has 'about 60% of its population currently living in informal settlements but occupying only 5% of the residential area' (Dafe, 2009: 16). Urban density varies enormously among the 360 inhabitants per square kilometre of Karen estate, and the 80,000 inhabitants of some parts of Kibera – a density comparable to cattle free lots (Davis, 2006: 95).

Since its creation in 1899, Nairobi's urban space was conceived as 'strongly exclusionary' (Anyamba, 2005). In the colonial political economy, Africans were considered only 'temporary workers who supposedly had permanent homes in the rural area' (Macharia, 1992: 225). Today, the cleavage between 'citizen and subject' (Mamdani, 1996) still appears to be the backbone of the state and the economic life. Politicians envisage 6-lane highways and 90-floor glass skyscrapers by 2030,[2] but most Nairobians survive in houses made of mud, iron sheets, wood and recycled plastic. It is a nightmarish environment where 'the exclusivist logic of the formal political economy ensures that thousands in the slums...remain marginalised' (Katumanga, 2005: 518). Opportunities are extremely different between the two 'cities': well-off Kenyans study in elegant campuses, find waged jobs in multinational companies or international agencies; however, slum dwellers struggle to earn a living from the so-called 'informal economy'. Hundreds of thousands of urban poor earn a few shillings to buy *ugali*,[3] beans and *sukumawiki*[4] from self-employment (e.g. street selling, garbage recycling, small-scale food processing, shoe-shining, petty manufacturers) or from waged jobs with oral contracts (e.g. export-oriented manufacturers, road repairing, transport).

Walking in the dusty peripheral roads, *matatu* and *makanga*[5] slowly become familiar to your eyes. This is a common encounter that is hard to get used to: dozens of big lorries with their bodies fully loaded with workers. This image might help the foreigner to realize what workers become in a hyper-capitalist environment such as Kenya: nothing more than a mere production factor. More specifically, the cheapest, since it seems to be infinitely abundant.

Nairobi is a city 'so fragmented that, instead of being a place where people meet and form social groups, it changes into a kind of archipelago, made up of many islands' (Floris, 2006: 19), with different standards of construction, different services and infrastructures and even different legal systems. Yet a network of economic exchange occurs across the urban space. As Warah (2008: 14) points out, Nairobi relies 'on the relatively cheap labour provided by slum dwellers to man...[its] factories, to construct buildings, to clean...[its] streets and to generally make the economy grow'. The so-called *jua kali*[6] becomes year-by-year more relevant in terms of employment creation,[7] and the state barely controls the flourishing of these economic activities. Consequently, the phenomenon has severe political consequences, such as the potential privatization of violence by organized groups that provide security to informal economic operators (Katumanga, 2005: 508).

In the absence of any kind of redistributive policies, labour rights and social protection, informal workers are able to cover a variety of needs (e.g. credit to run small businesses, insurance against business risks, education, health, funeral expenses) only by resorting to the common solution of aggregation into small clusters and groups. Marginalized individuals such as women, youths and poor people associate their strengths and limited resources to survive in the insecure and competitive environment of Nairobi's slums by creating and joining different kinds of self-help groups (SHGs). These groups provide the principal source of credit for informal economic operators and create a network empowering security of tenure, despite the inadequacies of the state or, more often, its perverse and pervasive patronage (Chesang, 2007).

SHGs are clusters of peers as well as cross-class associations, constantly formed from a common characteristic of the members which creates a mutual interest. Members may all be shoe-shiners, worshippers of a certain Pentecostal Church, come from the same rural 'home'[8] or live in the same area of a vast shanty town such as Kibera or Mathare Valley.[9] In all cases, a strong mutual trust among members pulls them together to share the small capital they have, discuss common issues and minimize the risk of being overwhelmed by the hostile environment. SHGs are often created with an income-generating idea such as to rear chicken, to make soap, to produce and market handicraft or to hire out a TV-room. Thus, my research aims to determine whether SHGs constitute an alternative form of work organization with respect to the mainstream capitalistic Kenyan scenario, or rather simply represent welfare associations.

## A theoretical framework for informal economy

The concept of the informal sector was coined in the early 1970s by Hart (1973) with a study of income opportunities in Ghana's urban economy. It underlined how the officially unemployed were actually self-employed in income-generating activities, where they could acquire skills that could later help them to find good quality jobs. The paper issued by the International Labour Organization (ILO) on 'Employment, Incomes and Equality', after its mission in Kenya (ILO, 1972), spread the term – analysing the rapid expansion of African micro-entrepreneurship in Nairobi. The ILO noted that those productive activities were not only marginal businesses but included profitable and efficient enterprises (King, 1996: 7; Chen et al., 2001: 3). Activities of the informal sector were typically defined by the following main characteristics: self-employment (with a high recourse to family workers), small-scale, labour-intensive technologies; facilitated entry (little capital and little or no bureaucracy required); low technical and professional skills; and a low level of organization (restricted access to organized markets, credit and services).

The concept received a mixed review from development scholars. Some argued that the persistence of informal activities in developing countries was due to the insufficient economic growth of these countries, therefore assuming that this part of the economy would disappear with modern industrialization.[10] Other observers, focusing on the lowest segment of the informal sector, maintained that it was a marginal phenomenon not linked to the formal economy. Due to a kind of misleading perspective, the notion of an informal sector did not capture much attention from mainstream development circles until the 1980s (Chen, 2006: 28–29).

Undoubtedly the term 'informal economy' is preferable to 'informal sector' since the two 'economies' are, indeed, so interlinked that it is incorrect to think of two separate sectors. Also, the term 'sector' would suggest a classification in terms of industry groups or commodity productive chains, and it is not possible to differentiate between formal and informal. Latouche (2004) suggests the term *société vernaculaire* to stress the relational networks that encompass the simple economical (and rational) market transaction. However, the term 'informal economy' tends to downplay the links, grey areas and interdependencies between formal and informal activities. The term 'informal economy' refers to all economic activities by workers and economic units that are – in law or in practice – not covered or insufficiently covered by formal arrangements. Therefore the informal workers do not enjoy any benefits from their labour (ILO, 2002a: 53)

With the Structural Adjustment Programmes (SAPs) imposed by the International Monetary Fund (IMF) and the World Bank (WB) to the developing countries, macroeconomic measures such as market deregulation, strong promotion for foreign direct investment and privatizations with consequent downsizing of public enterprising, contributed to an expansion of informal activities (Benería and Floro, 2006: 10). At the same time, minimalist-state logic came in vogue in several developed countries, increasing the insecurity of employment in the developed economies too (Henry, 1987). It appeared clear that informal activities were the only way of survival for disadvantaged individuals who could then try to maximize their only asset: their labour power (Chen et al., 2001: 14).

The expectation that the formal economy would automatically absorb the informal with economic growth was reversed and the notion of informal economy became more present in the literature, especially through the works of the neo-liberal Peruvian social scientist Hernando De Soto (1989, 2000). In a nutshell, he argued that the 'enormous population of marginalized laborers...is a frenzied beehive of proto-capitalists yearning for formal property rights and unregulated competitive space' (Davis, 2006: 179). A simplification of the bureaucratic procedures to obtain property rights and a widespread access to microcredit would be sufficient to guarantee the uplifting of hundreds of millions of 'plucky entrepreneurs' worldwide. This approach became the mainstream paradigm of the international institutions (WB and IMF among many) and the guideline for most of the international intervention by non-governmental organizations (NGOs) in the developing economies.

The advent of a globalized economy caused mounting recourse to the cost-cutting outsourcing of the productive process in the developing countries. Thus, the link between formal and informal appeared even more evident since many multinational companies subcontracted the production to smaller production units, some of which remained unregistered or informal (Piore and Sabel, 1984; Benería and Floro, 2006: 10–12). These processes revealed the inadequacy of the neo-liberal property-rights approach towards informal labour. When informal workers are waged, they do not need any facilitation to obtain property rights. On the contrary, they would benefit from an effective implementation of workers' rights, usually already formalized in national labour legislations. Thus, the term 'informal economy' appears more adequate for describing a widening range of labour relations, often not confined by self-employment labour (ILO, 2002b). From a definition based on 'enterprise characteristics', it was time to adopt an 'employment relations' definition (Chen, 2006).

Nowadays informal labour is estimated to account for the majority of new jobs in South America, Asia and for more than 8 out of 10 new jobs in Africa (Chen et al., 2001: 3). This notable shift from mass production to flexible, specialized production or sweatshop production had not been predicted, but it is a reality today, emphasized by the current global financial crisis. The grey zone between formal and informal tends to increase simultaneously with the decline of economic growth: formal jobs become rare and traditional forms of non-standard waged work (i.e. casual jobs) co-exist with self-employment (i.e. street vending or home-based work) and other forms of unregulated labour (Benería and Floro, 2006: 13–15).

Some observers declared that the concept of informal economy is simply too varied to be a meaningful concept, given its heterogeneity (Peattie, 1987). Nevertheless, a helpful definition, through its looseness, is the one comprising 'all forms of employment without secure contracts, worker benefits, or social protection' (Chen, 2006: 31). Informal labour encompasses both self-employment in informal enterprises and waged labour within informal employment relations. Thus, the term might be considered a multi-meaning concept, helpful to understand all the job agreements outside the rule of law, despite the legal output.

The possible, but not so widespread, overlap between the informal market and the black market contributes towards the criminalization of informality. Black markets occur with the marketing of prohibited goods, while informal ones usually deal only with legal outputs. Whereas most informal activities do not comply with registration at a national level, they are usually under para-legal agreements at a local level. Thus, it is extremely common that an informal self-run business may face a heavier taxation from city council agents, often in the form of fines and bribes, and/or from other, often non-legal, security-providing groups (Katumanga, 2005).

## Kenyan informal economy

Informal economy – in terms of self-employment not regulated by state control and without social benefits – was an already established pattern of resistance and survival during the colonial age. African reserves were conceived as pre-capitalist labour reservoirs for the capitalist settlers' economy, and the establishment of African self-managed businesses was strongly discouraged by the colonial administration (Clayton and Savage, 1974).

In postcolonial years, informality has not only been a widespread mode of production in Nairobi but also the dominant mode of city making. An insufficient economic growth compared to the strong population increase led to a rampant unemployment rate that encouraged people to migrate from rural areas to the urban centres. The city's population exploded, and Nairobi self-developed through the phenomenon of slumming, reaching the estimated 4 million mark in 2009. At least 60 per cent of the population lives in the slums: an invisible city according to official city maps, providing the cheapest housing and food supply for the hundreds of people that arrive every day from neglected rural areas.

Thus, it is not surprising that the term 'informal sector' was officially coined in Nairobi by the ILO researchers.[11] In the decade after independence the Kenyan urban space, which had been entirely a racially segregated colonial creation, developed a huge number of African micro-enterprises that appeared largely out of formal state control.

Their existence was necessary for the very survival of the bulk of the urban population; moreover, today the informal economy is so widespread that King (1996: 25) states that 'it is not the informal sector that is somehow special and extraordinary, but the formal sector, which encompasses such a small portion of the economically active population'.

A brief look at the most recent labour data supports the truth of this apparently paradoxical statement. In 2008, out of a total workforce that was estimated to reach almost 10 million (out of a total population of 38.3 million), formal – modern – employment was a reality for scarcely 2 million Kenyan workers. Moreover, the creation of new jobs is almost entirely performed by the informal economy. The perverse effects of the global financial crisis, combined with the post-election violence that ravaged the country between the end of December 2007 and March 2008, led to a decline in GDP growth from 7.1 per cent in 2007 to 1.7 per cent in 2008 (KNBS, 2009: 10). This notable decrease has negatively affected employment creation: the number of new jobs created decreased from 485,500 in 2007 to 467,300 in 2008. This fall has been extremely severe in the modern private sector, with the number of new jobs created decreasing from 74,000 in 2007 to 23,800 in 2008. This means a massive 67.8 per cent decrement (2009: 71).

The open unemployment rate is 10.5 per cent, which means that 1.3 million Kenyans are unemployed (UNDP, 2007: 1).[12] Nevertheless, despite the double-digit unemployment rate, the main problems of the national labour market are under-employment and under-payment. Despite participation in the labour market, poverty incidence amounts to 52 per cent in rural areas and 49 per cent in urban areas (Manda and Odhiambo, 2003). Among those working 1–27 hours a week (under-employed) nearly 70 per cent live in poverty. Among those working 28–39 hours per week, about 66 per cent are poor. 'Among the labor force participants working 40 hours or more per week, the percentage living in poverty does go down, to 46.1%. Still, this percentage remains very high' (UNDP, 2007: 2).

The most recent official data recognize that the majority of informal labour in Kenya – far from being only an urban phenomenon – is accounted for by jobs in rural areas. These figures notably differ from the data of the early 1990s, when the informal workforce still appeared to be especially urban (Ondiege, 1995: 2–3). Rural informal labour accounts for more than 60 per cent of the informal workforce: the figure is worth particular attention since small-scale farming and pastoralism are excluded. This means that the Kenyan countryside is witnessing a massive increase of small-scale shops, artisan activities and service micro-enterprises of which development is still related to the urban centres through circular migrations and exchanges with the urban markets. Urban informal labour is mainly concentrated in the capital city, Nairobi, even if its share is rising faster, comparatively, in the other major towns.

Nairobi would collapse without its informal economy networks. As Warah (2008: 14) points out, the city relies 'on the relatively cheap labour provided by slum dwellers to man... [its] factories, to construct buildings, to clean... [its] streets and to generally make the economy grow'. A real migration occurs every day at dawn when a large crowd of poor workers moves – usually on foot – from the informal settlements to the industrial areas or the wealthier estates. Furthermore, a considerable amount of services and facilities are offered at a very low price by informal economic operators, and even well-off Nairobians usually buy vegetables and fruits at informal kiosks.

Despite Nairobi remaining one of the biggest formal labour markets in Africa, a growing informalization has occurred in the formal sector as a constant trend since the 1980s. The establishment of Export Processing Zones (EPZs) on the outskirts of Nairobi, which were conceived to promote export-oriented industrial investments, has undoubtedly increased the informalization of employment and the exploitation of Kenyan labour (KHRC, 2004). Today, it is common to find people temporarily employed with *kibarua*,[13] even in formal big-scale businesses such as manufacturers producing for US-based companies such as Walmart, Jordache and Kmart.

The difference between the situation analysed in the 1970s by the ILO and the current informal economy in Kenya seems to be that today even the smallest economic activities are part of the global economy. For example, an informal tailor in Kisumu no longer competes with Kenyan garment industries, but has to produce at lower prices than Chinese textile factories and to compete everywhere with *mitumba*.[14] At the same time, a casual worker hired on a daily basis by a manufacturer in Athi River – whose management may be German or Indian – is likely to assemble products that will be marketed in a US discount store.

Nairobi – and the whole of Kenya – has increasingly become a series of islands of wealth and poverty that the state does not even attempt to bridge through taxation and welfare transfers. The informal economy appears, indeed, the only network connecting those areas – above all through exploitative dynamics.

In this scenario, labour is completely fragmented: there is no effective right to strike (KHRC, 2004: 32), security of tenure is always in doubt and there emerges a peculiar 'complex and exuberant sociability...made up of neo-clannish networks and cultural innovation' (Floris, 2006: 51). Despite strong familiar kinships, it is impossible to survive without the maximization of (fragile) social linkages. The choice to come together is, first of all, a consequence of exploitation and poverty, rather than a 'traditional' inheritance or an attempt to pursue alternative socio-economic models with respect to the leading capitalist framework. Lastly, it appears evident that the way informal economy is structured (thousands of similar self-run enterprises, dumping from big firms, volatile contracts when waged labour) undoubtedly facilitates the reproduction of capitalist hegemony (Leys, 1975).

## A brief political history of self-help in Kenya

Jomo Kenyatta – the first president of independent Kenya – developed an afro-socialist ideology, mainly based on a single concept: *Harambee*. This Kiswahili word, which still appears between the two lions on the Kenyan coat of arms, means 'let us pull together', referring to the frequent habit of traditional societies to demand members' energy and time for communitarian work.

In the first decades after independence, *Harambee* meant national cohesion, a constant memory of the struggle against the British, an alternative to Marxism and an incentive to support the local institutions through fund-raising and communitarian work. Specifically, the term took the meaning of 'voluntary contribution to development', often performed at huge public rallies where politicians or wealthy businessmen could demonstrate their affection to the local communities through generous cash grants. The *Harambee* movement 'became both an arena for exercising obligations and for interacting with the state at the local level, especially in making claims to state resources' (Ndegwa, 1998: 357). The phenomenon gave thousands of Kenyan communities the chance to build primary schools, boreholes, hospitals and roads, sometimes even holding local leaders to greater accountability. At the same time, it ended up diminishing 'the political rights of citizens...by reducing state-citizens interactions to economic concerns [often] emphasizing subservience in order to extract resources' (1998: 357).

This embryonic welfare state – albeit with few political rights – fell in deep crisis with the lowering of economic growth in the 1980s, and the subsequent SAP imposed by the global financial institutions. *Harambee* lost a great part of its vitality and often its character of voluntary contribution. The peak of absurdity was reached with President Moi, when 'fixed sums were deducted as contributions from the salaries of government employees and the money collected in this way was expended on grandiose – and useless – projects' (Munene, 2005: 29). *Harambee* has also become used by members of parliament to create political consensus in their constituency within a patron-client relationship often characterized by corruption and bribery (Thomas-Slayter, 1991: 306; Kibwana et al., 2001: 163).

If *Harambee* undertook a process of institutionalization and diminished its overall scale, the phenomenon of spontaneous groups and associations exploded as a direct consequence of the state withdrawal. As mutual clusters of citizens, SHGs were initially viewed as 'women matter', and thus they are sometimes still named 'women groups', despite the mixed membership. The primary goal of sharing risks, in a context of weak or inexistent social insurance and where risk is omnipresent (Fafchamps, 2008), contributed instead to their rapid increase in the country. Though sometimes they still coincide, nowadays SHGs and *Harambee* are distinct entities. The latter are extemporaneous fundraising rallies, held both for public and private needs,[15] the former are permanent associations with a clear organizational structure and a definite membership.

Research on self-help has indicated the constant characteristic of trust among the members as a catalyst factor for group formation (La Ferrara, 2002; Floris, 2006; Fafchamps, 2008). There are neither fixed functions nor fixed activities in a SHG. However, in Nairobi most of them are legally registered, and they have a fixed structure with an elected board composed of three officials: a chairman, a treasurer and a secretary. As a consequence, they tend to invariably follow one of two organizational schemes:

(1)  Chairman-led groups (see Figure 8.1), where the chairman is the unchallenged leader, being the founder and the main source of external resources (i.e. donors' contacts and funds, markets, innovation). The power is unequally distributed and the status gap (i.e. income, education, age) between the chairman and the rest of the group is typically wide in this kind of SHG.

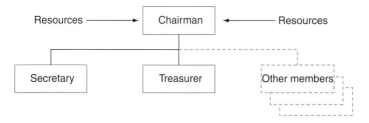

*Figure 8.1*   Self-help group (SHG) structure: chairman-led group

(2)  Officials-led groups, where the three officials constitute an effective committee, able to evaluate proposals and substantially influence the decision of the chairman. This usually comes from a different distribution of linkages with external resources, spread within the different group's members. The internal elections of officials usually generate an effective rotation of the three seats and power is undoubtedly more shared and fragmented. This type of SHG might bear more resemblance to a cooperative model (Figure 8.2).

As I will discuss in the following section, field experience has given me the sense that the majority of SHGs in Nairobi belong to the first category of organizational structure. In most cases, they are founded by a charismatic leader who holds the position of chairman for a long time; they often have a class cleavage which separates the leader from the rest of the group. Nevertheless, the other kind of SHG is not usually a *real* cooperative since it is extremely rare to find an SHG with full-time employment and complete profit-sharing agreements in place.

Summarizing, SHGs are spontaneous associative realities formed for welfare purposes by low-income workers striving to cover their basic needs within a network wider than their families. Created and run without any support from public institutions, the typical SHG in Nairobi has an average of 10–20 members[16] and offers three main services:

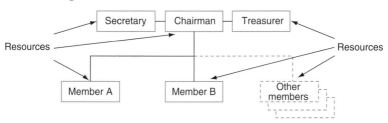

*Figure 8.2*   Self-help group (SHG) structure: officials-led group

(1) Provision of credit: usually through the so-called 'merry-go-rounds' – informal schemes of credit where every participant makes a regular (daily, weekly or monthly) contribution to a fund which is given to each contributor in rotation.

(2) Creation of social capital: every meeting usually provides a forum to share common issues and concerns such as health, education and often technical knowledge about work (Kinyanjui, 2006).

(3) Provision of income: an aspect that makes several SHGs close to communitarian micro-enterprises. A profit is made out of common income-generating activities (e.g. poultry/rabbit farming, garbage collection, soap making, tailoring, basket making, hiring of facilities [chairs, tents, rooms etc.]). Revenue sometimes allows a waged informal job to be offered to a member (often on rotation); profits usually stream into a fund which allows small loans to be financed (with interest) for extraordinary members' expenses (i.e. individual business development or family emergency needs).

There is no doubt that the primary roles of SHGs are welfare provision (in a context where the state is not able to provide basic social services) and credit provision (covering a constraint for small-scale self-managed activities). It is also clear that neither SHGs nor wider SHG clusters represent workers' associations with the capacity to defend labour rights at a national level. At maximum, they might enable members to raise their bargaining power – increasing the quality of their production (Kinyanjui, 2006). The point here at stake is whether SHGs constitute a kind of alternative form of work organization as micro-enterprises, managing their economic activities in a different way with respect to the mainstream capitalist framework.

## Are SHGs alternative micro-enterprises? An overview of Juhudi Zetu SHGs

A detailed evaluation of the Juhudi Zetu[17] programme has helped to deepen my knowledge of SHGs and to collect data and interviews. The goal of this programme, run by the Institute for Peace Development and Innovation (IPSIA),[18] was to support the transformation of SHGs towards self-managed social enterprises by providing training, network support and occasional cash grants to increase group capital. The vision was a network of social enterprises among different Nairobi informal settlements, with integration between welfare provision, income generation and sensitization to labour rights (IPSIA, 2007: 4). The specific means to achieve the programme's goals were multidisciplinary training (on business and management themes), provided by qualified university teachers and technical courses offered on request.

Leaving aside the specific evaluation of the impact of the Juhudi Zetu programme, I will, however, take advantage of the amount of data collected proceeding with an overview of the characteristics of the SHGs surveyed. The data, coupled with daily observation of their activities in the field, have enabled me to answer the research question on the potential alternative represented by SHGs as 'different' forms of work organizations.

Multiple research techniques were utilized to collect the data. The process of direct survey was conducted over a period of five months from May to September 2009. The primary sources used were IPSIA documents and the systematic collection of semi-structured individual interviews and group discussions. A more general participatory observation was carried out throughout the whole period that I spent in Nairobi (November 2008–October 2009).

The evaluation of the Juhudi Zetu programme gave me the opportunity to observe in depth the activities of a sample of SHGs spread over four different areas of Nairobi:

1. Athi River: a medium-sized township developed alongside the Nairobi–Mombasa highway. Its proximity to the two main routes of communication of the country (the highway and the international airport) has favoured the establishment of several EPZs whose informal workforce dwell in shanty informal settlements.
2. Baba Dogo: an informal settlement in the eastern periphery of Nairobi. It surrounds an industrial area where most of the workforce is hired as casual workers through informal employment agreements.
3. Kariobangi: one of the most densely populated quarters in Nairobi Eastland. In the 1980s it was designated as a light industrial area for *jua kali* enterprises (especially garages and metal works). The area is surrounded by some of the biggest slums of the city, such as Korogocho, Mathare Valley, Huruma and Dandora.
4. Riruta Satellite: a fast-growing low-income estate situated in the western periphery. All the SHGs of Riruta belong to the Kivuli Producers Association, a handicraft cooperative (wood carving, tailoring, batik and card making) created by Great Lakes refugees with the support of Koinonia, a local NGO.

*Table 8.1* Characteristics of the SHGs participating in the Juhudi Zetu programme

| Area of Nairobi | SHGs surveyed | Total members | Age (years) | Education (years) | Main characteristics |
|---|---|---|---|---|---|
| 1. Athi River | 12 | 170 | 42.8 | 6.7 | Women of Anglican Church of Kenya |
| 2. Baba Dogo | 11 | 197 | 29.1 | 7.3 | Students or self-employed |
| 3. Kariobangi | 7 | 132 | 27.7 | 6.1 | Students, self-employed or unemployed |
| 4. Riruta | 5 | 45 | 32.8 | 4.2 | Great Lakes refugees |
| Total/mean | 35 | 544 | 33.3 | 6.6 | N/A |

This case study is composed of 35 different SHGs (in total 544 members) whose main characteristics, grouped by each of the four Nairobi areas, are described in Table 8.1.

Each group was created from a common belonging which enabled mutual trust among the members. In only a quarter of the sample it was the same ethnic origin (25.7%); in most of the other SHGs it was the same religious belief (50.4%) or the same professional background (23.9%).

Despite often being defined as 'women groups', SHGs in Nairobi appeared almost equally composed of women (50.9%) and men (49.1%). A certain deviation from this value appears when considering the data from each area: in Riruta 91.1 per cent of members are men, in Athi River 76.5 per cent are women. This is probably due to the differences between the models in the two areas: while in Riruta the SHGs are mainly producers' associations, while in Athi River they serve especially as lending groups. However 23 SHGs in my sample (65.7%) are mixed in terms of gender. The mean age is 33.3 years, with a maximum in Athi River of 42.8 years and two under-30 years in Baba Dogo and Kariobangi. Education ranges between a minimum of less than 5 years in Riruta (where a dozen members are illiterate) and 7.3 years in Baba Dogo.

Out of the 35 SHGs surveyed, 26 (74.3%) were formally registered. All of them – even if not registered – had a fixed structure with a three-member executive committee composed of a chairman, treasurer and secretary. As already noted, most of them appeared to be founded by charismatic leader (the chairman) with the two other officials in a sub-ordinate position. Invariably income, social status and education are higher among officials than ordinary members. This suggests that the majority of SHGs surveyed had patron/client relations in place.

Characteristics common to the whole sample of SHGs are the regular money contributions of members and the presence of some form of mutual lending (merry-go-rounds or other more elaborate forms of interest lending). Within the sample, 26 SHGs (74.3%) run at least one income-generating activity (see Table 8.2).

Eleven SHGs (31.4%) also reported raising funds through sport events and art performances such as music, communitarian theatre (often funded by international NGOs), dancing and acrobatic shows (usually in connection with international tourism). The 8 groups that did not report any income-generating activity simply focus on credit schemes and risk-sharing initiatives.

I tried to deepen my analysis by collecting data on the 27 SHGs reporting to run at least one income-generating activity. The business might vary from production (e.g. small manufacture and handicraft such as wood carving, tailoring, batik and basket making) to petty trade (e.g. second-hand goods, cereals) and different kinds of services (e.g. garbage collection, plastic recycling, telecommunication).

*Table 8.2* Main source of group income for the SHGs participating in the Juhudi Zetu programme

| Source of group income | No. of SHGs | Percentage of the sample |
|---|---|---|
| Garbage collection and recycling | 7 | 20 |
| Small manufacturing/production and repair | 6 | 17.1 |
| Small retailers kiosk | 3 | 8.6 |
| Poultry farming | 2 | 5.7 |
| Soap making | 2 | 5.7 |
| Water selling | 2 | 5.7 |
| Chair/tent hire | 1 | 2.9 |
| *Simu Ya Jamii* (community phone) | 1 | 2.9 |
| Cyber cafe | 1 | 2.9 |
| Food preparation and selling | 1 | 2.9 |
| Biogas manufacture | 1 | 2.9 |
| No income-generating activity (only credit/sharing) | 8 | 22.9 |
| Total | 35 | 100 |

Those activities are usually managed in a way not dissimilar with respect to the so-called 'household micro-enterprises' that proliferate in the *jua kali* sector in Nairobi (WB, 2006: 31–33). The property of tools is usually collective, sometimes hired out by members, and other means of production are shared among members. Clearly, pricing is operated according to market fluctuations and this might lead to big fluctuations in revenues and profits. Decisions are taken by the leading committee (20 out of 27 SHGs), by the whole group (3 SHGs) or by the leader, after informal consultancy of other officials (4 SHGs); 21 out of 27 SHGs (77.8% of SHGs running income-generating activities) envisage plenary voting procedures for crucial extraordinary decisions.

The next analytical step was to investigate the modalities of work organization within each SHG. Subdivision of the production is common in the groups dealing with manufacturing and big orders (e.g. all the SHGs in Riruta, when working for international clients, craft different wood or tailor parts of their final products then assemble or paint them). From interviews and observation, a feature appeared constant: in the groups where the majority of members have sources of income other than the group (20 SHGs, 74.1% of productive SHGs), production is managed with strong mutual characteristics such as complete sharing of production means and profits (usually through a common fund used to finance personal loans). In the 7 SHGs (all the groups of Riruta, plus one in Baba Dogo) where members do not have a significant source of income other than the group activities, SHGs operate as clusters of self-entrepreneurs – sharing shelter, knowledge, main tools and sometimes market opportunities but not full entrepreneurial risk. When I tried to enquire about profit sharing in Riruta, the chairman of Kivuli Producers Association told me that 'we came together to share our skills, to increase our ability to produce for big orders...but nobody can survive without individual trade'. Since 'life in Nairobi is so expensive...everybody must struggle in doing his business', also because of the uncertainty of big international orders. Translated into the group account, this meant that each worker earned less than half of its money from the SHG, the rest from his/her self-employed work. I found a similar situation in all of the other SHGs analysed, without any example of complete profit sharing among the members. This might derive from the low degree of trust that a context so violent and opportunistic as Nairobi's slums creates in people in comparison to the strong mutual trust that characterizes rural relationships (Floris, 2006: 74–80).

SHGs in Nairobi rarely involve full-time work for their members. It is instead common to hire one or two employees (sometimes rotating among the members) and to cooperate part-time. A critical decision that the leading committees constantly manage is the set-up of rotation among members. Apart from the rare case of full-time hiring (always for a fixed salary), members take part in the activities of the group with fixed turns. Of the sample, 224 respondents (41.2%) spent less than 10 hours per week working for their SHGs, while 151 (27.8%) devoted between 10 and 20 hours per week; 99 (18.2%) worked between 20 and 30 hours per week and only 70 (12.9%, mostly in Riruta) worked more than 30 hours per week for the SHG. Those figures must be interpreted together with the multiple memberships recorded: a mere 6.1 per cent of the people interviewed belonged to just one SHG. Most people (43.4% in my sample) belonged to two SHGs, and 21 per cent to more than three. This can be a helpful metric of the main function of SHGs in Nairobi: informal workers try to maximize the risk insurance and credit provision functions of SHGs by multiplying the memberships to different SHGs. And this fact directly collides with the possibility of creating a coherent alternative work organization since production appears extremely fragmented.

It is possible to understand the fragmentation of labour that workers usually experience by observing a week in the life of Lucy Nduku, a member of the Noonkopir Market Women Group (a SHG from the Athi River area). Lucy works full-time in a hairdressing kiosk that she opened with her cousin Martha Wayua. The kiosk is open seven days per week, except on Sunday morning. She usually works from 7 a.m. to 8 p.m., but two evenings per week she leaves work at 5 p.m. to participate in the production of *kyondos*[19] with the Noonkopir Market Women Group. The members buy the semi-raw *sisal*[20] from farmers in *Ukambani*[21] then transport it – usually on a *matatu* roof – and work together in a rented iron sheet room to make baskets and other containers. Once a month, Lucy spends a whole day with another SHG member to fulfil their turn of marketing the production in Nairobi. The Noonkopir Market Women Group's membership allows Lucy to take part in a merry-go-round, receiving a sum of between 8000 and 10,000 ksh – depending on the sales – every two months. With this money, Lucy was able to expand her business, starting the sale of cosmetics in the hairdressing kiosk. Her cousin Martha is also a member of two other SHGs. In this way, they secure the weekly income of the shop without the need of a bank and assure a small credit every two weeks.

This example clearly shows that productive activities taking place within the SHG have, firstly, the aim of creating a small income to increase the size of a merry-go-round fund. Secondly, producing and trading goods increases the mutual trust among the members, allowing them to better cooperate at mutual lending. Production according to a different model, which might actually reduce the exploitation, is rather a background goal, since people are usually too busy struggling for their basic needs to experiment with new business models. When members produce together tools are usually shared, as is the space for work, and the marketing and strategic activities are undertaken as a common enterprise. Last but not least, members share the entrepreneurial risk, despite socio-economic cleavages often in place, by membership fees and extraordinary *Harambee* – undertaken to start-up new activities.

Nairobi is a hyper-individualistic labour market. People are pushed to compete against each other for tiny margins and the development of a collective attitude is usually very complicated. Workers rely on SHGs in their daily struggle for basic needs and welfare provisions but SHGs remain scarcely active in terms of alternative ways of organizing production and trade or in gathering workers to better defend their labour rights. Each individual relies on others to survive, through family ties and other social connections such as SHGs, but economic competition inhibits the development of cooperative models of production, where workers share – on a full-time basis – the experience of labour.

Furthermore, informal settlements are characterized by the widespread 'NGO-isation' (Hearn, 1998) that creates distortions and utilitarian behaviours. This kind of severe distortion contributes to the proliferation of associations – usually local NGOs but in some cases also workers' clusters and SHGs – apparently constituted only to raise grants from international donors. It is a fact, indeed, that many NGOs prefer to finance various sorts of 'communitarian development projects', instead of focusing on realistic business plans to start up an enterprise or cooperative. Against this background, it appears evident that the 'community self-help' model (Berner and Phillips, 2005) lying behind the bias towards SHGs is often a masked form of neoliberalism which prevents the formation of any real alternative to the status quo.

The evaluation of the Juhudi Zetu programme has often given me such an impression, since the formation of communitarian area-wide social enterprises (especially in Athi River, where a soap and detergent shop had been created with the support of IPSIA) appeared more a ratio-nal strategy to meet the NGO's expectation and take its cash grant than a real desire of the programme beneficiaries.

Nevertheless, the processes of wealth distribution and risk sharing operated by the groups surveyed confirmed the central role that SHGs play in the urban environment. Surely this role is primarily welfare, but production appears the main strategy – coupled with credit self-provision – chosen to support members' income. Thus, SHGs might represent a sort of socio-economic laboratory to understand how work will evolve in a hyper-competitive and fragmented environment such as the informal settlements of Nairobi.

## Conclusions

Nairobi is a global city that appears completely integrated in the global economy for tourists travelling from the airport to the Hilton before departing for a safari in the *Masai Mara*. Hundreds of cyber cafes are full of youths from morning to night and Barclays Bank signs can be seen on every corner. Globalization has definitely given a North American skyline to the Central Business District (CBD) – almost an island of wealth afloat the misery of Eastern Africa. In this context, informal workers struggle to survive, aggregating in groups and associations – so-called SHGs.

Today, it is evident that the urban/rural bifurcation of the African state is no longer a spatial reality. Rather, it is a clear class cleavage that cuts the whole society, both on the economic and political side. As Mamdani (1996: 297) points out, 'today it is informal [labour] that forms a class that is in civil society but is not of it'. The state continues to exercise its power in two different ways. In the 'modern' city as the major authority committed to defending the rights of private property with respect to the whole formal economy, comprising both urban services and capital-intensive rural activities (i.e. large-scale farming or tourism). And as only one actor – often not the most powerful – among several competitors seeking to maximize the grab of resources in the slums and in remote rural areas.

Against this background SHGs are, above all, a rational aggregation strategy to cover first survival needs. With regards to the possibility of SHGs representing alternative instances of work organizations, I have found at least three areas of criticism. Firstly, SHGs rarely provide the entire income for their members, thus they remain additional entities in the economic lives of their members. In most of the cases, they represent an addition to the meagre wages paid by a formal/informal capitalist firm or to the small profit of an informal self-run business.

Secondly, for all the cases surveyed, despite the fact that the sense of belonging and mutual trust appears extremely high, SHGs rarely represent *real* forms of mutual cooperatives with a complete sharing of production means, risks and profits. This is probably due to the deep cultural crisis that has taken place in Nairobi. While on the one hand, the last remains of 'traditional' values have disappeared, on the other hand, there is the continuous multiplication of hypnotic illusions, created by the mass media, uncritically mixing hip-hop music, wrestling and Hummers. In informal settlements, 'money has outclassed all of the values that people know and possess' (Floris, 2006: 27), increasing individualism, self-centredness and opportunistic behaviours that prevent SHGs to be taken as a first step through evolution into more structured and collective enterprises.

Lastly, my perception is that SHGs are always at high risk of exploitation within consensus dynamics by politicians and wealthy individuals. It is well known what *Harambee* has become through the decades in Kenya: 'a major arena of... politics [that] has shaped the structure of peasant-state relations' through a system of political patronage (Barkan and Holmquist, 1989: 359; Kibwana et al., 2001: 163). Therefore, rather than a coherent alternative to the exploitative system, SHGs might end up serving the interests of the already powerful and well-equipped 'big men' who rule the Kenyan economic and political life. In a nutshell, SHGs do not automatically represent 'democracy' despite having internal elections and voting procedures in place.

In addition, it is impossible not to mention the 'grey zone' which might lie between self-help and organized crime. As many observers have pointed out, self-help may transform into an ideology that further weakens the state power, creating wide spaces for patronage dynamics covered by the 'benefaction' mask (Davis, 2006). The result is a process of violence privatization, easy to start up through the basic services provided by SHGs, in an environment where unemployment is estimated to reach a rate as high as 46 per cent for the age-cohort of 15–24 years (WB, 2006: 29). SHGs might cover, in extreme cases, the cells of 'gangs and militant formations' such as *Talibans, Jeshi la Mzee, Jeshi la Embakasi* (all less famous but as violent as the well-known *Mungiki* sect) that 'could be hired by politicians for around 250 ksh [each youth] to unleash violence on their opponents' (Katumanga, 2005: 512). During my analysis, I found at least 6 SHGs that were seriously suspected to be linked with organized crime and gangs.

In summary, I found that the potentialities of strong SHGs are limited by political, cultural and economic factors. If political exploitation and cultural crisis are rather self-evident, the economic structure might be harder to understand. Low-income workers have limited means to find alternative ways of production, since the capitalist relations produce and reproduce by themselves – reducing any space for experimenting and developing new models. Informal workers persist with micro-capitalistic attempts at accumulation – aggregating through SHGs to cover their welfare needs – without exploring the possibility of evolving the same groups into more structured enterprises. I believe it is not the severe scarcity of resources that is the prime cause of lack of alternative development, but much more the strength of a socio-economic framework that – coupled with the client/peasant distortion at the backbone of the African state – vigorously curbs any sign of change.

The development of an integrated alternative full-time work organization, involving each member in profit sharing as well as in the enterprise management, might eventually evolve as some SHGs become conscious of the potentialities of the cooperative model. To this day, SHGs in Nairobi appear to be the vital minimum social cluster that consents to secure mutual welfare services, enhance the members' social capital and share income, credit access and risks among people that would otherwise be completely excluded. At the same time, SHGs appear to be the rational choice to maximize the opportunities to raise funds from international agencies and NGOs.

Finding ways of sharing the scarce resources remains the unique solution for survival. SHGs undoubtedly represent the rational solution to generate the few shillings that enable people to feed their children and to support their education. Despite probably not fully exploring their potential alternative dimensions – especially in terms of claims to political and labour rights – SHGs are already able to help slum dwellers in Nairobi in their daily battle against high food prices, lack of rights and insecurity. Without any doubt, they represent part of an alternative system that is going to arise in Africa.

SHGs might represent the first cells of an alternative model that, taking inspiration from Latin American experiences, allows small producers to ally against bigger competitors, creating situations of pricing stability and balancing the harsh competition that currently forces people to suffer severe labour exploitation. The degree and the modalities of the transformation are impossible to foresee. Probably the recently approved new Constitution will not change any part of the exploitation mechanism in Kenya; probably workers will remain fragmented for a long time. At the same time, it is possible to foresee a potential scenario of change where SHGs become closer to informal workers' associations and trade unions. In that case, workers would have a widespread network to defend and negotiate their rights and to demand a better share of production means (first of all land and water), thus experiencing a marked decrease of labour exploitation.

## Notes

1. I had the opportunity to do research in Nairobi for my MA from November 2008 to October 2009.
2. As declared on every document produced by the newly christened National Planning and Vision 2030 Ministry.
3. Maize white flour, the base of Kenyan diet.
4. A sort of cheap spinach. *Sukumawiki* literally means 'that pushes out the week'.
5. *Matatu* are the omnipresent 15-seat Japanese minibuses, *Makanga* are the rowdy *matatu* conductors.
6. Literally 'hot sun' in Kiswahili. The term, over the course of the 1980s, came to be used to refer to the artisans who were working in the open air, because of the absence of premises. Gradually, it was extended to refer to any kind of self-employment, becoming – despite its inadequacy – the Kenyan term for informal labour (King, 1996).
7. Informal economy is estimated to generate 9 new jobs out of 10 created in the country (KNBS, 2009: 2).
8. In Nairobi, as a legacy of the colonial prohibition for Africans to live in town, very few people do not have a rural area where they 'come from'. This does not imply that they were born there, but surely means that they have contacts with relatives and that they plan to bury their dead there (Floris, 2006: 91–94). This fact might appear insignificant, but it represents a constant incentive to join savings groups as unique sources of credit to cover high funeral expenses.
9. Two of the biggest informal settlements in Nairobi.
10. For example, see the Lewis two-sector development model (Lewis, 1954).
11. ILO (1972).
12. The open unemployment rate is 8.5 per cent in rural areas and 17.3 per cent in urban areas (UNDP, 2007: 17). Unemployment particularly affects youths, the least educated and women.
13. The daily oral contract traditionally in place only in informal enterprises or house-building.
14. The second-hand clothing coming from Europe and North America.
15. It is extremely interesting to observe how almost every meeting in Kenya – from a political rally to a birthday party, from a funeral dinner to the inauguration of a secondary school – seems to be organized on behalf of *Harambee* fundraising, even when it is evidently useless (Munene, 2005).

16. 14.22 and 14.75 are the mean values of the sample of two interesting economic studies on SHGs in Nairobi (La Ferrara 2002: 23; Fafchamps and La Ferrara, 2010: 30).
17. 'Our efforts' in Kiswahili.
18. Italian NGO related to ACLI (Christian Associations of Italian Workers).
19. Typical baskets of the *Kamba* culture.
20. A natural fibre derived from *Agave sisalana*.
21. An agricultural region south-east of Nairobi, homeplace of the *Kamba* people.

# References

Anyamba, T. J. C. (2005). *Nairobi's Informal Modernism*, URL: http://www.n-aerus.net/web/sat/workshops/2005/papers/3.pdf, 8 January 2011.
Barkan, J. D. and Holmquist, F. (1989). 'Peasant-State Relations and the Social Base of Self-Help in Kenya', *World Politics*, 41 (3): 359–380.
Benería, L. and Floro, M. S. (2006). 'Distribution, Gender and Labor Market Informalization: A Conceptual Framework with a Focus on Homeworkers', in *Rethinking Informalization. Poverty, Precarious Jobs and Social Protection*, L. Beneria and N. Kudva (eds), URL: http://ecommons.library.cornell.edu/bitstream/1813/3716/1/Rethinking%20Informalization.pdf, 8 January 2011.
Berner, E. and Phillips, B. (2005). 'Left to Their Own Devices? Community Self-Help between Alternative Development and Neo-Liberalism', *Community Development Journal*, 40 (1): 17–29.
Chen, M. A. (2006). 'Rethinking the Informal Economy: From Enterprise Characteristics to Employment Relations', in *Rethinking Informalization. Poverty, Precarious Jobs and Social Protection*, L. Beneria and N. Kudva (eds), URL: http://ecommons.library.cornell.edu/bitstream/1813/3716/1/Rethinking%20Informalization.pdf, 8 January 2011.
Chen, M. A., Jhabvala, R. and Lund, F. (2001). Supporting Workers in the Informal Economy: A Policy Framework, URL: http://www.wiego.org/papers/2005/unifem/11_ILO_WP_Chen_Jhabvala_Lund.pdf, 8 January 2011.
Chesang, G. (2007). 'Shoeshine Boundaries, Post-card Cities and the Villagisation of the City: The Shape of Urban Life in East Africa', in *State of East Africa 2007. Searching for the Soul of East Africa*, Aidan Eyakuze (ed.), SID, Nairobi-Roma.
Clayton, A. and Savage, D. C. (1974). *Government and Labour in Kenya 1895–1963*, Frank Cass, London.
Dafe, F. (2009). *No Business like Slum Business? The Political Economy of the Continued Existence of Slums: A Case Study of Nairobi*, URL: http://www.lse.ac.uk/collections/DESTIN/pdf/WP98.pdf, 8 January 2011.
Davis, M. (2006). *Planet of Slums*, Verse, London.
De Soto, H. (1989). *The Other Path: The Invisible Revolution in the Third World*, Harper and Row, New York.
De Soto, H. (2000). *The Mystery of Capital: Why Capitalism Triumphs in the West and Fails Everywhere Else*, Basic Books, New York.
Fafchamps, M. (2008). *Risk Sharing between Households*, URL: http://www.economics.ox.ac.uk/members/marcel.fafchamps/homepage/hbsoc.pdf, 8 January 2011.

Fafchamps, M. and La Ferrara, E. (2010). *Self-Help Groups and Mutual Assistance: Evidence from Urban Kenya*, URL: http://www.economics.ox.ac.uk/members/marcel.fafchamps/homepage/group.pdf, 8 January 2011.

Floris, F. (2006). *Puppets or People? A Sociological Analysis of Korogocho Slum*, Paulines, Nairobi.

Hart, K. (1973). 'Informal Income Opportunities and Urban Employment in Ghana', *The Journal of Modern African Studies*, 11 (1): 61–89.

Hearn, J. (1998). 'The "NGO-isation" of Kenyan Society: USAID and the Restructuring of Health Care', *Review of African Political Economy*, 75: 89–100.

Henry, S. (1987). 'The Political Economy of Informal Economies', *Annales of the American Academy of Political and Social Science*, 493: 137–153.

ILO (1972). *Employment, Incomes and Equality: A Strategy for Increasing Productive Employment in Kenya*, International Labour Organization, Geneva.

ILO (2002a). *Decent Work and Informal Economy*, International Labour Organization, Geneva.

ILO (2002b). *Women and Men in the Informal Economy: A Statistical Picture*, International Labour Organization, Geneva.

IPSIA (2007). *Juhudi Zetu Programme Concept Paper*, unpublished paper.

Katumanga, M. (2005). 'A City Under Siege: Banditry and Modes of Accumulation in Nairobi, 1991–2004', *Review of African Political Economy*, 106: 505–520.

KHRC (2004). *The Manufacture of Poverty: The Untold Story of EPZs in Kenya*, Kenya Human Rights Commission, Nairobi.

Kibwana, K., Kichamu Akivaga, S., Murugu Mute, L. and Odhiambo, M. (2001). *Initiatives against Corruption in Kenya. Legal and Policy Interventions, 1995–2001*, URL: http://www.clarionkenya.org/documents/initiatives.pdf, 8 January 2011.

King, K. (1996). *Jua Kali Kenya, Change and Development in an Informal Economy 1970–95*, James Currey, London.

Kinyanjui, M. (2006). *Institutions and Creativity in Jua Kali Enterprise Clusters in Kenya: The Case of Ziwani and Kigandaini*, IPAR, Nairobi.

KNBS (2009). *Economic Survey 2008*, Government Printer, Nairobi.

La Ferrara, E. (2002). *Self-Help Groups and Income Generation in the Informal Settlements of Nairobi*, URL: http://www.dagliano.unimi.it/media/WP2002_163.pdf, 8 January 2011.

Latouche, S. (2004). *Survivre Au Développement*, Arthéme Fayard, Paris.

Lewis, W. A. (1954). 'Economic Development with Unlimited Supplies of Labour', *Manchester School*, 22 (5): 139–191.

Leys, C. (1975). *Underdevelopment in Kenya. The Political Economy of Neo-Colonialism*, Heinemann, London.

Macharia, K. (1992). 'Slum Clearance and the Informal Economy in Nairobi', *Journal of Modern African Studies*, 2: 221–236.

Mamdani, M. (1996). *Citizen or Subject: Contemporary Africa and the Legacy of Late Colonialism*, Princeton University Press, Princeton.

Manda, K. D. and Odhiambo, W. (2003). *Urban Poverty and Labour Force Partecipation in Kenya*, URL: www.worldbank.org/urban/symposium2003/papers/odhiambo.pdf, 20 November 2010.

Munene, K. (2005). 'Sharing Among Africans', in *Social and Religious Concerns of East Africa*, G. J. Wanjohi and G. Wakuraya Wanjohi (eds), Wajibu, Nairobi.

Ndegwa, S. N. (1998). 'Citizenship Amid Economic and Political Change in Kenya', *Africa Today*, 45 (3–4): 351–368.

Ondiege, P. O. (1995). *Informal Sector Development Models and Assistance Programmes in Kenya*, Housing and Building Research Institute, Nairobi.

Peattie, L. (1987). 'An Idea in Good Currency and How it Grew: The Informal Sector', *World Development*, 15 (7): 851–860.

Piore, M. and Sabel, C. (1984). *The Second Industrial Divide*, Basic Books, New York.

Thomas-Slayter, B. (1991). 'Class, Ethnicity, and the Kenyan State: Community Mobilization in the Context of Global Politics', *International Journal of Politics, Culture and Society*, 4 (3): 301–321.

UNDP (2007). *An Employment-Targeted Economic Program for Kenya*, URL: http://www.ipc-undp.org/publications/reports/Kenya.pdf, 8 January 2011.

Warah, R. (ed.) (2008). 'The Development Myth', in *Missionaries, Mercenaries and Misfits. An Anthology*, AuthorHouse, Milton Keynes.

WB (2006). *Kenya. Inside Informality: Poverty, Jobs, Housing and Services in Nairobi's Slums*, World Bank Press, Washington.

# Index